"Like it or not, a brave new world replete with synthetic biology is now upon us. Rana's book will equip lovers of the truth to think Christianly in defense of that which corresponds to reality."

—**Hank Hanegraaff**, president, Christian Research Institute;
host, *Bible Answer Man* broadcast

"I tell my students that if scientists could produce life from completely nonliving materials, they would illustrate that such a feat requires lots of intelligent planning! In the spirit of Rana's earlier work (*The Cell's Design*), his *Creating Life in the Lab* beautifully details how intelligent divine planning—rather than unguided naturalistic processes—best explains the emergence of first life."

—**Paul Copan**, professor and Pledger Family Chair of Philosophy and Ethics,
Palm Beach Atlantic University; author of *Is God a Moral Monster?*

"I recommend Rana's book as an excellent resource for understanding in detail current developments in synthetic biology and origin-of-life research. It shows how these developments point toward rather than away from God the Creator."

—**Vern S. Poythress**, professor of New Testament interpretation,
Westminster Theological Seminary

"We are privileged to live in a time of unprecedented and accelerating scientific insights into the nature of the microcosm and the macrocosm. Significantly, this process has produced a growing wealth of evidences that require an intelligent agency as the inference to the best explanation. As Fazale Rana puts it in his significant new contribution to the growing literature on synthetic biology, to generate, sustain, and manipulate a living entity requires the intense involvement of highly intelligent beings. Rana's trenchant analysis of the characteristics of life, the conditions necessary for biogenesis, the information-rich biomacromolecules, and the attempts to synthesize artificial life is achieved with clarity and scientific rigor."

—**Kenneth Boa**, president of Reflections Ministries, Atlanta

CREATING
LIFE
IN THE
LAB

CREATING
LIFE
IN THE
LAB

HOW NEW DISCOVERIES
IN SYNTHETIC BIOLOGY MAKE
A CASE FOR THE CREATOR

FAZALE RANA

BakerBooks

a division of Baker Publishing Group
Grand Rapids, Michigan

Published by Baker Books
a division of Baker Publishing Group
P.O. Box 6287, Grand Rapids, MI 49516-6287
www.bakerbooks.com

Printed in the United States of America

Library of Congress Cataloging-in-Publication Data
Rana, Fazale, 1963–
      Creating life in the lab : how new discoveries in synthetic biology make a case for the Creator / Fazale Rana.
            p.   cm.
      Includes bibliographical references (p.   ) and index.
      ISBN 978-0-8010-7209-3 (pbk. : alk. paper)
      1. Synthetic biology—Religious aspects—Christianity. 2. Intelligent design (Teleology).
I. Title.
BL255.R37 2011
212′.1—dc22   2010036575

11   12   13   14   15   16   17   7   6   5   4   3   2   1

For Amy
Thank you for the life we have created together.

Contents

Illustrations

Acknowledgments

This book represents the sacrifice and hard work of many people, not just the author. I want to thank my wife, Amy Rana, and my children—Amanda, Whitney, and Mackenzie—for their love, encouragement, and understanding when this book project took "priority" over family matters.

Each member of the Reasons To Believe team has supported me with their friendship and encouragement in this endeavor, and I am grateful. Kathy and Hugh Ross deserve a special mention for their inspiration and the opportunities they have given me.

I especially want to acknowledge the editorial department who dedicated themselves to this book as if it were their own. Thank you Kathy Ross, Sandra Dimas, Marj Harman, Linda Kloth, Kyler Reeser, and Patti Townley-Covert for your expert editorial guidance and help with all the little chores that must be done during a book project. Thank you Jonathan Price and Phillip Chien for designing the many figures found in this book.

I'm indebted to Joe Aguirre, Dr. David Rogstad, Dr. Hugh Ross, Kenneth Samples, and Dr. Jeffrey Zweerink for our many stimulating conversations in the hallway and during lunch. These discussions helped to directly and indirectly shape the contents of this book.

I also want to thank my friends at Baker Books, especially Robert Hosack and Wendy Wetzel, for their efforts on this project and for their belief in our work at Reasons To Believe.

1

Waking Up in Frankenstein's Dream

I entered with the greatest diligence into the search of the philosopher's stone and the elixir of life; but the latter soon obtained my undivided attention.

Victor Frankenstein in *Frankenstein* by Mary Shelley

Science is one of my great loves. But that wasn't always the case. During high school, I really didn't care for science at all. The only reason I took classes in biology and chemistry was because they were recommended for college.

When I enrolled at West Virginia State College (now University), I discovered the school didn't offer the pre-med major I wanted. So to prepare for medical school, I had to choose between chemistry and biology as my major course of study.

Chemistry seemed the best option. My thinking was that if I didn't make it into medical school, I'd have an easier time finding a decent job with a bachelor's degree in chemistry, especially where I lived in the Kanawha River valley, with chemical plants lining the banks of the Kanawha River.

Before college, science was merely a means to an end. But that changed when I took my first college class, an introduction to biology, during the summer before my freshman year. I still remember trudging up several flights of stairs to the top floor of the old science building day after day for six weeks. My reward for reaching the top was sitting for long hours in the hot, humid lecture hall and laboratory—without air-conditioning. The miserable stickiness, however, soon seemed nothing compared with the elation I felt as I unexpectedly stumbled upon a new direction for my future.

It all began with a simple but profound question: what is life? This question tops the usual list of topics addressed in introductory biology. It makes sense. If someone wants to learn about *life*, then it's helpful to know what exactly biologists mean when they use the word.

I was astonished to find that scientists do *not* know how to define life. They can list the characteristics common to all life, but they cannot really define it. My surprise soon turned to curiosity. And that curiosity became an obsession. I wanted to know:

- What is life?
- How does life operate at its most fundamental level?
- How did life begin?

Biochemistry held the greatest potential to answer my questions. Becoming a physician no longer interested me. I wanted to be a biochemist. I wanted to understand as much as possible about the fundamental features of life, especially at its most basic level—the molecular level.

Science became more than a means to an end. For me, it became the end, in and of itself.

The Diligence of Discovery

In my introductory biology course, I learned about two landmark discoveries— each reported in 1953 and each related to the questions that gripped me on

What Is Biochemistry?

Atoms and molecules form the basic chemical components of matter. Chemists study the structure of matter and the transformations it undergoes. They expend considerable effort to characterize the structure of molecules and learn how their configurations change when they react with one another. Ultimately, chemists want to relate structural and transformational qualities of molecules to the macroscopic (large-scale) structure and behavior of matter.

Biochemistry is the application of chemistry to biological systems. It's the study of the molecules (proteins, DNA, RNA, carbohydrates, and fats) essential to life. Biochemists want to understand the structure of these molecules and how they undergo change when reacting with each other. They seek to relate the structure of biomolecules and their chemical reactivity to higher-order biological structures and processes.

that first day of class. These discoveries have set the course for biochemists since then.

Collecting the Cellular Parts

First, James Watson and Francis Crick unveiled the structure of DNA (deoxyribonucleic acid),[1] the biomolecule that carries genetic information within its architecture. Insight into DNA's structural makeup reveals how genetic information is transferred from parent to offspring. Watson and Crick's discovery launched the molecular biology revolution.

As part of this revolution, biochemists have made enormous strides toward understanding the operation of life at its most basic level. We now have fairly complete knowledge about the chemical composition of the cell's structure and contents, and we know how living systems extract and convert energy from the environment for use in their various operations. We are beginning to grasp the relationship between the structural and functional features of biomolecules. And we've learned how the cell stores and manages the information needed to carry out life activities. The molecular basis for inheritance and the chemical processes responsible for cell division have been fully disclosed. Researchers can describe how life—with all its constituent parts—operates at its most fundamental level.

As the second decade of the twenty-first century begins, the second question in my "big three" list has been answered, for the most part. But my other two questions remain: what is life, and how did it begin?

Lightning Strikes

The same year Watson and Crick reported their findings on DNA's structure, Stanley Miller, Nobel Laureate Harold Urey's student at the University of Chicago, published the results of his now famous spark discharge experiments.[2] In an effort to discover how life could arise from nonliving chemical systems, Miller sent an electrical discharge through a mixture of hydrogen, ammonia, and methane gases, plus water vapor. When all traces of oxygen were carefully removed from the experimental setup, the spark produced amino acids and other organics.

The Miller-Urey experiment represented the first step toward experimental verification of a hypothesis (the Oparin-Haldane hypothesis) that suggested how life could have arisen from nonlife (see "The Oparin-Haldane Hypothesis," p. 16). A series of similar experiments by other scientists soon followed.[3] These studies seemed to provide repeated validation of Oparin and Haldane's ideas. Thus began the origin-of-life research program as a formal scientific discipline. Giddy with Miller's amazing success, many scientists predicted the origin-of-life question would soon be fully answered.[4]

The Oparin-Haldane Hypothesis

Russian biochemist Alexander I. Oparin and British geneticist J. B. S. Haldane independently provided their detailed hypotheses for abiogenesis (life from nonlife) in the 1920s. Though neither initially accepted nor widely disseminated, the Oparin-Haldane hypothesis became the chief organizing principle in origin-of-life research throughout the 1970s and, in some ways, persists today.[5] For the first time, this hypothesis cast the mechanism for life's beginning in the form of a detailed scientific model.

Both Oparin's and Haldane's models proposed stepwise pathways from inorganic systems likely present on primordial Earth to the first living entities. Oparin and Haldane each postulated an early Earth atmosphere devoid of oxygen and dominated by reducing gases—hydrogen, ammonia, methane, and water vapor. Energy discharges within this gas mixture presumably generated prebiotic molecules. These compounds would then have accumulated in Earth's oceans to form the primordial soup where, over time, stepwise chemical reactions purportedly led to the first life-forms.

Even though their models were eventually connected, Oparin and Haldane differed regarding the intermediate step(s) to life. Oparin viewed them as protein aggregates. Haldane regarded the transitional molecular system as a large self-replicating molecule.

Optimism characterized the next few decades of research into how life began. Excitement grew as Sidney Fox achieved another important milestone.[6] Fox and his group coaxed amino acids to condense to form "proteinoids." Some of these compounds, closely related to proteins in structure, were able to catalyze, or assist, chemical reactions. Fox and his co-workers observed that under certain conditions, "proteinoids" aggregated to form microspheres. These microspheres superficially resembled cells.

As origin-of-life research matured, though, the optimism of earlier decades gave way to growing pessimism. Intractable problems surfaced, fueling frustration (see *Origins of Life*, which I wrote with Hugh Ross, for details). Initially, origin-of-life studies focused on finding possible chemical routes to the formation of life's molecular building blocks. By the mid-1980s and 1990s, the quest had become all the more challenging as scientists began to assess the operation of these chemical pathways in light of conditions on early Earth. Research also began probing the geochemical and fossil records of the oldest rocks—data that established tight time constraints for origin-of-life scenarios. Further, researchers began applying information theory to the origin-of-life question and, as a consequence, struggled to account for what has been recently learned about life's minimal complexity.

Still No Answers

With much respect for their laudable achievements, I think it is safe to say that origin-of-life researchers are little, if any, closer today to answering my question about life's beginning than they were fifty years ago when Stanley Miller first conducted his experiments. Significant resources have been brought to bear on the origin-of-life question, and yet no genuine progress has been made toward understanding how life originated.

Despite disappointment and frustration, the quest to explain life's start through some form of chemical evolution continues. Scientists rightfully assert that the problem is much more challenging than originally conceived. Meanwhile, they remain convinced that enough money, effort, and time will eventually lead to the breakthroughs needed to explain the emergence of the first life-forms by natural processes alone.

Traditionally, origin-of-life researchers have taken one of two complementary approaches in their investigations: the bottom-up or the top-down approach.

The bottom-up strategy uses lab techniques to identify pathways that could lead to the formation of biologically important compounds from materials present on early Earth. This tack involves discovery of physicochemical processes that can produce (1) self-replicating molecules and (2) mechanisms capable of generating molecular complexes and aggregates that could have led to the first protocells.

The top-down approach starts with life as we know it today—contemporary life—and works backward to determine what first life must have been like long ago. Since the end of the 1990s, with the emergence of a new biochemical research program called genomics, this approach has gained some momentum. Genomics involves sequencing and characterizing the entire genetic content, or genome, for certain organisms. Origin-of-life researchers mine the growing database of microbial genomes to gain insight into the properties of life's last universal common ancestor (LUCA), as well as into first life's complexity, life's minimal complexity, and the origin of the various biochemical processes observed in the cell.

Cultivating Life in the Lab

Amid mounting problems associated with both bottom-up and top-down research, some scientists have opted for a completely different approach to explaining life's origin. They hope to construct life in the lab.

These scientists see the attempt to produce synthetic and artificial life in the lab as a means to shed light onto the pathways that supposedly led to life's origin. In doing so, their expressed hope is to provide the ultimate validation for the notion that life can emerge from nonlife—even if they can't be sure that what they accomplish has any real bearing on the actual events that took place.

To his credit, origin-of-life researcher and Nobel Laureate Jack Szostak acknowledged in an interview with the *Harvard University Gazette*,

> If we make something everyone agrees is alive, that would provide a plausible scenario for the great event [the origin of life]. But, because the trail is billions of years cold, we'll never really know for sure if we're right.[7]

Many of the initial efforts toward creating life in the lab have focused on developing self-replication—molecules that can "reproduce" by making copies of themselves. (DNA can be considered a self-replicating molecule because it directs its own reproduction.) Most biochemists consider self-replication a central feature of life. Accordingly, any molecule that can self-replicate would represent an important milestone in the transition from inanimate to animate. In *Life's Origin*, veteran origin-of-life researchers Alan Schwartz and Sherwood Chang highlight this point:

> Today, many researchers would probably agree that a particularly critical event in the origin of life was the appearance of self-replication in some set of information-containing molecules (such as, for example, primitive nucleic acids or proteins).[8]

Thus far, researchers have had only limited success, at best, in identifying a self-replicating molecule that might have been the first self-replicator on Earth.[9] This is not to say that researchers haven't produced self-replicating molecules. They have—just not molecules with any realistic relevance to the origin of life.[10]

One of the first successes at creating self-replicating molecules came from the laboratory of Reza Ghadiri, a chemist at the Scripps Research Institute in La Jolla, California. Ghadiri, winner of the Feynman Prize in Nanotechnology (1998), and his colleagues managed to construct peptides (small protein-like molecules) that can self-replicate.

Beyond Reach

The clever, innovative designs of Ghadiri's molecules exemplify science at its best. So I was excited for the opportunity to hear Ghadiri speak at the 1999 conference of the International Society for the Study of the Origin of Life (ISSOL).[11] The boldness of his opening comments riveted my attention.

Ghadiri unabashedly announced that the goal of his lab was to create something more than self-replicating peptides—he planned to create life. Despite Ghadiri's esteemed reputation, his announcement was met with noticeable skepticism by the origin-of-life researchers in the audience that day. His self-replicating peptides, though truly remarkable, fell a long way short of even the simplest imaginable life-form. The lofty goal of creating life in the lab seemed a far-off, perhaps unattainable dream to most researchers back in 1999.

Suddenly within Reach

Less than a decade later, however, the prognosis for producing life at the lab bench has dramatically changed. During the summer of 2007, science journalist Seth Borenstein sent a shock wave through the scientific community and beyond with the headline, "Artificial Life Likely in 3 to 10 Years."

In his article, Borenstein reported on the work of several scientists working to create artificial life in the lab, a venture that appears more and more promising. According to Mark Bedau, the chief operating officer of the biotechnology company Protolife (Venice, Italy), all that's needed to construct artificial life is:

1. A membrane or boundary;
2. A genetic system that controls the function of the "life-form" and allows it to reproduce;
3. A means to extract energy from the environment.

At the time the article was written, Szostak, at Harvard University, expressed optimism that the first two steps were well within grasp. In fact, he optimistically predicted that within six months, creation of an artificial cell membrane from relatively simple fatty acids would be achieved. [12]

Borenstein's report was just one of many. Public interest in the pursuit of artificial life has been stirred by recurring articles documenting the stepwise progress of Craig Venter (who headed Celera Genomics, the private company that sequenced the human genome in competition with the public program[13]) and Hamilton O. Smith (a winner of the 1978 Nobel Prize in Physiology or Medicine for the discovery of restriction enzymes, an indispensable breakthrough in molecular biology). Together they're attempting to engineer a synthetic bacterium. Venter, Smith, and their collaborators report that they have (1) identified the minimum genetic requirements for life; (2) synthesized the genomes of two simple microbes from basic chemical constituents; and (3) figured out how to insert a synthetic genome into a bacterial cell.[14] They have been able to combine all these steps to create a synthetic version of a bacterium.[15] All that's left is to use their methodology to make a novel, artificial genome and implant it into a bacterial cell, and the research team will have created the first artificial organism.

A New Life-Form

The efforts of Szostak, Ghadiri, Venter, Smith, and many others to make artificial life fall into a new discipline of science known as synthetic biology. One of the most exciting and rapidly growing areas of research, synthetic biology represents a fusion of chemical and genetic engineering with more traditional work in biology. The goal is to make novel forms of life.

As with traditional origin-of-life research, scientists working in synthetic biology approach the problem in two fundamentally distinct yet complementary ways: top down and bottom up. The top-down approach, exemplified by Venter and Smith's efforts, involves reengineering existing life-forms to carry out novel processes. The bottom-up approach, highlighted by Szostak's work, focuses on building artificial life-forms by assembling them from biomolecular building blocks one step at a time.

From my vantage point, it looks as if scientists are genuinely on the verge of creating artificial and synthetic life-forms from both the bottom up and the top down. And the timetable suggested by Borenstein seems realistic.

A Marvel or a Menace?

The very real prospect of scientists' creating life in the lab conjures up images of the fictional Victor Frankenstein and the monster he created. It also raises all sorts of theological and ethical questions.

Scientists pursuing the creation of artificial and synthetic life claim these novel life-forms will not only shed light on the origin-of-life question but also benefit humanity. Venter and Smith want to engineer a synthetic bacterium that can generate hydrogen gas, providing a renewable form of clean energy. Accomplishing this breakthrough could go a long way toward resolving the energy and climate crises.

At the same time, one can't help but ask, "Is it right for human beings to play God?" "Is it safe to create artificial and synthetic life?" "What if the creators of these novel life-forms lose control of their creation, as Frankenstein did, and unleash a disaster of biblical proportions?" "How should we balance the potential benefits of this emerging biotechnology with the real possibility of danger?"

For many Christian theists, the genesis of novel life-forms by human hands raises other troubling questions: "Will the creation of artificial and synthetic life-forms mean there's no need for God, as the Creator?" "Will this development validate the theory of evolution for the origin of life?"

These questions, concerns, and implications have not been lost on atheists and agnostics. In his interview with Borenstein, Mark Bedau declared, "Creating protocells has the potential to shed new light on our place in the universe.

This will remove one of the few fundamental mysteries about creation in the universe and our role." He also stated, "We are doing things which were thought to be the province, in some quarters, of God—like making life."[16]

Living the Dream

These mysteries have motivated my research as a biochemist. They've also motivated me to write this book. Though the race for artificial and synthetic life may seem misguided and unwise and is commonly perceived as a threat to Christianity, I'm convinced it may well prove otherwise. Rather than validating an evolutionary explanation for the origin of life, the successful attempts to modify and even make new life in the lab will compellingly demonstrate that life's origin and transformation could not have happened apart from the work of an intelligent agent. This book explains why.

In the process, we cannot avoid the question, "What is life?" For scientists striving to create life in the lab, this question becomes even more important than it was for an inquisitive college student. To know if they have succeeded in making life in the lab, researchers must have a clear understanding of what life is and what it isn't. Chapter 2 considers how the inability to define life impacts attempts to explain life's beginnings and to develop artificial life. Chapter 3 marks the beginning of a section updating each of the leading endeavors to make artificial and synthetic life in the lab. This chapter explores the top-down approach to synthetic biology, detailing the work of Venter and Smith. Chapter 4 describes some of the most intriguing efforts to date to modify existing life and thus create biochemically foreign life-forms. Chapter 5 examines the bottom-up approach to synthetic biology based on the chemistry of living systems as we know them. Chapter 6 continues this theme, narrating research efforts to create, from scratch, life as we *don't* know it—synthetic life-forms based on biochemistries other than those found throughout the living realm.

Each of these chapters concludes with comments on how the discussed work could impact the origin-of-life question, especially as related to such issues as intelligent design and the Christian view of creation.

Because there are many similarities between the bottom-up quest for artificial life and the bottom-up scenarios for the origin of life, a third section segues from discussion of synthetic biology to its implications for life's origin. Chapter 7 provides an outline of some of the hypotheses researchers propose to account for the bottom-up appearance of life. Chapter 8 sets the stage for understanding life's beginning as a creation event rather than as the work of undirected physicochemical processes. The role of researchers as intelligent designers in successfully modeling the supposed steps in the pathway to life's beginning is the focal point of this chapter.

Chapters 9 through 13 examine some of the key stages thought to have brought about life's initial appearance. These chapters critically evaluate whether these steps could have occurred on early Earth apart from the intervention of the biblical Creator.

The epilogue concludes by reflecting on the implications, from a Christian point of view, of creating artificial life.

By necessity, this book involves cell biology and biochemistry. I've done my best to keep the technical details to a minimum and to avoid jargon. Still, to fully appreciate the significance of synthetic biology and the origin-of-life question, some of the technical complexity surrounding the topic remains unavoidable. Throughout the book, the background information necessary to understand each topic appears prior to discussion of that topic. An appendix functions as a primer on biochemistry.

Now let's delve into this chilling question: are scientists about to awaken Frankenstein's monster?

2

Life Is like Music

The untaught peasant beheld the elements around him, and was acquainted with their practical uses. The most learned philosopher knew little more. He had partially unveiled the face of Nature, but her immortal lineaments were still a wonder and a mystery. He might dissect, anatomise, and give names; but, not to speak of a final cause, causes in their secondary and tertiary grades were utterly unknown to him.

Victor Frankenstein

I grew up in the seventies, and rock music was a big part of my life. Later, I was surprised to discover the music that defined my generation didn't just arise out of nowhere. Instead, the sounds I listened to day and night traced their roots back to the African American musicians of the early 1900s. Rock music was born from the blues. And some of my favorite artists (The Allman Brothers, Jeff Beck, The Jimi Hendrix Experience, Eric Clapton, Foghat, Led Zeppelin, Lynyrd Skynyrd, The Marshall Tucker Band, Steve Miller Band, and ZZ Top) had one foot firmly planted in that genre.

This new insight prompted me to find out more. And my love affair with a truly American art form began. I was like Frankenstein's monster hearing music for the first time—"sounds sweeter than the voice of the thrush or the nightingale"—as he secretly peered from his hovel into the cottage of a peasant family. To this day, I can't get enough of the blues.

My wife, on the other hand, can't stand those soulful sounds, or at least a steady stream of them. There's no accounting for musical taste. What's a symphony to one can be a noisy cacophony to another. Because music is perceived subjectively, tastes vary from person to person—and culture to culture. In fact, what is even recognized as music differs from person to person and culture to culture.

Though philosophers, musicologists, and scientists have tried, no one can adequately define music. Some say it's organized sound. Others claim music is a language of sorts, a means to communicate moods, emotions, impressions, and concepts. Others argue that music is sound with aesthetic qualities. Cognitive scientists maintain that music is a distinct mode of sensory perception. And adherents to postmodernism assert that the definition depends exclusively on the social context. Others give up trying to define music and resort merely to listing common characteristics of all styles.

Music isn't the only thing hard to define. Biologists face a similar problem in their attempts to define life. According to origin-of-life researcher Antonio Lazcano, "Life is like music; you can describe it but not define it."[1]

What Is Life?

This difficulty doesn't mean philosophers, origin-of-life researchers, biochemists, biologists, chemists, and even physicists haven't tried to answer the question. Since the 1850s, science has yielded a rich history of attempts to find an agreed-upon definition. In his book *Between Necessity and Probability*, astrobiologist Radu Popa collected about a hundred definitions that range from practically incomprehensible to tongue-in-cheek. Sampling a few helps shed light on some of the difficulties associated with defining life.[2]

> Life is characterized by maximally-complex determinate patterns, patterns requiring maximal determinate templets for their assembly. . . . Biological patterns are determinant patterns, and the uniquely biological templets have stability, coherence, and permanence. . . . Stable templets—reproducibility—was the great leap, for life is matter that learned to recreate faithfully what are in all other respects random patterns.[3]

> Patterned after Theodosius Dobzhansky . . . life is what the scientific establishment (probably after some healthy disagreement) will accept as life.[4]

> (a) A terrestrial living entity is an ensemble of molecular-informational feedback-loop systems consisting of a plurality of organic molecules of various kinds, coupled spatially and functionally by means of template-and-sequence directed networks of catalysed reactions and utilizing, interactively, energy and inorganic and organic molecules from the environment. (b) A living entity is an uninterrupted succession of ensembles of feedback-loop systems evolved since emergence time to the moment of observation.[5]

Just as wave-particle duality signifies microscopic systems, irreversibility and trend toward equilibrium are characteristic of thermodynamic systems, space-symmetry groups are typical for crystals, so do organization and teleonomy signify animate matter. Animate, and only animate matter, can be said to be organized, meaning that it is a system made of elements, each one having a function to fulfill as a necessary contribution to the functioning of the system as a whole.[6]

It's alive if it can die.[7]

Without consensus about how to distinguish between living and nonliving entities, many biologists give up the effort and become like music enthusiasts who resort merely to listing common characteristics, features shared by all life on Earth. Instead of providing a definition for life, they merely describe it.

The Descriptive List

Certain overarching properties are common to all life (at least life as known on Earth). Before describing life, I'd like to present a few key tenets that apply to all living entities.

1. Life is made up of atoms combined to form molecules.

Like all matter, life consists of atoms. The most common elements found in living systems are carbon, hydrogen, oxygen, nitrogen, sulfur, phosphorus, and metals such as sodium, potassium, and iron. These chemical elements combine to form a wide range of macromolecules that then interact to form life's basic structures. Through their chemical reactivity, some of these molecules are responsible for the processes essential to life.

The major classes of macromolecules are proteins, made by linking together smaller molecules (amino acids) and the nucleic acids (DNA and RNA) which are formed by joining together smaller molecules called nucleotides. The appendix provides a more detailed description of the structure and function of proteins and nucleic acids. It also includes a description of the molecules that form cell membranes.

2. Life is made up of cells.

According to the cell theory, cells are the fundamental units of life. They are the smallest entities that can be considered "life." As a corollary, all organisms consist of one or more cells.

Most life-forms on Earth are single-celled. Multicellular organisms (plants, animals, and fungi) are made up of specialized cells that carry out the many activities necessary to life.

An idealized cell is defined by a cell boundary or membrane. This structure separates the cell's interior from the exterior surroundings. The cytoplasm—made up of water, salts, and organic molecules—forms the cell's internal matrix.

By the mid-1950s, biologists recognized two fundamentally distinct cell types: eukaryotic and prokaryotic. Eukaryotic cells contain a nucleus, organelles, and internal membrane systems. Organelles are large structures embedded within the cytoplasm that carry out specific functions for the cell. A membrane, similar to the cell membrane, surrounds most organelles. The nucleus houses the cell's genetic material (DNA). As with other organelles, a membrane also surrounds the nucleus. Most eukaryotic cells are between 5 and 40 microns across. (A micron is a millionth of a meter.) Unicellular protists and multicellular fungi, plants, and animals are examples of eukaryotic organisms.

Prokaryotic cells are typically about 1 micron in diameter. These cells appear to be much simpler than eukaryotic cells. Apart from a cell boundary, prokaryotes possess no visible defining features—no nucleus, organelles, or internal membranes. The genetic material of prokaryotes consists of "naked" DNA that resides in the cytoplasm. Bacteria and archaea are prokaryotic organisms.

3. Life obeys the laws of chemistry and physics.

As recently as the 1800s, many scientists, even Louis Pasteur, believed in a "vitality" unique to life. This force supposedly distinguished life at the molecular level from inanimate matter. Vitalists argued that the chemical processes inside a cell could not be achieved anywhere else. They maintained that because of this vital force certain compounds could be produced only by living organisms, not by inorganic processes.

Over time, German chemists largely debunked this view. Friedrich Wöhler showed that urea, a compound made by living organisms, could be made from an inorganic material (ammonium cyanate) in the lab. The vitalist claim that the life-essential process of fermentation could take place only within the cell also proved untrue. Lab work by Eduard and Hans Buchner showed that an enzyme extracted from yeast could cause fermentation.

Life also adheres to the laws of thermodynamics. The first law states that the total energy of the universe must remain constant. As is the case for any process, the activities of living organisms can neither create nor destroy energy.

The second law of thermodynamics requires that energy undergoes a change from a high quality to a low quality any time a process takes place. The net result is that the overall entropy of the universe increases. (Entropy is a measure of energy quality; the higher the quality, the lower the entropy.) Often a decrease in order is associated with an increase in entropy. In other words, under certain conditions systems tend to become disordered over time. All living entities are characterized by a high degree of order and organization (see "Life Is Organized," p. 27).

This quality doesn't mean life defies the second law of thermodynamics. Instead, a flux of energy into living systems establishes and maintains order, preserving their highly organized state. As a consequence of the energy flow into living systems, the surroundings become less ordered, and the overall entropy for the universe increases.

In addition to agreeing upon these tenets, life scientists have developed a universally recognized list of characteristics possessed by all life on Earth.

Characteristic 1: Life Is Organized

Living entities are highly structured, whether simple single-celled creatures or complex multicellular organisms. Within cells, myriad large molecules interact to form subcellular architectures, and chemical reactions are organized into pathways and networks. (See appendix, p. 199).

A Vital Force?

Many who take the position that life stems from the work of a Creator hold to some form of vitalism, whether explicit or implicit. While they may not directly espouse a classical form of this belief, adherents to it still seem to regard life's basic operations as more than the outworking of physicochemical processes. They see life—animate matter—as possessing a unique property stemming from the Creator that makes it distinct from the material that makes up the inanimate realm.

To date, I've seen no compelling evidence for vitalism of any type. Biochemists have discovered that, all things being equal, molecules—in fact entire biochemical systems—behave identically whether inside the cell or in a test tube. And this behavior can be accounted for by applying the laws of physics and chemistry.

The rejection of vitalism in no way undermines the case for a Creator. The following analogy might help me make my point. Consider life to be like an automobile engine. A car's motor runs in accord with the laws of physics and chemistry. No vital force is necessary to make an automobile work or to describe its operation. Still, the laws of physics and chemistry don't explain how the engine originated. A motor's defining features clearly must stem from the work of an intelligent agent, such as an automotive engineer. While the laws of physics and chemistry readily explain the operation of biological and biochemical systems, those laws cannot account for life's beginnings.[8]

Many in the scientific community confuse these two points. Life scientists often think that because biological systems function in mechanistic ways, a Creator is not needed to account for their origin. Yet there is no reason to think these two ideas are connected. Understanding the operation of a system is not the same as explaining where it came from.

While a vital force is unnecessary for life's operations, life can still be understood as coming from the work of a creative agent.

In multicellular organisms specialized cells secrete molecules into the extra-cellular space. These molecules are organized into an extracellular matrix. Several different types of specialized cells reside and interact within this matrix to form tissues. They combine in specific ways to form organs, and different organs work conjointly to form the systems that make up complex multi-cellular plants and animals.

Characteristic 2: Life Is Chemically Distinct from Its Environment

The same atoms make up living and nonliving systems. These atoms, how-ever, occur in different proportions and exist as different molecules within living organisms. In fact, the molecules that constitute an organism are generally produced by that organism.

Characteristic 3: Life Is Homeostatic

Life actively works to maintain its chemical distinction. This state of main-tenance is called homeostasis, which means "staying the same." In spite of what the term seems to imply, homeostasis involves dynamic processes in which the organism draws matter and energy from the environment, transforms it into the appropriate chemical composition, and expels waste and heat into the milieu. These ongoing transactions result in an organism with a stable chemical composition.

Characteristic 4: Life Takes Energy and Matter from the Environment and Transforms Them

Organisms can absorb energy from the environment in the form of sunlight or chemical energy and transform it into alternate forms of chemical energy, mechanical energy, electrical energy, and heat. Through this process, the trans-formed energy is used along with matter taken from the environment to power life-essential operations like building and maintaining bodies, reproducing and generating motion, and so forth.

Creatures that turn sunlight into energy are photoautotrophs, while those that use chemical energy are chemoautotrophs. Heterotrophs obtain energy by eating other organisms and organic foodstuff.

Characteristic 5: Life Responds to Stimuli from the Environment

Response to various stimuli helps life gain access to food and energy and avoid harmful materials and circumstances. The stimuli that elicit these re-sponses vary considerably. Plants grow toward sunlight, predators detect the presence and motion of their prey, honeybees are attracted to flowers, worms sense decaying remains of an animal, and even bacteria swim toward nutrients in their surroundings.

Characteristic 6: Life Reproduces

All life has the capacity to replicate itself with high fidelity. Organisms produce offspring nearly identical to themselves, generation after generation. (Slight variations in descendants result from genetic changes and differing environments.) Some single-celled organisms reproduce asexually by dividing in two. Others reproduce sexually by combining genetic material to yield offspring. As part of the reproductive process, some organisms undergo a complex process of growth and development.

Characteristic 7: Life Is Adapted to Its Environment

Living organisms are exquisitely suited to their surroundings. Their anatomical, physiological, and behavioral properties allow them to make the most of a particular environment while avoiding its inherent dangers.

Characteristic 8: Life Evolves

Organisms can change as their environment changes. This ability occurs through mutations in their genetic material. In rare circumstances, these mutations can create new biochemical and biological traits. If these new characteristics impart a greater ability to survive, the organism will reproduce more effectively. Over time, this new trait will take hold in the population, transforming the species.

Evolutionary change takes place at four distinct levels. Microbial evolution, the first level, involves transformations in viruses, bacteria, archaea, and single-celled eukaryotes—changes such as the acquisition of antibiotic resistance in bacteria. Microevolution is the second level and refers to evolutionary variation within a species in response to selection pressures and genetic drift. One example includes the peppered moth's change in wing color.

Speciation is the third level of evolutionary change. In this case, one species gives rise to another closely related sister species. A well-known example is the evolution of the finches of the Galapagos Islands. The ancestral finch species came to the Islands, then diversified into closely related species that vary in size and beak shape in response to different ecological niches on different islands.

Evolutionary biologists and most creationists agree that an abundance of evidence exists for microbial evolution, microevolutionary changes, and speciation. Biological evolution at these three levels is well documented and largely noncontroversial.

Controversy about biological evolution centers primarily on the fourth level: macroevolution. This term refers to the creative potential for large-scale biological changes. Evolutionary biologists assert that over vast periods of time, the processes that generate microevolutionary changes and speciation can yield large-scale transformations (e.g., whales from a raccoon-like creature or birds from dinosaurs).

Creationists and intelligent design proponents remain skeptical of evolution at this level.[9] I include myself among those skeptics. My view is that while organisms can adapt to changing environments and other selective pressures, they cannot evolve in dramatic ways. In other words, a Creator must be responsible for life's origin and history, and biological and biochemical systems show every indication of having been intelligently designed.

Regardless of an individual's position on macroevolution, one of life's defining features is that it does evolve, at least to a limited extent.

The Importance of Defining Life

The fact that philosophers, musicologists, and scientists cannot define music deters no one from experiencing music's impact to the fullest. In the same way, the inability of biologists to define life has never prevented anyone from studying and developing a rich understanding of it. Still, attempts to define life are not merely academic. They have practical importance in a number of scientific arenas.

An agreed-upon definition of life is essential to origin-of-life researchers' understanding—at least in a general sense—of how life might have emerged from a nonliving system. Without it, attempts to describe the origin of life *on Earth* merely target entities with the same characteristics as contemporary life and probe the chemical evolutionary means by which they may have come into being. Unless life is adequately defined, these Earth-centric efforts cannot successfully yield a general theory of abiogenesis.

This problem has become more pronounced as astrobiologists begin earnestly searching for life beyond Earth. For the most part these scientists must look for biomarkers that correspond to life as we know it. However, they readily admit the inadequacy of this approach because life radically different from Earth's could, in principle, exist on bodies in our solar system (and elsewhere).[10] Without a definition, it's impossible to know if life can exist on planets such as Mars, Venus, and Mercury or on moons like Jupiter's Europa or Saturn's Titan. Though it's unlikely Earth life could exist on these bodies, perhaps some unknown form could. There is simply no way to know without a robust definition.

Scientists hope that attempts to create artificial and synthetic life will help them focus on more clearly defined targets in their search for life on other planets (or other objects) in our solar system. Creating nonnatural life-forms should lead researchers to a better understanding of how life differs from inanimate matter and may even move the scientific community closer to a definition.

To create artificial and synthetic life, scientists must first develop a much more complete understanding of life's most fundamental systems. More comprehensive knowledge will permit researchers to alter these biochemical systems in nonnatural ways or to create nonnatural analogs. Such activities will help stake out the boundaries between life and nonlife.

Ironically, the same problems that confront origin-of-life investigators and astrobiologists bedevil scientists trying to create artificial and synthetic life in the lab. If they can't define life, how will they know when they have made artificial life, particularly if it begins to deviate from life as we know it?

This point is important to keep in mind. When scientists claim to have created novel life-forms, validation of their assertions will depend on life's definition. If a researcher defines life as a self-replicating entity, he will declare the invention of a self-replicating molecule to be the generation of a new life-form. If, on the other hand, a researcher defines life more comprehensively, this accomplishment will be viewed as no more than the invention of a molecule with interesting properties. The standard to evaluate the creation of artificial and synthetic life must be consistent.

It is safe to say, however, that the inability to define life won't stop scientists from trying to create it. The next several chapters describe some of the work already done and discuss what these efforts mean. At the top seems the best place to start.

3

Blessed by a New Species

A new species would bless me as its creator and source; many happy and excellent natures would owe their being to me. No father could claim the gratitude of his child so completely as I should deserve theirs.

Victor Frankenstein

Many readers readily recognize Victor Frankenstein as the real monster of Mary Shelley's story. As a young student, Victor arrogantly eschews the advice of his mentors and obsesses about uncovering the secrets of life. Secluding himself from virtually all human contact, Frankenstein finally achieves his goal: the creation of a monster. Then, almost immediately, he's repulsed by the very creature he labored to create.

Frankenstein takes no responsibility whatsoever for the monster he's made. Instead of caring for his creation, the scientist flees his lab, leaving the thing to its own devices. Neglect and rejection eventually turn the creature into an evil being intent on destroying its maker.

Suffering intense remorse, guilt, and shame for what he's done, Frankenstein refuses to tell anyone about the monstrous results of his efforts. His secrecy brings tragedy and grief to many people. First, his brother is murdered and then his own bride on their wedding night as the monster exacts its revenge. Again Frankenstein becomes obsessed—this time with the destruction of what he created. Ultimately, his deep hatred brings about Frankenstein's own demise.

Through it all, this driven scientist evokes some measure of sympathy. He is a tormented soul who loses everything and everyone dear to him. He pours himself into his work and destroys his own life in the process.

A Modern-Day Frankenstein?

In 2008, *Time* magazine voted Craig Venter among the world's one hundred most influential people. He is one of the most prominent scientists of the last decade. He is much admired and yet, at the same time, much despised by people inside and outside the scientific community. Venter, a scientific maverick who thinks big and has little patience for the bureaucracy that characterizes many scientific programs, has played a major role in the emerging science of genomics, making friends and enemies along the way. Venter's notoriety began in the early 1990s when he used express sequence tags to identify several thousand human brain genes.[1] Within a few months of this major breakthrough, the number of human genes known to the scientific community increased by thousands. However, when Venter filed patents on these newly discovered genes, he outraged many people.[2]

Later in the decade Venter left the National Institutes of Health (NIH) and took over The Institute of Genomic Research. Though a grant application to fund his work was denied because scientific reviewers thought his approach was impossible, Venter assembled a team of researchers who perfected the shotgun sequencing of genomes.[3] The team then used this technique to sequence an organism's (*Haemophilus influenzae*) entire genome for the first time. They followed that success by generating the genome sequence for the fruit fly *Drosophila melanogaster*, another key breakthrough.[4]

In 1999, Venter helped form Celera Genomics, a private company. There this maverick scientist generated even more controversy. In spite of naysayers who once again claimed it couldn't be done, Venter's team successfully applied shotgun sequencing to the human genome and entered into an intense competition with the publicly funded Human Genome Project.

Celera's approach brought faster progress than the one employed by the public project. With the goal of completing the human genome sequence first and constructing a privately owned human genome database, Venter's company charged a subscription fee for access to their sequences. This attempt to capitalize on the human genome data—the genetic blueprint of human beings—angered many in the scientific community. They believed the human genome data should be free. Still, Celera's successful use of shotgun sequencing forced the public project to adopt this technology, speeding up the completion of the human genome sequence in 2000.

Venter moved on from there to form the J. Craig Venter Institute. One of its projects is to develop and apply metagenomics techniques for assessing the genetic diversity of microbial communities in the world's oceans.[5] Using his own personal yacht, Venter circumnavigates the globe to sample ocean water. Then his team uses shotgun sequencing methods to identify the genes present. From this data, researchers gain insight into the types and numbers of microbes distributed throughout the world's oceans. Most in the scientific community consider these efforts significant and worthwhile.

Once again, however, Venter has generated a mixture of excitement and horror among the scientific community and the public at large with the announcement that he, like Victor Frankenstein, has decided to create life in the lab.

To accomplish his goal, Venter has founded Synthetic Genomics Inc. This new company is devoted to making artificial, nonnatural life—microbes that have commercial utility, particularly for the production of ethanol, hydrogen, and other forms of renewable energy. Scientists who, like Venter, pursue the creation of artificial and synthetic life claim these novel life-forms will benefit humanity. If Venter accomplishes the desired breakthrough, it could go a long way toward resolving the energy and climate crises.

Still, the very real prospect of scientists creating life in the lab raises all sorts of questions. Is such work tantamount to human beings playing God? Will Venter and his colleagues, like Frankenstein, lose control of their creation and unleash unintended disaster? Will the genesis of novel life-forms by human hands eliminate the need for a Creator, giving support to evolutionary explanations for the origin of life?

Many believers and skeptics alike think that if scientists create life in the lab, then there must be nothing special about life itself. The origin of life, therefore, might have easily taken place on early Earth without God's involvement.

This chapter describes Venter's work at Synthetic Genomics Inc. and explores what his team's efforts mean in terms of the creation-evolution debate. Understanding what these researchers are trying to accomplish and what they have achieved thus far seems a good place to begin.

Driven to Create

Venter and his co-workers first became interested in creating artificial life as they began work to determine the minimum genome for life. This effort requires exploring an organism's entire hereditary information stored in the nucleotide sequences of DNA. Regions of these sequences, called genes, house the data used by the cell's machinery to construct proteins.

Proteins take part in virtually every biochemical process and play a critical role in nearly every cell component. Cataloging the number and types of proteins present in an organism gives biochemists important insight into that organism's structures and operations. Venter's team hopes that identifying the minimum genome will reveal life at its most fundamental level.

In their attempts to determine the minimum genome, Venter's group focused their attention on *Mycoplasma genitalium*. Possessing only about 480 gene products, this microbe, a bacterium that parasitizes the human genital and respiratory tract, has possibly the smallest known genome.[6] Thus *M. genitalium* serves as a model system to determine the bare minimal requirements for life. This genome can also help scientists indentify which biochemical systems are "nonnegotiable," absolutely essential for an entity to be recognized as life.

Venter and his colleagues reasoned the bare essential genome is likely even smaller, and they may be correct. They discovered that a significant fraction of this parasite's genome is dedicated to mediating interactions between the parasite and its host and can be considered nonessential to a strictly minimal life-form.

To ascertain the minimum number of genes needed for life, Venter's team used a "knock-out" approach. This experimental protocol involved using both the random and systematic mutation of *M. genitalium* genes to determine those that are indispensable. (Biochemists refer to these procedures as knock-out experiments.) If a gene is unnecessary, *M. genitalium* will grow after the gene is experimentally mutated.

Once the essential genes have been determined by knocking out the nonessential genes, Venter's team hopes to confirm its result by preparing a synthetic minimal genome and introducing it into a cell to see if it grows. In the process of identifying the minimum genome, the group recognized that they are just a few short steps away from making artificial life in the lab.

Let's Take It from the Top

Venter and his collaborators are using a top-down approach to create an artificial life-form. After stripping a naturally occurring microbe down to its bare essence, they plan to generate a nonnatural life-form by adding nonnative genes to the minimal genome. The major stages in this effort include:

1. Systematically eliminating genes from the *M. genitalium* genome to identify the essential genes;
2. Synthesizing the minimal genome from scratch starting with nucleotides;
3. Introducing the minimal genome into the cytoplasm of an *M. genitalium* cell (or the cell of a closely related microbe) that has had its original genome deleted;
4. Initiating the growth and replication of the organism that harbors the synthetic genome.

Completing these steps will lead to the creation of a nonnatural organism. Venter and his group have already named the anticipated microbe *Mycoplasma laboratorium.*

Once created, *M. laboratorium* will supply a genetic foundation on which Venter's team can build. They plan to incorporate additional genes into the minimal genome and thereby produce proteins that can generate hydrogen or other commercially and biomedically interesting compounds. By separately adding an ensemble of different genes to the minimal genome, these researchers could, in principle, make a wide array of artificial microbes, each with distinct metabolic capabilities exploitable for biomedical, agricultural, or industrial applications.

Checking In

Venter's team has made remarkable progress toward their goal of producing *Mycoplasma laboratorium.* Already, they have identified the essential gene set, which consists of about 380 genes.[7] In addition, they have synthesized the entire genome of a wild-type *M. genitalium* strain from scratch and cloned the entire genome in yeast.[8] They have done the same for the microbe *Mycoplasma mycoides*, an organism that harbors about 1,000 genes in its genome. They have also transferred the wild-type *M. genitalium* genome into a closely related *Mycoplasma* species.[9] In a parallel set of experiments, they have also transferred a synthetic version of the *M. mycoides* genome into *Mycoplasma capricolum*, transforming the recipient into a synthetic version of *M. mycoides.* Each milestone stands as a significant scientific accomplishment. The only thing left for Venter's team is to put all these steps together: synthesizing, cloning, and transferring a synthetic genome into a *Mycoplasma* cell. This will be a technically challenging feat, but it seems within reach.

Venter's team has worked hard at each stage. Their success has depended upon their expertise in carrying out detailed and sophisticated laboratory procedures. More importantly, these researchers have displayed remarkable creativity and strategic brilliance in the process of identifying the minimal gene set and synthesizing the entire *Mycoplasma* genome.

The effort required for the scientists to get to this point and, ultimately, to create *M. laboratorium* has huge theological and philosophical significance. In short, the work and ingenuity necessary to create artificial life in a top-down manner suggests that life cannot be created or transformed in any appreciable way apart from tremendous intelligence, diligence, and care.

Highlighting some of the technical challenges associated with the achievements accomplished thus far and describing key steps in "bestowing animation on lifeless matter" illustrates the important role intelligent agency plays in the genesis of life.

Crafting a Genome

To achieve the total synthesis of the entire M. *genitalium* genome, Venter's team didn't rush into the lab and start throwing nucleotides into test tubes, carrying out chemical and enzymatic reactions. Instead, they carefully devised a synthesis strategy. They decided to build the genome by first synthesizing small pieces of DNA and then assembling these pieces into increasingly larger sections using chemical, biochemical, and *in vivo* methods until the entire genome was cobbled together.

The Strategy

To appreciate their efforts, consider the generation of a synthetic version of the M. *genitalium* genome. Before beginning any lab work, Venter's team started at the drawing board. They carefully parsed the sequence of the entire genome into cassettes (or fragments) about 5,000 to 7,000 nucleotides (abbreviated as "bp" for base pairs) in size. Then, the researchers carefully delineated the boundaries between cassettes, making sure the demarcations would reside between genes. The team also carefully designed the cassettes so the sequences between two adjacent pieces of DNA overlapped by about 80 bp. This strategic plan allowed them to piece together the M. *genitalium* genome in a manageable way.

Once the cassette map was developed, the researchers executed the synthesis and assembly in stages. This work required the use of:

1. Chemical and physical methods to synthesize and purify about 10,000 short pieces of the genome, each approximately 50 nucleotides in length (automated DNA synthesizers conducted these operations);
2. Enzymes to biochemically combine the chemically made fragments into 101 larger fragments about 5,000 to 7,000 nucleotides in length that corresponded to the cassettes mapped out at the drawing board stage;
3. Enzymes and the bacterium *Escherichia coli* to combine the 100 larger fragments into four fragments about 140,000 nucleotides in size;
4. Yeast to combine the four fragments into the entire genome.

Each stage demanded intricate planning and execution.

Chemical Synthesis and Purification

Chemical synthesis of DNA refers to the nonbiological, chemical production of small segments of DNA called oligonucleotides. With state-of-the-art methods, chemical synthesis can reliably generate these oligonucleotides up to about 200 bp in size using automated procedures.

The capability to chemically synthesize DNA has been a long time in the making. Related experiments began in the 1950s. Thanks to the efforts of some of the world's most prominent chemists over the last half century, that capability has advanced through several key milestones.

DNA consists of chain-like molecules known as polynucleotides. The cell's machinery links four different subunit molecules—the nucleotides adenosine (A), guanosine (G), cytidine (C), and thymidine (T)—together to form individual polynucleotide chains. Two polynucleotide chains align in an antiparallel fashion, twisting around each other to form the well-known DNA double helix.

An individual nucleotide has several different chemical groups that can react with each other to form a bond with another nucleotide. Yet in DNA, the nucleotides must be linked together in a specific way to form the polynucleotide strands. The enzymes that constitute the part of the cell's machinery responsible for producing DNA manifest such a high degree of specificity as to ensure that the linkages form in the correct manner. In a test tube without enzymes present, the nucleotides will react with each other to form a *variety* of linkages. Combining them in this way yields polynucleotides with a mishmash structure having no biological use.

To avoid this problem, chemists devised a strategy of using carefully selected chemical groups to block these reactive sites. The blocking groups were designed to fit the unique chemistry of each reactive group. Chemists can selectively remove the blockers at the appropriate times during the reaction sequence to make specific chemical groups available to react. After the total synthesis of the oligonucleotides has been affected, the remaining blocking groups are then removed.

If these reactions are conducted in solution, a purification step must be included after each nucleotide is added to the growing oligonucleotide chain. To get around this cumbersome process, chemists devised an approach using a solid support to anchor the oligonucleotide chain during the reaction sequence. The first nucleotide is attached to a solid material that has been packed into a column. Chemicals can then be poured into the column to initiate reactions with the next nucleotide in the chain. When the reaction is complete, the column is washed. Unreacted materials and undesired chemicals are removed from the column, while the oligonucleotide remains attached. This approach not only eliminates a costly purification step but also increases the accuracy of the synthesis.

The specific steps for the chemical synthesis of oligonucleotides include:

1. Attaching the first nucleotide to a solid support after deblocking the appropriate group;
2. Removing the appropriate protecting group from the attached nucleotide in the first position to allow it to react with the next nucleotide in the

oligonucleotide sequence that, in turn, has had the appropriate blocking group removed;

3. Allowing the nucleotides to react under carefully controlled conditions;
4. Adding a chemical cap to any unreacted oligonucleotides (necessary because a small percentage of the nucleotides don't react with the attached oligonucleotide chains);
5. Stabilizing the linkage between the two nucleotides with an oxidizing agent;
6. Washing away unreacted nucleotides;
7. Repeating steps 2 through 6 until the entire oligonucleotide has been constructed;
8. Cleaving the oligonucleotide from the solid support;
9. Removing all the blocking groups;
10. Purifying the oligonucleotide, which is absolutely critical to ensure the accuracy of the biochemical recombination step.

Biochemical Recombination

Once the chemical synthesis and purification of the 50 bp in size oligonucleotides has been completed, they need to be linked together to form the 5,000 to 7,000 bp cassettes diagrammed on the *M. genitalium* genome map. To make these oligonucleotides link together both accurately and efficiently, chemists must rely on enzymes to carry out the recombination process.

Biochemists can't just throw DNA fragments into a test tube with a mixture of enzymes and get the desired recombinations. Instead, they must painstakingly formulate a strategy that selects the appropriate enzymes based on their catalytic properties, design the oligonucleotides (prior to the chemical synthesis step) so they are compatible with the enzymes, and devise a reaction scheme that will yield the desired recombination product.

The procedure Venter's team used to recombine the 50 bp oligonucleotides into fragments about 5,000 to 7,000 bp in size was previously worked out by putting together the entire genome (5,386 bp in size) of a bacterial virus. It entailed:[10]

1. Treating the oligonucleotides with the enzyme T4 polynucleotide kinase, an enzyme that modifies the ends of the oligonucleotides so they could take part in the next stage of the reaction.
2. Treating the end-modified oligonucleotides with *Taq* ligase, an enzyme that combines smaller oligonucleotide fragments into larger ones, preparing them for the next stage of recombination. This combination step required the oligonucleotides from each of the DNA strands to pair up with each other in the appropriate way. To make this happen, Venter's

team had to carefully design the sequences of the 50 bp oligonucleotides made by chemical synthesis.

3. Performing a polymerase cycling assembly of the paired and ligated oligonucleotides. Again, the success of this step depended on the careful design of the sequences of 50 bp oligonucleotides made by chemical synthesis. This clever procedure used enzymes (DNA polymerases) to assemble small-paired DNA fragments into larger ones. The paired oligonucleotides did not fully overlap one another, so single-stranded regions existed. The DNA polymerases filled in those gaps, eliminating the overlap and in the process joining the fragments together, extending their size. The polymerase cycling assembly had to be repeated between 35 and 70 times to build fragments between 5,000 and 7,000 bp in size.

4. Performing a polymerase chain-reaction amplification of the fully assembled DNA pieces (5,000 and 7,000 bp in size). Not only did this part of the process generate numerous copies of the fully assembled DNA pieces, but it was designed in such a way as to allow *only* the fully assembled DNA pieces to be amplified and to eliminate any partially assembled DNA.

Once the 101 pieces of the 5,000 to 7,000 bp cassettes were assembled, they were further combined in three stages to form four pieces of DNA about 144,000 bp in size. These large fragments correspond to one-fourth the *M. genitalium* genome. Again, these parts of the assembly operation required careful planning and execution.

The first stage involved assembling neighboring cassettes in groups of four (1–4, 5–9, 10–13, etc.) along with a piece of DNA from the bacterium *E. coli* to form pieces of the *M. genitalium* genome about 24,000 bp in size. This stage of the assembly yielded twenty-five fragments, 24,000 bp each.

The specific steps for this stage included:

1. Treatment of the 5,000 to 7,000 bp oligonucleotides with an enzyme (a 3' exonuclease). This enzyme removed pieces of DNA from each of the DNA strands that were part of the paired oligonucleotides to expose overlapping sequences;

2. Allowing the oligonucleotides to incubate for a period of time under exacting conditions so the neighboring cassettes could assemble;

3. Treatment of the assembled oligonucleotides with a polymerase and ligase to fill in the missing nucleotides (removed as a result of the exonuclease treatment) and link the assembled cassettes together.

The assembled cassettes were also joined to a piece of DNA from the bacterium *E. coli*, a different piece for each of the individual 24,000 bp cassettes.

This bacterial DNA allowed the researchers to import the DNA into *E. coli* so it could be cloned and amplified for the next stage.

After the DNA was cloned and amplified, the bacterial DNA was released from each 24,000 bp fragment. These fragments were now ready for the next stage of assembly.

Stage two involved joining three adjacent 24,000 bp pieces of DNA to form 72,000 bp fragments using the same enzymatic protocol as was used in the first stage of assembly. Stage three involved combining two adjacent 72,000 bp pieces to form fragments 144,000 bp in size.

At this point in the assembly, the researchers hit a wall. They discovered that the use of enzymes and *E. coli* was no longer feasible because this microbe couldn't handle larger DNA fragments. So to finish the genome assembly, the researchers turned to yeast.

In vivo *Recombination in Yeast*

The choice of the yeast *Saccharomyces cerevisiae* to complete the assembly of the *M. genitalium* genome was judicious. This organism has the capacity to take up extremely large pieces of foreign DNA when combined with a yeast-compatible DNA.

Instead of using enzymes in a test tube to complete the genome assembly, Venter's team used the yeast's own intracellular biochemical machinery to assemble the final pieces of the genome before cloning it. To their delight, the scientists discovered they didn't have to assemble the genome in a stepwise fashion, first joining together two quarter genomes then two half genomes. Instead, they could induce the yeast to take up all four pieces of the genome simultaneously to affect the assembly. The capacity of *S. cerevisiae* to take up several pieces of DNA and assemble them all at once has intrigued Venter's team with the possibility that added efficiencies could be built into their approach to total genome synthesis and assembly.

Recently Venter's team showed that stages two through four can be eliminated. Instead of relying on enzymatic recombination plus the cloning in *E. coli* to successively produce pieces of DNA 72,000 bp and 144,000 bp in size, scientists can use yeast to recombine the twenty-five 24,000 bp DNA fragments generated at stage one of the assembly process.[11]

The complete chemical synthesis and assembly of the entire *M. genitalium* genome affected by Venter's team at Synthetic Genomics Inc. is a tremendous scientific achievement. This work was voted by the editors of *Science* as one of the top ten scientific breakthroughs of 2008 because it paves the way to better understand the minimum requirements for life. It is also a key technology for creating novel, nonnatural life-forms with commercial and biomedical use. With this ability scientists are positioned to synthesize, starting from nucleotides, a completely artificial genome that consists of the minimal gene set identified when Venter's team subjected *M. genitalium* to knock-out experiments.

Introducing a New Genome

Once the synthetic genome is made, Venter's team will need a way to transfer it into a *Mycoplasma* cell that has had its genome deleted. Recent work suggests that, under the right conditions, this transfer is possible. Venter and his collaborators were able to induce the bacterium *Mycoplasma capricolum* to take up the entire genome isolated from the closely related microbe *Mycoplasma mycoides*. (Both of these bacteria are surface parasites, like *M. genitalium*.)

Once this transfer took place, the original *M. capricolum* genome seemed to disappear, yielding a microbe identical to *M. mycoides*.[12] The researchers referred to this newly discovered process as genome transplantation.

Molecular biologists have known for decades that bacterial cells can take up DNA by a variety of mechanisms. In all cases, however, the newly acquired DNA recombines with the host cell's genetic material instead of replacing it. To create an artificial cell using the approach adopted by Venter and his team, the synthetic DNA has to completely replace the recipient's DNA. A few investigators have tried to get bacteria to take up the genome of another microbe but, at best, have met with only partial success. These mixed results most likely stem from fundamental differences between the microbes.

Venter and his collaborators sidestepped this problem by carefully choosing the bacteria for the genome transplantation procedure. They selected *Mycoplasma capricolum* and *Mycoplasma mycoides* for a number of strategic reasons. These closely related microbes are more likely to be able to accept one another's genome. They also have small genomes, making their genetic material easier to handle. Larger genomes tend to be fragile and break during laboratory manipulations. Additionally, *Mycoplasma* cells have no cell wall, only a cell membrane, making it easier to get DNA into the cells.

Because no one had ever successfully transplanted a genome from one microbe to another, Venter's team had to go through a painstaking process of developing a procedure to do so. They discovered that getting *M. capricolum* to take up the isolated *M. mycoides* genome required special treatment of the cells.

The researchers developed a protocol for incubating the cells in a carefully designed solution containing controlled levels of salts before exposing the *M. capricolum* cells to DNA isolated from *M. mycoides*. This regime had to take place at a specific temperature and involved a process of lowering the solution's pH throughout the incubation period. The scientists also found that pretreatment of the cells with calcium chloride and polyethylene glycol was critical for genome transplantation. And they discovered they could optimize genome uptake by fine-tuning the cell levels and the concentration of DNA during the exposure time.

After exposing *M. capricolum* cells to *M. mycoides* DNA, the researchers grew the *M. capricolum* cells in the presence of the antibiotic tetracycline. A gene that encodes for an enzyme that protects the cell from the harmful effects of tetracycline was incorporated into the *M. mycoides* genome. Any cells that took up the *M. mycoides* genome would be able to grow in the presence of the antibiotic, thus providing the researchers with a means to select cells containing the transplanted genome.

To their surprise, Venter and his colleagues discovered that after the *M. mycoides* genome was assimilated by *M. capricolum*, the cells lost their native genetic material. By performing sequencing studies on the DNA isolated from the cells that grew in the presence of tetracycline, the researchers confirmed that the transformed cells harbored no *M. capricolum* genes. They also demonstrated that the proteins produced by the transformed cells were uniquely made by *M. mycoides*.

Venter's team soon discovered that this methodology lacks robustness, however. It failed to work when they tried using a synthetic genome or transplanting a *M. genitalium* genome into *M. pneumoniae*.

These difficulties have motivated the researchers to improve on their genome transplant methodology.[13] While working to enhance the genome transplant procedure, they also decided to develop procedures that will allow them to add genes to minimal genomes. Once again, they worked with *M. mycoides* and *M. capricolum* and were able to isolate the genome from *M. mycoides* after inserting specialized DNA sequences into it, transfer the genome into yeast, engineer the genome in yeast, isolate the engineered genome from yeast, alter it with a special enzymatic treatment that increased transplantation efficiency, and transplant it into *M. capricolum*, transforming this microbe into *M. mycoides*.

Though conceptually straightforward, this methodology relies on a clever strategy that borders on genius to make it work. It also requires a large team of highly skilled molecular biologists to perform detailed laboratory manipulations. It is safe to say that this methodology is intelligently designed and is dependent on intelligent agents to execute it.

Before the *M. mycoides* genome was isolated and transplanted into yeast, Venter's team added a piece of DNA into the genome (called a *vector*) containing a number of specialized yeast sequences. The vector enabled the yeast cells to recognize and replicate the bacterial genome and allowed the researchers to manipulate the *M. mycoides* genome inside of yeast. The vector also contained genes that imparted the bacterium with resistance to tetracycline, thereby enabling the scientists to select *M. mycoides* cells that had successfully incorporated the vector into their genome. The team grew the microbes in growth media that contained the antibiotic. Only the cells with the vector added to their genome can grow, ensuring that the researchers are working with the desired microbes.

After incorporating the vector into the *M. mycoides* genome, the researchers isolated it and used it to transfect yeast cells. Because of its specialized DNA sequences, the genome functioned as a plasmid (an extra piece of DNA that exists independently from yeast chromosomes) inside the yeast.

Introducing the *M. mycoides* genome into yeast served two critical purposes: First, the final steps for the synthesis of genomes take place inside yeast, so it allowed the researchers to develop a more realistic and practical method. And second, yeast provides an environment for the researchers to modify and engineer the genome. To illustrate this point, they deleted a gene from the *M. mycoides* genome through a sequence of carefully designed and executed steps.

Once they had engineered the *M. mycoides* genome in yeast, they isolated it and attempted to transplant it into *M. capricolum* cells. Initially, they were unsuccessful. They reasoned that perhaps *M. capricolum* restriction endonucleases were digesting the *M. mycoides* DNA, frustrating the process.

Restriction endonucleases cut both strands of DNA at specific nucleotide sequences, called restriction sites. These restriction endonucleases protect the cell from foreign DNA, like viruses, by cutting the invading DNA into fragments.

These vital biomolecules occur in conjunction with proteins (called DNA methylases) that attach methyl groups to the same DNA sequences that would normally be cleaved by restriction endonucleases. When these sequences are methylated, restriction endonucleases cannot cut them. Restriction sites of the bacterial DNA are methylated to protect the bacterial DNA from being chopped up by its own restriction endonucleases. Foreign DNA, however, is not afforded this same protection.

To test the idea that *M. capricolum* restriction endonucleases were interfering with the genome transplantation process, the team did three separate experiments. The first involved deleting the genes for restriction endonucleases from the *M. capricolum* genome, leaving it without protection against foreign DNA. The second and third involved treating the engineered *M. mycoides* genome isolated from yeast with cell extracts from *M. capricolum* and purified methylases from *M. capricolum*, respectively. Both treatments methylated the restriction sites of the engineered *M. mycoides* genome, protecting it from the *M. capricolum* restriction endonucleases.

In all three cases, the researchers were able to successfully transplant the engineered *M. mycoides* genome isolated from yeast into *M. capricolum*, and in many instances, the newly transplanted genome took over, transforming *M. capricolum* into *M. mycoides*. The team confirmed their success by sequencing the genome isolated from the cells that were transformed from *M. capricolum* into *M. mycoides*.

This work now sets the stage for Venter's team to generate a synthetic genome derived from the minimum gene set of *M. genitalium* and introduce it into a closely related *Mycoplasma* species, transforming it into an artificial life-form dubbed *Mycoplasma laboratorium*. To demonstrate their readiness, Venter and his team made a synthetic version of the *Mycoplasma mycoides* genome, starting with the four nucleotides that make up DNA, and transplanted it into *Mycoplasma capricolum*. The net result: *M. mycoides*, 2.0.[14]

Claiming the Gratitude

Venter and his associates are on the cusp of one of the biggest breakthroughs in the history of science: the creation of a completely synthetic life-form. Though this organism will be based on a minimum gene set derived from *M. genitalium*, it will be unlike anything that exists in nature. And this novel life-form is only the beginning.

The *M. laboratorium* genome will provide a platform for adding genes that will impart specific metabolic capabilities for biomedical and commercial use. It's easy to envision an entire ensemble of *M. laboratorium* strains, each one capable of unique metabolic properties. The possible therapeutic applications for such life-forms are nearly endless.

The new biotechnology pioneered by Venter and his team at Synthetic Genomics Inc. has the potential to transform our world in unimaginable ways. Far from producing a modern-day Frankensteinian nightmare, Venter's technology will truly benefit humanity. It's exciting to see what for so long seemed like science fiction become science reality.

Even more thrilling is the way Venter's work benefits those skeptical of the evolutionary paradigm—people who believe life must stem from the work of a Creator. The soon-to-be realized creation of *M. laboratorium* strengthens the case for intelligent design in two ways, and perhaps more.

Intelligence Required

Despite how conceptually simple the steps may seem to reengineer a life-form from the top down, the amount of intellectual effort put forth by Venter's team has been astounding. Each part of the process required careful planning and expert execution of laboratory procedures by highly trained chemists and molecular biologists. Remember that to assemble the chemically synthesized DNA pieces into increasingly larger DNA fragments required Venter's team to select the appropriate enzymes based on their catalytic properties, design the oligonucleotides (prior to the chemical synthesis step) so they would be compatible with the enzymes, and devise a reaction scheme that could yield the desired recombination product.

Venter and his colleagues even had to give careful thought to the organisms selected—the bacterium *E. coli* and the yeast *S. cerevisiae*—to facilitate genome assembly in the final stages. The scientists also had to deliberate about which bacteria to use in the genome transplantation experiments.

Additionally, these researchers depended on the accomplishments of the scientists who came before them. The technology to chemically synthesize oligonucleotides represents a remarkable technical accomplishment resulting from the dedicated efforts over the last half century of some of the best scientists in the world (including Nobel Laureates). Without these brilliant minds and remarkable achievements, Venter's team would have had no hope to carry out the total synthesis of the *M. genitalium* genome.

Given the effort that went into the synthesis of the total *M. genitalium* genome, it's hard to envision how unintelligent, undirected processes could have generated life from a prebiotic soup. Though not their intention, Venter and his colleagues have provided empirical evidence that life's components and, consequently, life itself must spring from the work of an intelligent Designer.

Over 200 years ago, Darwin's theory of evolution was advanced as a way to explain the mystery of mysteries—the origin of species. Darwin proposed that life began through natural selection. Who could have known that soon

Using Used Parts

As remarkable as it will be when Venter's team succeeds in creating artificial life, it's important to resist viewing their accomplishment as more than it is. Headlines describing this work give the impression that these researchers are generating life solely from building-block materials. In reality, when Venter and his colleagues succeed, they will *not* have made life from "scratch." Instead, they will have merely remodeled an existing life-form to generate a novel creature.

An analogy might help demonstrate what Venter's team will have accomplished when they create *M. laboratorium*. A microbe can be considered similar to an automobile. Venter's team is, in essence, functioning as curious auto mechanics who disabled the parts of an automobile engine, one at a time, to identify the components that must be present for it to run. (This imagery corresponds to the work Venter's team has done to determine the minimum gene set.)

Once the mechanics identified the minimal parts list, they bought the essential engine parts from a "parts store" and assembled them. (This step corresponds to the synthesis of the *M. genitalium* genome.) Then they removed the motor from a perfectly working car and put their minimalist engine into the vehicle to see if it would run. (This step corresponds to the introduction of the synthetic genome into a cell that had its genome removed.) When all these steps work, then the auto mechanics have not only confirmed that they properly identified the minimal engine parts but also produced a novel automobile.

after the 150th anniversary of his book, *The Origin of Species,* scientists would be on the verge of originating new species—not by undirected processes but rather by precise methods and procedures intelligently designed and expertly executed.

The Minimum Requirements

Venter's quest to make *M. laboratorium* began with an experiment designed to identify the minimal gene set and understand life's minimum complexity. As his team continues to hone in on the minimum number of genes and the essential biochemical systems necessary, life's complexity in its minimal form becomes all the more striking. The preparation of *M. laboratorium* will provide important confirmation that minimal life requires hundreds of genes. And this kind of complexity strongly indicates that life requires a Creator. (For more information, see my book *The Cell's Design.*)

Venter's quest for artificial life has brought the immense complexity of life in its bare essential form into focus. And as he and his collaborators make *M. laboratorium* and derive additional microbes from it, life's minimal complexity will become even more rigorously established.

Although much recent attention has focused on the efforts of Craig Venter and his collaborators at Synthetic Genomics Inc., they are not the only scientists trying to make nonnatural life-forms. A number of other molecular biologists and synthetic biologists have already succeeded at reengineering life from the top down. In fact, these efforts have been underway since the early 1970s. The modified life-forms produced through these efforts possess the capability to generate proteins and engage in metabolic activities they naturally would not. Although less ambitious than Venter's venture, this research is just as provocative. The next chapter explains why.

4

Treading in the Steps Already Marked

> So much has been done, exclaimed the soul of Frankenstein—more, far more, will I achieve: treading in the steps already marked, I will pioneer a new way, explore unknown powers, and unfold to the world the deepest mysteries of creation.
>
> Victor Frankenstein

When Frankenstein created his monster, he had help. True, he worked in secret—alone in his laboratory, day and night, refusing to let even his closest friends know what he was up to. But if it hadn't been for the scientists who went before him, he couldn't have discovered the "cause of generation and life" or the techniques to animate "lifeless matter." Each predecessor was his collaborator. Each provided small clues to the mystery.

So Much Has Been Done

Like Frankenstein, Craig Venter wouldn't be in position to create a novel life-form if not for the work of the scientists who preceded him. One such researcher is Hamilton Smith. His involvement in creating artificial life traces back to the late 1960s, when Venter was just starting college. Doing research at Johns Hopkins, Smith and his students studied restriction endonucleases, a newly discovered class of enzymes. At the time, Smith had no inkling of his work's significance for the entire discipline of molecular biology.

Endonucleases are a general class of enzymes that chew up DNA. Restriction endonucleases are a special subset that don't break down DNA indiscriminately. Instead, these enzymes cleave it at highly specific locations along the DNA chain. Hamilton Smith was the first to recognize this property, and subsequently he identified and described the cleavage site used by a restriction endonuclease in the bacterium *Haemophilus influenzae*. His concern was merely to do good biochemistry, nothing more.

About a decade later, much to his surprise, Smith along with Werner Arber and Daniel Nathans won the 1978 Nobel Prize in Physiology or Medicine for the discovery and applications of restriction endonucleases. These enzymes have nearly limitless utility as "tools" in molecular biology. Indispensible for DNA sequencing, gene cloning, and genetic engineering, these technologies ushered in the molecular biology revolution and became stepping stones to numerous breakthroughs, including the creation of artificial life in the lab.[1]

Sadly, for Smith the Nobel Prize became more of a curse than a blessing.[2] Upon hearing he'd won this coveted award, Smith became physically ill—not from excitement but from fear. His debilitating shyness kept him hiding in the lab, working on experiments instead of interacting with people. At Johns Hopkins, he struggled with being a teacher because he was so uncomfortable standing in front of students. Smith knew that as a Nobel Laureate, he'd become the focus of ongoing public attention, and he feared he couldn't handle the limelight.

Countless invitations to speak came, along with requests to serve on advisory boards for biotech and pharmaceutical companies. Students flocked to Smith's laboratory wanting to work for him.

These distractions became overwhelming. Because he was no longer able to focus on research, Smith's genius was lost. He rapidly devolved into an ordinary scientist who gradually became all but forgotten by the scientific community—until he met Craig Venter.

Though very different from each other, these two nonconformists struck up a friendship in the early 1990s after an encounter at a scientific conference. Their alliance has since become one of the most fruitful scientific collaborations of all time. Venter gave Smith an environment—first at The Institute for Genomic Research (TIGR), later at Celera, then with The J. Craig Venter Institute and Synthetic Genomics Inc.—that rekindled his genius.

Now Venter's right-hand man, Smith has been a key collaborator in: (1) developing the shotgun approach for whole genome sequencing; (2) applying this technique to sequencing the genomes of a host of organisms including human beings; (3) identifying the minimum gene set; and (4) generating the artificial bacterium, *Mycoplasma laboratorium*.

Hamilton Smith is one among countless other scientists who've paved the way for Venter. Since the late 1970s, molecular biologists and biochemists have used the tools and methods of molecular biology to engineer microbes, modifying their genetic makeup so these creatures can engage in biochemical activities that are unnatural for them. Most of this work involves isolating a single gene from one organism and adding it to the genome of a microbe, producing a genetic chimera. Nobel Laureate Paul Berg first accomplished this feat in 1972.

Shortly afterwards, Herbert Boyer and Stanley Cohen inserted the gene for human insulin into a bacterium. Their efforts coaxed the microbe to produce insulin at will. This genetically engineered protein now provides an important source of insulin for treatment of diabetes.

Today, these genetic manipulations have become routine and are the basis for the biotechnology industry. Though far less ambitious than the program Venter, Smith, and their collaborators are pursuing, this work still has the same outcome: the generation of life-forms that do not occur in nature.

So Much Yet to Come

Synthetic biologists have moved beyond simply adding isolated foreign genes into the genomes of microbes. These researchers are aggressively striving to introduce entire metabolic pathways into bacteria and yeast. In some cases, they are even attempting to engineer novel, unnatural metabolic systems. Researchers such as Peter Schultz have gone one step further: expanding the genetic code, perhaps the most important metabolic system in the cell, the system that governs protein manufacturing operations. By engineering an expanded genetic code, researchers can now make proteins containing non-natural amino acids, proteins not found in nature.

These top-down efforts carry important ramifications for biomedicine and practically endless commercial applications for agriculture and industry. At the same time, this work will help scientists develop a better understanding of life's basic chemical operations—another worthy goal.

While the work of Venter and his colleagues draws more attention, these equally important projects tend to fly below the radar. And attempts to re-engineer life are no less provocative. They too raise philosophical and theological questions about the limits of science and the origin and evolution of life. When a human gene was introduced into a bacterium for the first time in the 1970s, Paul Berg and other scientists called for a two-year moratorium on such work. They called for an examination of both ethical and safety issues involved in recombinant DNA (DNA combined from two different organisms). They wanted regulations and guidelines put in place before further work continued.

The science behind genetic engineering, the design of novel metabolic pathways, and the expansion of the genetic code warrants attention. So do the theological and philosophical implications. What does the creation of artificial life-forms through genetic engineering mean for the creation-evolution controversy? If scientists can engineer novel, nonnatural metabolic pathways and expand the genetic code does that negate the exceptional design of the genetic code found in nature? Is God no longer necessary to explain life's origin and diversity? Does man's achievement prove that metabolic systems and the genetic code can arise and change through natural evolutionary processes, or is there more here than meets the eye?

Material to Success

Compared to Craig Venter's big-science operation or smaller-scale attempts to reengineer microbes with novel metabolic pathways, the insertion of a single gene into an organism's genome now seems fairly trivial. These procedures have become almost turnkey. But incorporating isolated genes into an organism's genome became routine only because many researchers worked tirelessly over the last few decades to perfect these methods. In reality, genetic engineering requires a well-developed experimental strategy and careful execution of that strategy in the lab. This capability ultimately stems from the insight of molecular biologists who recognized the utility of enzymes, such as restriction endonucleases and ligases, and of extrachromosomal pieces of DNA found in bacteria.[3]

The Genetic Engineering Tool Kit

Several decades ago, microbiologists discovered within bacteria small circular pieces of DNA (plasmids) that exist independently from their chromosomes. Plasmids harbor a variety of genes, some associated with antibiotic resistance. Bacteria can exchange plasmid DNA with each other, and through this conjugation process, drug-resistant microbes can transfer the genes responsible for antibiotic resistance to other bacteria.

Molecular biologists soon realized that if they could splice genes into plasmid DNA, they could introduce novel genes into microorganisms. This laboratory technique would allow scientists to genetically engineer bacteria with the capacity to produce proteins they couldn't otherwise produce. When restriction endonucleases were discovered, Daniel Nathans recognized that these enzymes provided the tools necessary to insert pieces of foreign DNA into plasmids. For this profound insight, Nathans shared the Nobel Prize with Smith.

Strategic Cuts

Shortly after identifying restriction endonucleases, biochemists learned that these proteins play a role in protecting bacteria from viruses. When viruses inject their DNA into the cell, the viral DNA takes over the cell's machinery, forcing the microbe to make more copies of the virus using genes housed within the viral DNA.

Because restriction endonucleases cut up this DNA at specific restriction sites, the cell's machinery can distinguish between the invading viral DNA and DNA belonging to the bacterium. This ability permits these remarkable enzymes to defend bacteria against invading pieces of foreign DNA without destroying their own in the process. If the restriction endonucleases instead cleaved the DNA randomly, bacteria would not be protected.

Bacterial DNA also has restriction sites. But these sites are methylated (methyl groups attached to the DNA) by enzymes known as methylases. (Each restriction endonuclease has a corresponding methylase.) Protective methyl groups prevent the restriction sites in the bacterial genome from being cleaved. Viral DNA is not protected and thus is vulnerable to attack by the restriction endonucleases.

A large number of restriction endonucleases have been isolated from a host of bacteria. Each individual type cleaves DNA at a unique restriction site. This ensemble of enzymes produces a tool kit used by molecular biologists for genetic engineering, allowing them to select the right restriction enzyme for the job.

When restriction endonucleases cut DNA, they form "sticky ends." Because the cleavage of the DNA double helix doesn't take place at the exact same spot for each individual strand, one strand ends up longer than the other. This overhang creates a sticky end that will match another one produced when the same restriction endonuclease cuts another piece of DNA.

This property allows molecular biologists to use a restriction endonuclease to isolate DNA from one organism and combine it with DNA from another organism that's been treated with the identical restriction enzyme. Once the sticky ends match up, molecular biologists use ligase (an enzyme) to seal the DNA molecules together, forming recombinant DNA.

Introducing a Gene into a Bacterium

When molecular biologists want to insert a gene into a microbe with the goal of expanding its biochemical capability, the first step is to select the appropriate restriction endonuclease that can cleave sequences upstream and downstream from the target gene. Once isolated from its natural source, the gene needs to be spliced into the appropriate plasmid DNA. A plasmid is chosen that will be readily taken up by the host bacterium.

To ensure that the restriction endonuclease will cut the plasmid of choice, molecular biologists genetically engineer it to include a synthetic piece of DNA with a sequence that includes restriction sites for a large number of restriction endonucleases. This engineered portion of the plasmid is called a polylinker. Its specially designed DNA sequence permits researchers to insert practically any gene into the plasmid using any restriction endonuclease depending on which restriction sites are available adjacent to the gene.

Molecular biologists also engineer the plasmid by introducing DNA sequences that control, at will, the inserted gene's expression. These promoter and operator sequences allow the cell's machinery to read the information harbored in the inserted gene and use it to make proteins. Promoters and operators also permit molecular biologists to turn genes "on" and "off" at appropriate times. In this way the genetically engineered microbe can operate as a factory controlled by biotechnologists, producing desired protein products as the bacterium grows and divides in fermentation vessels.

Researchers also ensure the plasmid has an origin of replication. This special sequence of DNA allows the bacterium's biochemical machinery to make copies of the plasmid during cell division. As the cell divides, so does the plasmid that carries the gene of interest—partitioning between the daughter cells. If the plasmids did not divide along with the cell, eventually the inserted gene would be diluted out of the bacterial population.

In addition, molecular biologists genetically engineer plasmids to carry a gene that makes them resistant to antibiotics. Incorporating an antibiotic resistant gene into the plasmid allows scientists to select the bacteria that have taken up the plasmid containing the foreign gene. Once a plasmid has been engineered, molecular biologists expose it to the host bacteria. Some take up the plasmid, others don't. By growing the microbes in the presence of an antibiotic, only those cells that have taken up the plasmid with the gene for antibiotic resistance will grow. So lab workers can know they are using bacteria with the inserted gene.

An Insatiable Desire for More

Genetic engineering involves far too many details to present here. Nor is there enough space to describe some of the specific laboratory manipulations associated with each step of the genetic engineering process. Suffice it to say, the preparation of recombinant DNA and the incorporation of it into a host microbe depend on highly skilled laboratory workers carrying out exacting procedures in the lab. This brief overview of the procedures for introducing novel genes into bacteria should help convey the ingenuity that undergirds what has now become a routine laboratory protocol—an operation that modifies microbes to behave in nonnatural ways.

While biotechnologists want to introduce single genes into bacteria to get these microbes to produce proteins with biomedical or commercial use, scientists want to use bacteria to do even more. In recent years, molecular biologists have moved beyond inserting single genes into bacteria. They are now racing to reengineer entire metabolic pathways.

Metabolism involves reactions of small molecules. For example, compounds such as glucose and other sugar molecules are broken down into smaller molecules to provide energy for the cell's operations. Multiple metabolic reactions produce small molecules used by the cell's machinery as building blocks to assemble proteins, DNA, the RNAs, and cell membrane bilayers. Some metabolic activities prepare materials the cell no longer needs (cellular waste) for elimination. Other reactions detoxify materials that could be harmful to the cell.

By engineering novel metabolic pathways, synthetic biologists can enable microbes to produce a far greater variety of materials than would be possible by introducing just a single gene (into bacteria) that produces a single protein. In recent years enough effort has gone into this area of synthetic biology to make commercial processes using metabolically reengineered microbes a reality.[4]

The potential benefits of metabolic engineering abound. Developing renewable energy and new medicines represent just two among many. These examples help demonstrate the intellectual effort and careful laboratory manipulation required to successfully reengineer metabolic pathways.

Pioneering a New Way

In the ongoing quest for affordable sources of renewable energy to power automobiles, ethanol has been considered a possible fuel. However, its use stirs controversy for several reasons:

1. Ethanol can't serve as a total replacement for gasoline. It has to be blended with petrol.
2. The cost of ethanol production exceeds the value of the energy it provides.
3. Because corn is one of the chief sources of ethanol, its use raises concerns about a reduced food supply and increased costs.
4. Some researchers have suggested switch grasses and celluloses as better options, but cost-effectiveness has yet to be determined.

These problems have led to consideration of other alternatives. One possibility is the use of alcohols with five or more carbons (C5 alcohols). C5 to C8 aliphatic alcohols are more similar to gasoline than ethanol (which is a C2 alcohol). These compounds are also much less water soluble, a characteristic that makes them easier to distill from water. (Ethanol has high water solubility.)

One approach to generating C5 to C8 aliphatic alcohols in an environmentally friendly and cost-effective way is to use microbes. Some bacteria have metabolic pathways that produce alcohols, but the compounds generated are smaller than the desired C5 materials. Recently researchers engineered a novel, nonnatural metabolic system in the bacterium *Escherichia coli* capable of producing nonnatural alcohols promising for use as alternative fuels.[5]

Relentless Efforts

Metabolic processes within the cell's interior are often organized into a series of chemical reactions that transform a starting compound into a final product via a series of small, stepwise chemical changes. Each step along a metabolic route is facilitated by an enzyme that mediates the chemical transformation.

Reengineering metabolic pathways to produce nonnatural materials such as C5 alcohols involves hurdling numerous obstacles. One difficulty stems from the limited set of metabolic pathways and metabolites found in living systems. This constraint gives biotechnologists only a few ways to use biochemistry to make nonnatural materials, but bioengineers have taken advantage of these few metabolic pathways by feeding nonnatural ingredients to cells.

Even this approach has limitations, however. Due to the specificity of the enzymes that catalyze metabolic routes, many nonnatural compounds won't interact with the metabolic machinery in a way that chemically transforms them into the desired product. For example, the Ehrlich pathway is the only well-studied route known to form aliphatic alcohols. While it can be exploited to make alcohols by feeding amino acids to microbes, this metabolic pathway generates only alcohols smaller than C5.

To overcome this barrier, researchers faced the need to find a way to expand metabolic pathways, thereby extending the chemistry and the range of metabolites that can be processed—an extremely daunting task. Metabolic pathways operate using the collective function of multiple enzymes working sequentially in conjunction with one another. So the task of building upon the existing chemistry of a metabolic pathway calls for reengineering the entire enzyme collective.

Diligent Experimentation

To create a novel pathway capable of generating alcohols larger than C5 in *E. coli*, researchers relied on a common metabolic process to add carbon atoms to metabolites. Scientists reasoned they could take advantage of certain enzymes that use acetyl-CoA as a substrate to make a C6 alcohol. Existing metabolic pathways such as the tricarboxylic cycle, glyoxylate cycle, mevalonate pathway, and leucine biosynthesis use the compound acetyl-CoA as the source for carbon addition.

Researchers noted that the compound 2-keto-isovalerate could be converted to the larger compound 2-keto-isocaproate through a three-step elongation pathway that makes use of acetyl-CoA. This reaction sequence is catalyzed by the enzymes dubbed LeuA, LeuC and LeuD, and LeuB (which are 2-isopropylmalate synthase, isopropylmalate isomerase complex, and 3-isopropylmalate dehydrogenase, respectively). Scientists reasoned that these enzymes could generate 2-keto-4-methylhexanoate from 2-keto-isovalerate. Once 2-keto-4-methylhexanoate formed, they recognized that this compound could be converted to 3-methyl-1-pentanol (a C6 alcohol) by the sequential action of the enzymes KIVD (2-keto-isovalerate decarboxylase) from the bacterium *Lactococcus lactis* and ADH6 (alcohol dehydrogenase) from the yeast *Saccharomyces cerevisiae*. To make the starting material, 2-keto-isovalerate, scientists speculated that they could use the intrinsic metabolic capacity of *E. coli* to make 2-keto-3-methylvalerate, a related compound.

With this strategy worked out, the researchers redesigned some of the key enzymes in the nonnaturally constructed metabolic pathway. They made strategic use of structural data for the enzyme and substrates along with detailed knowledge of the reaction mechanisms to rationally replace amino acids in the binding and active sites of KIVD and LeuA. Substitutions were made so the reengineered enzymes would preferentially operate on the nonnatural metabolic intermediates 2-keto-4-methylhexanoate and 2-keto-isovalerate.

After mapping out the novel metabolic pathway on paper and producing these reengineered versions of LeuA and KIVD, researchers went into the lab to try out their newly devised capability to generate C6 alcohols via *E. coli*. First they constructed three synthetic plasmids (circular pieces of DNA that can harbor genes and be taken up by bacteria). These plasmids contained sets of genes with the information to make the enzymes involved in the production of C5 to C8 alcohols. Two of the plasmids were comprised of genes already present in the *E. coli* genome. The third contained novel genes that encoded the proteins LeuA, LeuB, LeuC and LeuD, KIVD, and ADH6.

Extra genes present in the bacterium resulted in the desired overproduction of enzymes needed to generate key metabolites for the production of the C6 alcohol. By introducing two plasmids with genes already found in *E. coli,* the researchers ensured that most of the foodstuff consumed by the bacteria (glucose) would be metabolized to produce the C6 alcohol.

The plasmids were also designed to include a promoter. This on-off control switch allowed the researchers to turn on the plasmid genes by feeding the bacteria with a specific sugar (lactose). Using this approach, the researchers succeeded in producing relatively high levels of the C6 alcohol. This work opens up the possibility of using bioengineering of metabolic pathways in microbes as a way to generate alternative sources of energy. At the same time, it illuminates the ingenuity required to introduce a novel, nonnatural metabolic pathway into a bacterium.

Synthetic Biology to the Rescue

Drug-resistant infectious agents present as much concern as the energy crisis. Particularly troubling is malaria. *Plasmodium falciparum* threatens three hundred to five hundred million people around the world each year, killing about one million annually. Increasingly, medical providers encounter drug-resistant strains of the malaria parasite.[6] However, newly developed combination therapies employing artemisinin can kill these strains at nearly a 100 percent rate.

Artemisinin is a natural product extracted from sweet wormwood. This compound is in short supply and extremely costly, thus beyond the reach of the world's poorest populations. Chemical synthesis of this compound remains difficult and expensive.

In the face of this challenge, a team of researchers headed by Jay Keasling of the University of California, Berkeley, turned to synthetic biology. They genetically engineered yeast to produce artemisinin via a nonnatural metabolic pathway.[7] The yeast, *Saccharomyces cerevisiae*, naturally possesses a way to produce the compound farnesyl pyrophosphate. Researchers use this compound as the starting point to make artemisinin.

The metabolic route, the mevalonate pathway, yields farnesyl pyrophosphate. Starting with acetyl CoA, three enzymatic reactions sequentially add four carbon units and hydrogen (to acetyl CoA) to produce mevalonate. In turn, mevalonate produces farnesyl pyrophosphate through a sequence of five enzyme-catalyzed reactions.

In yeast, an enzyme called squalene synthase normally converts farnesyl pyrophosphate to squalene, which enters into a metabolic pathway that leads to the production of sterols. For their purposes, the researchers needed to prevent squalene from forming, or else it would siphon away the farnesyl pyrophosphate essential to making artemisinin. So they added a promoter sequence to the gene that codes for squalene synthase. By adding the amino acid methionine to the yeast, they could switch off (or turn down), at will, the activity of the gene for squalene synthase.

The researchers also wanted to enhance the production of farnesyl pyrophosphate so the modified yeast strain could make as much artemisinin as possible. To do this they introduced a genetically engineered copy of 3-hydroxy-3-methyl-glutaryl-coenyzmye A reductase into the yeast. This protein is a key enzyme in the pathway that produces farnesyl pyrophosphate. This extra copy increased production of the key compound.

In addition, researchers added genes from the sweet wormwood plant. The first gene incorporated into *S. cerevisiae* was amorphadiene synthase. In sweet wormwood, this enzyme normally converts farnesyl pyrophosphate into amorphadiene. This reaction is the first in the metabolic pathway that makes artemisinin.

The researchers also needed to identify other genes in sweet wormwood responsible for making artemisinin from amorphadiene. To do this, they analyzed a database containing DNA sequences of genes that code for enzymes that could conceivably oxidize amorphadiene. Once the desired gene was identified, researchers cloned it, producing enzyme molecules and confirming the enzyme's biochemical properties.

Scientists then introduced this gene into the yeast and engineered it to be under the control of a promoter that turns on the genes when the yeast is exposed to the sugar galactose. This regulation allowed lab workers to control the production of artemisinin.

Remarkably, these genetically engineered strains produced the same amount of artemisinin per unit biomass of yeast as the sweet wormwood plants. The big difference: the yeast only took a few days to grow instead of several months.

This work promises to make artemisinin combination therapies a real possibility. It also provides a way to decouple artemisinin production from the vagaries of climactic variability, ensuring a reliable supply of the drug.

The ability of researchers to engineer *E. coli* for the generation of C5 to C8 alcohols and *S. cerevisiae* for the production of artemisinin rests on work started in the 1960s by Hamilton Smith and other researchers. Both studies exemplify the striking ingenuity and strenuous effort required by genetic engineering. Research teams used their understanding of the metabolic capabilities of living systems to carefully map out plausible pathways. Using detailed knowledge of chemistry, they redesigned key enzymes from a variety of sources to engineer a new pathway. Highly trained researchers carefully selected appropriate microorganisms to harbor the exquisitely designed nonnatural metabolic routes. This elite group of men and women also cleverly conceived and constructed the plasmids to transfer the necessary genes and regulate their activity in *E. coli* and *S. cerevisiae*.

If not for decades of accumulated knowledge and insight, this ability to engineer novel, nonnatural metabolic pathways wouldn't exist. The ability to reengineer organisms to carry out novel, nonnatural metabolic processes is a truly remarkable scientific achievement. The significance of this type of work for developing biomedical and biotechnology applications cannot be overemphasized. The prospect of reengineering the cell's protein manufacturing machinery by expanding the genetic code is even more astounding. Provocative from the standpoint of what humankind can accomplish, this lab work also has implications for the question of life's origin.

Exploring the Unknown

To appreciate the scientific effort to expand the genetic code, a basic understanding of the code's structure and role in governing protein synthesis is essential. At the same time, this background helps us appreciate the ingenuity of researchers in developing laboratory protocols that allow life's vital metabolic systems to be reengineered. (For readers unfamiliar with biochemistry, the appendix of this book provides help in understanding the ensuing discussion.)

The Genetic Code

For all intents and purposes, the genetic code is universal among all living organisms. Cells use this set of rules to relate the nucleotide sequences of DNA to the specific amino acid sequences that make up proteins.

Combinations of three consecutive nucleotides (codons) form the fundamental genetic coding units. Sixty-four codons comprise the entire genetic code. Because the code needs to specify twenty amino acids, some of the codons are redundant, which means different ones may signify for the same amino acid. Up to six different codons specify some amino acids—others use just one. Table 4.1 presents the universal genetic code.

TABLE 4.1
The Genetic Code

5' End	U		C		A		G	
U	UUU	Phe	UCU	Ser	UAU	Tyr	UGU	Cys
	UUC	Phe	UCC	Ser	UAC	Tyr	UGC	Cys
	UUA	Leu	UCA	Ser	UAA	End	UGA	End
	UUG	Leu	UCG	Ser	UAG	End	UGG	Trp
C	CUU	Leu	CCU	Pro	CAU	His	CGU	Arg
	CUC	Leu	CCC	Pro	CAC	His	CGC	Arg
	CUA	Leu	CCA	Pro	CAA	Gln	CGA	Arg
	CUG	Leu	CCG	Pro	CAG	Gln	CGG	Arg
A	AUU	Ile	ACU	Thr	AAU	Asn	AGU	Ser
	AUC	Ile	ACC	Thr	AAC	Asn	AGC	Ser
	AUA	Ile	ACA	Thr	AAA	Lys	AGA	Arg
	AUG Met(Start)		ACG	Thr	AAG	Lys	AGG	Arg
G	GUU	Val	GCU	Ala	GAU	Asp	GGU	Gly
	GUC	Val	GCC	Ala	GAC	Asp	GGC	Gly
	GUA	Val			GAA	Glu	GGA	Gly
	GUG Val(Start)		GCA	Ala	GAG	Glu	GGG	Gly
			GCG	Ala				

Note: The first nucleotide of the coding triplet begins at the 5' end of the sequence, as seen in the left-most column. The nucleotides in the second position can be read from the row across the top of the table. The nucleotide in each codon's third position (the 3' end) can be read within each box. For example, the two codons, 5' UUU and 5' UUC, which specify phenylalanine (abbreviated Phe), are listed in the box located at the top left corner of the table.

Some nucleotide triplets, called stop codons or nonsense codons, always occur at the end of the gene, informing the protein manufacturing machinery where the protein chain ends. These codons don't specify any amino acids. (For example, the codon UGA is a stop codon.) On the other hand, start codons play a dual role in the genetic code. These codons not only encode amino acids but also "tell" the cell where a protein begins. For example, the codon GUG not only encodes the amino acid valine but also specifies the starting point of the protein chain.

Protein Synthesis

The genetic code governs the metabolic process that produces proteins. The cell's protein-manufacturing machinery consists of three main components: messenger RNA (mRNA), transfer RNA (tRNA), and ribosomes. All interact to form an assembly line process that generates proteins.

Transfer RNA (tRNA), like mRNA, consists of a single RNA strand. Unlike mRNA, tRNA adopts a precise three-dimensional structure critical for protein synthesis.[8] As the single tRNA strand folds into its three-dimensional shape, four segments of the tRNA strand interact. This structure gives tRNA a clover leaf shape in two dimensions (see figure 4.1). Bending the clover-leaf and twisting the paired regions yields the overall L-shaped architecture.

Transfer RNA molecules bind amino acids and carry them to the ribosomes.[9] This process makes the amino acids—the starting materials for protein production—available to the cell's protein-producing machinery. Each of the twenty amino acids used by the cell to form proteins is attached to at least one corresponding tRNA molecule. An activating enzyme, called an aminoacyl-tRNA synthetase, links each amino acid to its specific tRNA carrier. Each tRNA and amino acid partnership has a corresponding activating enzyme specific to that pair.

The amino acid binds to one end of the tRNA "L." The other end of the tRNA (the anticodon) "reads" the manufacturing instructions found in mRNA. An anticodon consists of a three-nucleotide sequence that pairs with a codon's complementary nucleotide sequence in mRNA.

Each tRNA's anticodon matches a codon in mRNA. Since each tRNA binds a single and specific amino acid, the codon-anticodon pairs serve as the cellular hardware that implements the manufacturing instructions for protein production.

Ribosomes also play a central role in protein synthesis. These subcellular entities bind and manage the interactions between tRNA and mRNA.[10] Ribosomes also catalyze or assist the chemical reactions that form the bonds joining amino acids together in protein chains.

Ribosomes consist of proteins and RNA molecules called ribosomal RNA (rRNA). Two subunits of different sizes combine to form a functional ribosome. In bacteria, the large subunit contains two rRNA molecules and about thirty different protein molecules. The small subunit consists of a single rRNA molecule and about twenty proteins. The rRNA molecules act as scaffolding to organize the myriad ribosomal proteins.

FIGURE 4.1

Structure of tRNA

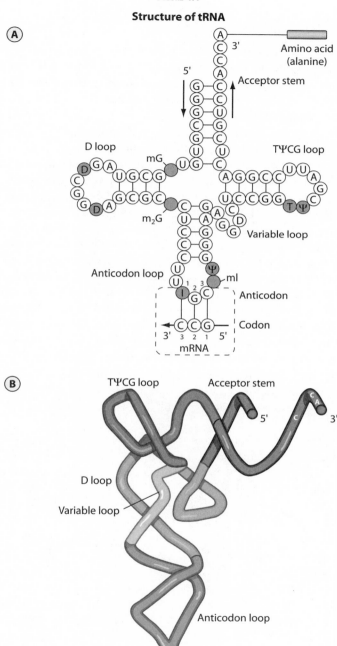

The single tRNA strand folds to form its three-dimensional shape when four segments of tRNA pair. This pairing produces a cloverleaf shape in two dimensions. Bending the clover leaf and twisting the paired regions yields an upside-down L-shaped architecture.

Expanding the Genetic Code

Even though the genetic code specifies only twenty amino acids, proteins contain well over one hundred different amino acid residues. These residues (which expand the chemistries available to proteins) are derived from the twenty amino acids in this way: after amino acids are incorporated into the protein chain at the ribosome, enzymes chemically alter some of them at specific locations in the protein chain, generating novel amino acids as a result. This process is called posttranslational modification.

Synthetic biologists and biochemists also want to make artificial proteins with more than twenty amino acids. Additional amino acids would permit scientists to make novel, nonnatural proteins with chemical properties that extend beyond what's possible in nature. Instead of chemically modifying amino acids that have already been incorporated into the protein chains, synthetic biologists hope to reengineer microbes in such a way that their genetic code specifies nonnatural amino acids in addition to the natural twenty.

So far, synthetic biologists have been able to modify separately the genetic code in *E. coli*, yeast, and mammal cells so that more than thirty nonnatural amino acids are incorporated into proteins produced by the cell's machinery. These expanded genetic codes have been engineered by a variety of means. The following discussion outlines only one of them. For interested readers, descriptions of the other methods can be found in the scientific literature.[11]

The efforts to expand the genetic code are quite involved. Even a simplified overview of the methodology can be demanding for the uninitiated. For those readers that become bogged down in the details, skip the "Stretch!" section on pages 64–65.

This protocol has been used to separately expand the genetic code to recognize over thirty different nonnatural amino acids. Researchers have already shown that this technology can be used to engineer novel proteins with chemical capabilities that extend well beyond what is currently possible with the twenty naturally occurring amino acids.[12] The potential utility of this biotechnology for humanity's benefit seems almost limitless.

Cells that possess an expanded genetic code are truly artificial life-forms that have people talking about "life as we don't know it." But in the midst of all the exhilaration and anticipation of what this new synthetic biology milestone could lead to, it's important to recognize all the effort that went into reaching it. As even this summary overview makes clear, expanding the genetic code of an organism requires detailed understanding of the molecular biology and biochemistry of protein synthesis, advanced working knowledge of the "tool kit" and protocols associated with genetic engineering, innovative techniques, and elegant strategies. Such insight represents the hard work of generations of scientists, each building on the work of their predecessors.

Creation's Deepest Mysteries Unfold

Well before the vision for *Mycoplasma laboratorium* was cast, molecular biologists had already created artificial life-forms from the top down using genetic engineering. Though not nearly as ambitious as the work by Venter and his team, since the early 1970s scientists have been successfully introducing foreign genes into a whole host of organisms. These inserted genes result in creatures that make proteins not produced naturally.

This work set the stage for much more extensive genetic engineering. Synthetic biologists can now genetically engineer organisms so extensively as to produce nonnatural metabolic systems encoded by several genes, not just a single isolated piece of DNA. Perhaps the pinnacle of achievements in genetic engineering has been the expansion of the genetic code for production of organisms with the capacity to manufacture proteins containing nonnatural amino acids.

As someone persuaded by the evidence that life must stem from the hand of a Creator, I find these top-down efforts to modify life and create nonnatural life-forms intriguing. This work provides empirical demonstration that unless intelligent agents are directly involved, life cannot undergo any significant transformation at the biochemical level.

If not for work based on decades of accumulated knowledge, brilliant ingenuity, and strategic planning toward a specific goal, researchers would never have been able to design novel, nonnatural metabolic pathways or add to the genetic code. Even the engineering of *E. coli* to make C5 to C8 alcohols represents a scientific marvel.

And yet, researchers didn't create this metabolic pathway from scratch; rather, they pieced it together using modified enzymes from a variety of sources. The same is true for the reengineering of yeast to make artemisinin and the efforts to expand the genetic code. It's fair to say that these novel metabolic processes were intelligently designed—or more appropriately, intelligently modified. In fact, biochemists describe this type of work as rational design.

Configuring artificial metabolic systems raises provocative questions: Is it reasonable to assume that life's chemistry originated and evolved through undirected processes given the heroic effort that went into reengineering existing metabolic systems to make C5 to C8 alcohols or artemisinin? Does the creativity that undergirds the work to expand the genetic code suggest that the universal genetic code originated by undirected means? On the contrary, to conclude that biochemical systems owe their existence to the direct involvement of intelligent agency seems more rational to me.

Still, many scientists (appropriately) search for some type of naturally occurring mechanism by which metabolic pathways emerged. What helps spur

Stretch!

To expand the genetic code, synthetic biologists must modify tRNA molecules and their corresponding aminoacyl-tRNA synthetases so that the enzymes attach nonnatural amino acids to the tRNA molecule with high fidelity. They also have to reassign a codon so it recognizes the modified tRNA molecule.

Additionally, researchers need to ensure the modified tRNA is not accidently recognized by the other aminoacyl-tRNA synthetases in the cell. If it is, the modified tRNA will bind the wrong amino acid. Scientists also need to ensure the modified aminoacyl-tRNA synthetase doesn't add the nonnatural amino acid to other tRNA molecules normally associated with one of the twenty amino acids specified by the genetic code.

One reason molecular biologists have focused these intricate engineering efforts on the bacterium E. coli is that this microbe's genetics and protein synthetic machinery are well understood. Plus, these researchers know how to manipulate its genetic systems.

To expand E. coli's genetic code to include nonnatural amino acids, some researchers use a stop codon called an amber codon. This coding triplet doesn't specify an amino acid. Instead, the amber codon tells the cell's machinery where the gene, and consequently the protein, ends. E. coli has a special type of tRNA, called a suppressor tRNA, that recognizes and binds to the amber codon. This tRNA doesn't normally latch on to any amino acids. By binding to the amber codon, the suppressor tRNA prevents other tRNAs from inadvertently binding to the stop codon, a quality control measure that ensures proteins are made without error.

Researchers have learned how to prevent unwanted cross talk between the engineered cell components (tRNAs and aminoacyl-tRNA synthetases) and those occurring naturally. They need to use suppressor tRNAs from another microbe. The best source of these alternates turns out to be organisms belonging to life's Archaea domain. Archaeans are single-celled microbes that superficially resemble bacteria but differ fundamentally at the biochemical level.

The strategy to expand the genetic code in E. coli involves producing a collection of tRNAs that are variants of a suppressor tRNA isolated from an archaean. This collection of tRNAs is referred to as a library. The genes for these tRNAs are individually incorporated into separate plasmids, and the entire library is introduced into E. coli. These plasmids are randomly taken up by the bacterial cells.

Additionally, all the E. coli cells are coaxed into taking up a plasmid containing a mutated gene for the enzyme barnase, a protein that breaks down tRNA molecules. The barnase gene is altered to contain the amber codon in the middle of its sequence.

them on are numerous examples of microbes that appear to have spontaneously undergone changes that impart new metabolic capabilities.[13]

Perhaps one of the most interesting and high-profile cases is the evolution of the ability to digest nylon by the microbe *Flavobacterium* sp. KI72.[14] Researchers have discovered forms of this bacterium in the wastewater of plants that

This inserted codon prevents the dismantler protein from being produced. If any of the naturally occurring aminoacyl-tRNA synthetases accidently adds an amino acid to any of the mutated suppressor tRNA molecules, then the mutated barnase gene will be expressed and the protein will cleave RNA inside the cell and kill it. The only cells that can survive contain suppressor tRNA molecules that won't interact with the naturally occurring *E. coli* charging enzymes.

These surviving cells are, in turn, exposed to plasmids harboring a mutated gene for the protein β-lactamase. This enzyme protects the cells from the harmful effects of antibiotics such as penicillin. Like the mutated barnase gene, the β-lactamase gene is altered to contain the amber codon in the middle of its sequence. This protein will be produced only if the modified tRNA binds an amino acid by the archaean aminoacyl-tRNA synthetase.

At this point, the modified *E. coli* microbes are grown in the presence of an antibiotic. If their tRNA is recognized by the archaean aminoacyl-tRNA synthetase, they survive.

The next step in this protocol involves altering the archaean aminoacyl-tRNA synthetase so it attaches a nonnatural amino acid to the modified tRNA. To do this, a library of modified archaean aminoacyl-tRNA synthetases is created. These libraries are introduced into *E. coli* along with a plasmid containing a mutant gene for the enzyme chloramphenicol acetyltransferase. This protein deactivates the antimicrobial agent chloramphenicol. The amber codon is inserted into the DNA sequence of chloramphenicol acetyltransferase gene. A pool of the nonnatural amino acids is made available for the modified archaean aminoacyl-tRNA synthetases. Those charging enzymes that can attach the nonnatural amino acid to the modified tRNA will be able to produce chloramphenicol acetyltransferase, allowing cells that harbor these modified biomolecules to grow in the presence of this antimicrobial agent.

Those cells that survive this stage of the procedure are subjected to another challenge. In this case, a plasmid harboring an altered barnase gene is inserted into the bacteria with an amber codon in the middle of the gene's DNA sequence. These cells are grown without any of the nonnatural amino acid available. If the modified archaean aminoacyl-tRNA synthetase accidently attaches one of the naturally occurring twenty amino acids to the modified tRNA, the barnase gene is produced and the cell dies. This filter prevents the modified archaean aminoacyl-tRNA synthetase from transferring the wrong amino acid to its tRNA partner. These last two steps are repeated several times to fine-tune the operation of the archaean aminoacyl-tRNA synthetase.

manufacture nylon. This synthetic polymer didn't exist before 1935. At some point between nylon's first use and the mid-1970s, these bacteria acquired the ability to use the components of nylon as a food source. It turns out this acquired metabolic capability resulted from the spontaneous emergence of two enzymes that can break down by-products of nylon production.

Though provocative, this evolutionary event falls short of supporting the notion that all metabolic systems can be explained as the outworking of evolutionary processes. In nearly all similar examples to date, including those cited in the references that follow, the expanded metabolic capabilities resulted from mutations in a single gene that either altered the amount of protein produced or modified a preexisting protein to give it new catalytic range or function. In the case of the nylon-eating microbe, a frameshift mutation—an extremely rare event—appears responsible for the generation of the two enzymes.

Such changes are not surprising given the large populations of microbes in both nature and in the laboratory, where evolutionary changes are detected under controlled conditions. Mutations are almost always harmful or neutral. Seldom are they beneficial. In the case of frameshifts, these mutations almost always destroy the function of the protein encoded by the gene. However, if *enough* opportunities are provided, random mutations (even those as devastating as frameshift mutations) can generate functional proteins by chance.

These probabilities apply in nearly every example of the evolutionary emergence of new metabolic capabilities. Yet more often than not, the newly acquired metabolic capabilities amount to little more than minor modifications to preexisting biochemical pathways. To say it another way, these changes are examples of biochemical microevolution.

Frequently, the new enzymes responsible for new capabilities function suboptimally. For example, the two enzymes that make nylon components available to the feed cell operate with much less efficiency than typical enzymes. Still, the ability to digest nylon components, even if inefficiently, represents an advantage for organisms living in wastewater loaded with these compounds.

Spontaneous emergence of new metabolic capabilities observed in nature or in the lab is a far cry from engineering microbes to make C5 to C8 alcohols, produce artemisinin, or expand the genetic code. To my knowledge, no one has ever seen the spontaneous emergence of a completely novel metabolic pathway. Such an event would require the evolution of an ensemble of new genes appropriately regulated to express the right numbers and kinds of proteins so the pathway operates more effectively in the larger context of the cell's biochemical operations. As for expansion of the genetic code, the multitudinous difficulties seem sufficient evidence that this set of rules must be the product of a mind.

Nevertheless, many scientists maintain there is nothing particularly special about the universal genetic code found throughout the living realm. According to science writer Carl Zimmer, "This research has pushed the debate over the genetic code to new ground. No one can argue that life's twenty amino acids are the only ones that can make life possible."[15]

As I argue in my book *The Cell's Design*, however, the structure of the universal genetic code—and the choice of the twenty amino acids specified by its rules—is notably optimized.[16] This optimization is so extreme, in fact, that I consider it one of the most compelling lines of evidence that life must stem from the work of a Creator.

Based on this optimization, most scientists have concluded that the rules of the genetic code cannot be a frozen accident. If a genetic code were assembled through random biochemical events, it would not possess nearly ideal error-minimization properties. So researchers argue that a "force" shaped the genetic code. Yet instead of considering the possibility of a supernatural explanation for the genetic code's origin, these scientists appeal to natural selection. That is, random events operated on by the forces of natural selection over and over again, somehow, in relatively short order, produced the genetic code's error-minimization capacity.[17]

While many researchers assume natural selection shaped the genetic code, other scientific work suggests otherwise. In 1968, Nobel Laureate Francis Crick convincingly argued that the genetic code could not have undergone significant evolution.[18] The rationale for his position is simple. Any change in codon assignment would lead to changes in amino acids in *every* protein made by the cell. This wholesale change in protein sequences would yield a large number of defective proteins. Nearly any conceivable change to the genetic code would prove lethal to the cell.

Although fully aware of Crick's work, some scientists still argue for a natural-process explanation of the genetic code's optimal design based on the existence of non-universal genetic codes. While the genetic code in nature is generally regarded as universal, some non-universal genetic codes exist— genetic codes employing slightly different codon assignments. Presumably these non-universal codes evolved from the universal one. Therefore, some researchers assert genetic code evolution is possible. These same scientists also point to the ability of synthetic biologists to expand the universal genetic code beyond the standard twenty amino acids as further support for this notion.

For the most part, however, the codon assignments of the non-universal genetic codes are nearly identical to those of the universal genetic code. Only one or two exceptions exist. It's best to think of the non-universal genetic codes as rare deviants from the universal.

Does the existence of non-universal codes imply that wholesale genetic code evolution is possible? Careful study reveals that the codon changes observed in the non-universal genetic codes always occur under extremely limited and specific circumstances: (1) they tend to happen in relatively small genomes, such as mitochondrial genomes; and (2) they involve either stop codons or codons that occur at low frequencies in their particular genome. Changes in assignment for such codons could occur without producing a lethal scenario, because only a small number of proteins in the cell or organelle would experience an altered amino acid sequence. So it appears that limited evolution of the genetic code *can* take place, but only in special circumstances.[19] These deviant codes represent merely another instance of microevolutionary change at a biochemical level.

Even if the genetic code could change over time to yield an optimal set of rules, there was not enough time for evolution to occur.[20] Biophysicist Hubert Yockey determined that natural selection would have required exploration of 1.40×10^{70} different genetic codes to hit upon the universal genetic code found in nature. Yockey estimated 6.3×10^{15} seconds as the maximum time available for the code to originate. Natural selection would have had to "evaluate" roughly 10^{55} codes per *second* to find the code.[21] Put simply, natural selection lacked the time.

Other work places the genetic code's origin as coincidental with the origin of life. Operating within the evolutionary paradigm, a team headed by renowned origin-of-life researcher Manfred Eigen estimated the age of the genetic code at 3.8 ± 0.6 billion years.[22] Current geochemical evidence places life's first appearance on Earth at 3.86 billion years ago.[23]

In the face of such challenges, some scientists suggest that the genetic code found in nature emerged from a simpler code that employed codons consisting of one or two nucleotides.[24] They propose that, over time, these simpler genetic codes eventually expanded to yield the universal genetic code based on coding triplets. The number of possible genetic codes for coding triplets far exceeds that for codes based on one or two nucleotide codons. This reduced coding capacity, they argue, makes code evolution more likely from a naturalistic standpoint.[25] Again, the success synthetic biologists have enjoyed in expanding the genetic code to include nonnatural amino acids supports some scientists' confidence in this idea.

One complicating factor for such proposals, however, arises from the fact that simpler genetic codes cannot specify twenty amino acids. Rather, they are limited to sixteen. Thus, the first life-forms would have had to make use of proteins consisting of no more than sixteen different amino acids. Because some proteins found in nature, such as ferredoxins, are produced with only thirteen amino acids, the idea that the genetic code found in nature arose from a simpler code would seem to garner some observational support. Yet proteins such as ferredoxins are atypical. The vast majority of proteins require all twenty amino acids.

The extensive effort required to expand the genetic code further frustrates the idea that it evolved from a simpler code. If not for the brilliance and skill of synthetic biologists and molecular biologists, expansion of the genetic code to include nonnatural amino acids would be impossible. Again, it seems more likely, based on direct, empirical evidence, that biochemical systems require the work of intelligent agency to come into being and undergo significant change.

However, attempts to generate artificial life from the top down are not the only approaches synthetic biologists are taking. Some look to create life from the bottom up, assembling it from molecular components. The next two chapters describe these efforts and explore how this approach might lead to life in the lab.

5

Becoming Acquainted with the Principals—
and Principles

> I alighted, and was conducted to my solitary apartment, to spend
> the evening as I pleased. The next morning I delivered my letters of
> introduction and paid a visit to some of the principal professors.
>
> Such were my reflections during the first two or three days of
> my residence at Ingolstadt, which were chiefly spent in becoming
> acquainted with the localities, and the principal residents in my
> new abode.
>
> Victor Frankenstein

During my elementary school years, my father was chairman of the physics department at West Virginia Institute of Technology (WVIT). We lived next door to this small school, and its campus became my playground. The faculty, staff, and students all knew me and watched out for me—for better or for worse. On at least a few occasions some disapproving member of the college community escorted me to my father's office to make him aware of some mischief I had perpetrated. But most days were fun.

Because of my childhood experience, I usually feel comfortable in a college setting. When I walk onto a college or university campus—even if for the first time—I tend to feel at home right away.

I must admit that wasn't the case my first few days at Ohio University. As I started graduate school there in biochemistry, my excitement and anticipation mingled with fear that I might not be good enough to earn a PhD, and it nearly overwhelmed me. But when I settled into my dorm room, got to know some fellow students and faculty members, and got started with my research project, I began to relax and feel at home once again.

The only time since then I remember feeling uncomfortable on a university campus was a few years ago when I took a short drive to the California Institute of Technology in Pasadena to hear origin-of-life researcher Jack Szostak lecture to faculty and students in Caltech's biophysics program. Though I'd been to the Caltech campus many times before, on this occasion I couldn't shake the feeling that I didn't quite belong. Departmental seminars are normally intimate affairs with only members of that program attending. With so few people in the audience, everyone would recognize me as an outsider.

The fact that I couldn't figure out how to get into the lecture hall added to my discomfort. With the main entrance closed due to construction, I walked around the building several times looking for a way in and thinking, *Here I am on the campus of one of the premier universities in the world—home to numerous Nobel Laureates, ground zero for some of the most important scientific breakthroughs in all of human history—and I can't even figure out how to get into a building.* Sheepishly, I asked a passerby for help.

My desire to hear Szostak outweighed my discomfort. I'd read about his work in peer-reviewed scientific journals. And his efforts to create life in the lab sparked many of the stories widely circulated and discussed among science enthusiasts. Headlines such as "Harvard Scientists Doing God's Work"[1] fueled my expectation that this brilliant man might be arrogant and egocentric. But to my pleasant surprise, I found Jack Szostak to be a soft-spoken, cautious researcher who, though fully aware of the significance of his work, also humbly recognized the difficulties he faces in creating a synthetic life-form.

Despite huge obstacles, Szostak and his collaborators at Harvard University have made significant strides toward that goal. Using an approach very different from Venter's, Smith's, and others' top-down strategy for reengineering life, Szostak's group starts from the bottom up. They begin with simple chemicals and look for ways to combine them into increasingly complex supramolecular entities. Called protocells, these assemblies serve as models for simple cells.

Szostak's team consists of several groups of scientists engaged in this task. Because this team has done what seems the most comprehensive work to date, this chapter focuses mainly on their efforts. Some of the more significant research of other groups also receives attention, particularly that which represents important milestones. (For further reading, see a recently published treatise on the creation of protocells.[2])

What does the creation of artificial life-forms from the bottom up look like? Why do some observers and commentators describe this work as "God's work"? The best way to begin addressing these questions is to outline the strategy researchers are using to create life in the lab from the bottom up.

Putting Life's Parts Together

To create protocells—artificial life—from "scratch," synthetic biologists strive to assemble increasingly sophisticated ensembles and aggregates of molecules with the hope they will eventually begin to operate as living systems. Because no suitable definition for life exists, synthetic biologists have no choice but to try to construct supramolecular complexes that manifest as many characteristics of terrestrial life as possible (see chapter 2). Once they produce something with the essential features, they will have created protocells that are arguably "alive."

Synthetic biologists working at a molecular level to make life from the bottom up need to understand the structure and physical properties of biomolecules and learn how their functions translate into the different characteristics biologists consider universal to all life-forms. Much of this understanding has accumulated over several decades of intensive work. A few examples of what's been discovered illustrate how this knowledge can be used to construct protocells. (Note: For readers unfamiliar with biochemistry, the appendix of this book provides some background.)

Cell Membranes

One of life's key properties is its ability to maintain a chemical composition distinct from the life-form's environment. From a biochemical standpoint, this chemical distinctiveness is established, in large measure, by the membrane that surrounds the cell separating the interior from the exterior. Without that boundary, life could not retain a chemical makeup different from its surroundings.

Biochemists have learned that under certain laboratory conditions, compounds that help make up the cell membrane, such as phospholipids, can form spheres with an internal cavity. These structures are called vesicles. Superficially, a vesicle resembles cells and serves as the foundation for constructing protocells. The membrane segregates materials located in the vesicle's cavity from the environment outside it.

The membrane plays a key role in yet another process. As life draws energy and materials from the environment, transforming and using this matter, proteins embedded in the membrane function as channels and transporters. They move nutrients and wastes back and forth across the cell membrane. The membrane is also the location for metabolic processes that harvest energy for the cell's use.

In order to create protocells, synthetic biologists must figure out not only how to form vesicles but also how to allow transport across vesicle boundaries. These tasks require manipulating the chemical structure of the amphiphiles that form vesicle walls or incorporating pore-forming proteins into the vesicle membrane.

Researchers must also develop protocells with the ability to generate energy to power chemical and physical processes within the vesicle's interior. This goal is most easily achieved by introducing energy-generating proteins into the vesicle membrane.

The ability of a cell to respond to stimuli from the environment also resides with the cell membrane. Proteins called receptors respond to chemical and physical signals and communicate the conditions in the cell's surroundings to the metabolic processes inside the cell. Synthetic biologists must also, then, incorporate receptors into the membranes of vesicles that they can, in turn, use as a tool to regulate and control the protocell's activity.

Reproduction

Biochemists have learned that the cell's ability to reproduce itself, by dividing into two identical daughter cells (in principle), fundamentally resides in the structure of DNA, the molecule harboring the cell's genetic information (see appendix, page 201).

The first step in cell division involves the replication of DNA. This process results in the generation of two identical molecules that are then partitioned between the daughter cells by the cell's machinery. Each receives the full complement of genetic information. Biochemists refer to the process of DNA replication as "template-directed" and "semiconservative." Template-directed means nucleotide sequences of the parent DNA molecule function as a template, directing the assembly of the DNA strands in the two daughter molecules. Semiconservative means that after replication, each daughter DNA molecule contains one newly formed DNA strand and one strand from the parent molecule.

Conceptually, template-directed, semiconservative DNA replication entails the separation of the original DNA double-helix into two single strands. By using the base-pairing rules, each strand acts as a template guiding the cell's machinery as it forms a new DNA strand with a nucleotide sequence complementary to the original strand.

In their quest to make artificial life from the bottom up, synthetic biologists must find ways to encapsulate DNA, RNA, or some other complex information-harboring molecule within vesicles. The encapsulated genetic material can (in principle) direct the production of proteins within a vesicle's interior. If synthetic biologists can get genetic material to replicate within the confines of a vesicle, that accomplishment would set the stage (in principle) for replication of the protocell. All that is required is to coax the vesicle to split into two, with each daughter molecule finding its way into the daughter vesicles.

Step by Step

Origin-of-life scientist and synthetic biologist David Deamer has summarized the strategy to make protocells in his step-by-step delineation of the way he thinks various "parts" need to be put together to generate the simplest possible life-form.[3] These steps include:

1. Assembly of boundary membranes;
2. Formation of energy-capturing capabilities by the boundary membrane;
3. Encapsulation of macromolecules (like proteins, RNA, and DNA) within the boundary membrane;
4. Introduction of pores into the boundary membrane that can funnel raw materials into the interior space;
5. Production of systems that allow the macromolecules to grow;
6. Generation of catalysts that speed up the growth of the encapsulated macromolecules;
7. Provision for the macromolecules to replicate;
8. Introduction of information into one set of macromolecules that directs the production of other macromolecules;
9. Development of mechanisms to cause the boundary membrane to subdivide into two smaller systems that can grow;
10. Production of the means to pass information-containing macromolecules to the daughter products of the subdivision process.

Considering all that's involved, Deamer noted, "Looking down this list, one is struck by the complexity of even the simplest form of life."[4] This complexity means that synthetic biologists have their work cut out for them. Let's take a look at some of their progress, focusing on the accomplishments of Szostak's group.

Starting at the Bottom

Since the mid-1990s, Szostak's lab has pursued three main lines of investigation, each one critical for achieving the steps Deamer lists as the pathway to creation of artificial life.[5] Szostak's team has focused intense effort on:

1. Getting vesicles to grow and divide;
2. Generating genetic material that can replicate and evolve within the interior of vesicles;
3. Producing artificial proteins, by both making them from scratch and reengineering them from nature.

As the researchers achieve results in each of these areas and then successfully integrate them, they will produce protocellular systems that, by some definitions, could be classified as living entities.

The program Szostak and his collaborators are engaged in builds on the accomplishments of membrane biophysicists. In the process of studying the fundamental structural and functional properties of cell membranes and their components, earlier, pioneering researchers developed methods to:

1. Produce vesicles from purified phospholipids;
2. Entrap biomolecules within vesicle interiors;
3. Incorporate purified proteins into the walls of vesicles.

These systems are usually studied as models for cell membranes. But the cell membrane models can also be considered a preamble to the construction of protocells.

Synthetic biologists begin by trying to capitalize on the vesicle-forming properties of phospholipids to construct protocells. During the late 1990s, membrane biophysicist and origin-of-life researcher Pier Luigi Luisi led a team that conducted one of the first experiments with significant results.[6] These researchers encapsulated ribosomes and other biomolecular components necessary to carry out protein synthesis inside vesicles made up of purified phospholipids. Using this system, the scientists produced a model protein (polyphenylalanine) within the vesicle—a significant step toward creating a protocell that displays life properties.

Other synthetic biologists have looked for ways to design protocells from simpler amphiphiles such as fatty acids. Part of the reason for using fatty acids is that they are more versatile than phospholipids. Fatty acid vesicles display more varied behavior than those made from phospholipids. Luisi and David Deamer both pioneered this approach. (And these origin-of-life researchers have crossed over into synthetic biology.) The desire to understand how cell membranes originated and evolved has motivated Luisi and Deamer, along with their collaborators, to spend years exploring these questions. (Chapter 13 details the work on the origin of cell membranes and its implications for the creation-evolution controversy.)

Luisi, Deamer, and Szostak all have come to recognize that insights gleaned from their own and others' studies on the origin of life have direct application to the creation of protocells from the bottom up. (And conversely, these researchers also realize that attempts to make life in the lab shed light on how life may have originated.)

Within the past decade, Deamer's group has demonstrated that fatty acids can assemble into bilayers to form vesicles. This process occurs under highly specific conditions (low salt, specific pH values, etc.) and at specific temperatures and concentrations, all of which depend on the identity of the fatty acid.[7] (See chapter 13 for more details.)

Luisi's team has demonstrated that vesicles formed from certain types of fatty acids can grow if fatty acids are added to the vesicles. This addition enlarges the vesicles until they become unstable and fissure into two daughters. The researchers have also used fatty acid vesicles to encapsulate enzymes such as polynucleotide phosphorylase. This interesting enzyme can use the compound adenine diphosphate (ADP) to build an analog to DNA: polyadenylic acid.[8] Researchers consider this accomplishment proof that genetic material can be replicated within vesicles—a preliminary step toward generating self-replicating protocells.

Bringing the Components to Life

Szostak's group built on this foundational work with the goal of making life-like protocells. In their effort to develop processes to make vesicles from fatty acids, they demonstrated that allowing fatty acids to interact with mineral surfaces helps improve the efficiency of the vesicle formation process.[9]

Szostak's team has yet to address a critical issue confronting synthetic biologists: vesicles made from fatty acids have marginal long-term stability. Unless exacting conditions are maintained, these vesicles readily collapse. (This problem also exists for vesicles made from phospholipids and other amphiphiles.) Currently, no method has been developed that can form stable, long-lasting vesicles. Researchers must be able to make stable vesicles in order to create artificial life. Boundaries are the means for ensuring that life remains chemically distinct from the environment.

Szostak and his colleagues have extended Luisi's work by exploring ways to get vesicles to reproducibly grow and divide. In fact, a significant amount of Szostak's lab effort has been devoted toward this end. While his team has confirmed that the addition of fatty acids to vesicles prompts them to grow, they've also developed a mechanistic understanding of how this process works.[10]

Luisi's team has observed vesicles fissuring after growth, presumably due to instability. This division process is insufficiently robust and reliable to sustain cell division in protocellular systems. Szostak's team has addressed this issue and developed a way to drive vesicle division after growth. Their methodology involves extruding (pushing) the expanded vesicles through pores. This process—growth by addition of fatty acids, followed by division by extrusion—can be repeated indefinitely, allowing researchers to mimic two key properties of life and, in effect, to produce multiple generations of protocells.[11]

Researchers have also succeeded in encapsulating RNA within fatty acid vesicles.[12] RNA, like DNA, can function as genetic material. Scientists have figured out a way to allow RNA molecules within the vesicles to become catalytically active. This important breakthrough means that metabolic processes mediated by enzyme-like materials can take place within the vesicle interiors of protocells, a necessary capability to sustain lifelike activity.

Szostak's team also noted that encapsulation of RNA within the interior of vesicles actually promotes growth because it exerts osmotic pressure on the vesicle walls.[13] This stress makes it easier for fatty acid molecules to become incorporated into the vesicle bilayers and thus drive growth. What's more, researchers observed that the RNA is retained within the vesicle's interior after the division process mediated by extrusion through a filter.[14]

In other experiments, researchers encapsulated clay minerals in vesicles, along with RNA, and have observed that the vesicles retained the clay and RNA during the growth and division process. This result is significant because other investigators have demonstrated that clay can be used as a catalyst to generate RNA from its building blocks. (Chapter 11 describes this work in detail in light of the origin-of-life question.)

Finding an Energy Source

Many researchers have been looking for ways to generate power for pro-tocell activities using vesicles made from phospholipids. Knowing that cells use pH differences across membranes as a way to harvest energy for their biochemical operations, a team of investigators incorporated into the bilayers of phospholipid vesicles a large compound that absorbs light energy and generates a pH difference across the vesicle boundary.[15] By also adding the enzyme complex F_0F_1 ATP synthase into the vesicle bilayers, they were able to use the pH difference to power the production of a compound called ATP. This biomolecule is used by the cell to temporarily store energy for cell use.

Szostak's group has discovered a simpler way to generate the pH difference. They found that growth of vesicles made from fatty acids naturally generates a difference in pH across the inner and outer surfaces of the vesicle membrane.[16] This work suggests that a source of energy can be made available for protocells simply through the growth and division process.

Permeability and Stability

Szostak's group discovered yet another unexpected benefit of using fatty acids rather than phospholipids to make vesicles. Fatty acid vesicles are much more permeable, allowing compounds to cross the boundary more easily. Phospholipid bilayers are notoriously impermeable, especially to compounds such as amino acids and nucleotides. The permeability of fatty acid vesicles means researchers can design protocells that extract and transform material from their surroundings without having to introduce transporters into the vesicle membranes.

Szostak's team further demonstrated that vesicles made from fatty acids permit the sugar ribose, a key component of RNA, to make its way into the vesicle's interior.[17] Activated nucleotides (the building blocks of RNA and DNA) also made their way through the bilayers of fatty acid vesicles.[18] Taking advantage of this property, they designed systems in such a way that activated nucleotides, once inside the vesicles, could combine to form short DNA chains using a previously encapsulated strand of DNA as a template.

In addition, the researchers found another useful property of vesicles made from mixtures of specific types of fatty acids (monounsaturated) and other related compounds (fatty alcohols and monoglycerides). This mixed vesicle system displayed unexpected stability as the environmental temperature was cycled between water's freezing and boiling points.[19] Such a discovery represents an important advance for at least two reasons. First, vesicles formed from fatty acids are only stable at certain temperatures, with the identity of the fatty acid dictating the stable temperature regime. If these vesicles find themselves outside of the stable temperature regime, they fall apart. Szostack's team found a way to enhance the robustness of protocells to temperature changes.

Second, this advance allows scientists to chemically replicate DNA within the vesicle interior. To reproduce DNA, the double helix has to unwind, allowing enzymes that copy DNA to access each strand. Inside the cell, other enzymes unwind and separate the DNA strands. But this unraveling also occurs when DNA is heated. Thermal energy unwinds the DNA double helix, exposing the strands. This exposure permits researchers to replicate DNA within the vesicle's interior. Once encapsulated, heating unwinds the DNA so that enzymes such as DNA polymerase can access the single strands and copy them, thus generating copies of the DNA molecule *without* the vesicles breaking apart from the heat. In this scenario, the nucleotide building blocks needed for the replication process can be added to the solution surrounding the protocells and diffuse into the vesicle's confines.

Manufacturing Reproduction

Szostak and his collaborators are also working to identify molecules that might serve as self-replicating genetic material (similar to DNA) housed within the interior of vesicles. The objective is to coordinate the growth and division of the vesicles with the replication of the genetic material, resulting in protocellular entities that could be considered alive.

As a reminder, DNA is the molecule that comprises the genetic material in practically all life-forms on Earth. While several synthetic biologists are looking for ways to incorporate DNA within protocells along with the enzymes needed to direct its replication,[20] Szostak's group is taking a different tack. They are looking to identify molecules that might be simpler genetic systems easier for synthetic biologists to manipulate.

One system they've focused on is RNA, with the aim of developing a self-replicating version of this biomolecule. To date origin-of-life researchers and synthetic biologists have had only limited success in this effort. (The quest to identify self-replicating RNA molecules is discussed in chapter 11 as part of the bottom-up attempt to explain life's origin.) So some researchers have worked to develop nonnatural, artificial genetic systems structurally distinct from DNA.[21]

Finding Alternatives

Recent focus centers on two other systems: glycerol nucleic acids (GNA) and phosphoramidate glycerol nucleic acids (pGNA). Instead of using ribose or deoxyribose as part of their backbone, as do RNA and DNA respectively, these molecules use glycerol. Szostak's team has shown that GNA can serve as a template to build a complementary DNA strand using DNA polymerase enzymes, and conversely, DNA provides a template to construct short GNA strands, again using certain types of DNA polymerases. This work provides a starting point for designing novel, nonnatural genetic systems distinct from DNA and perhaps simpler.

Szostak and his colleagues are also attempting to reengineer proteins found in nature as well as to design novel proteins from scratch.[22] The purpose of

---

A Giant Step toward Artificial Life

One of the most interesting pieces of work in the bottom-up venture to create artificial life was reported in 2004 by a team of researchers from the Rockefeller University in New York City.[23] These scientists produced phospholipid vesicles that could take ribonucleotides and amino acids from the environment and use them as building blocks to produce proteins encoded in a piece of DNA. This protein production could be sustained for up to four days.

To accomplish this feat, the researchers devised a way to encapsulate the cytoplasmic contents of the bacterium *Escherichia coli* within phospholipid vesicles. These contents include biochemical equipment that reads information harbored in the DNA molecule and uses it to make proteins. The scientists also entrapped in the vesicles pieces of DNA containing two genes. One encodes the protein α-hemolysin, which forms pores in cell membranes. The other gene encodes the green fluorescent protein (GFP), a protein that fluoresces green when light is shined on it.

The enriched vesicles were then able to make α-hemolysin, forming pores within the vesicle bilayer that allowed ribonucleotides and amino acids to enter and sustain protein production. These vesicles also produced GFP for up to four days, as evidenced by the emission of green light.

These results may have important biochemical utility. The approach allows researchers to devise and make proteins, treating protocells as tiny bioreactors. It also represents an important milestone toward the creation of artificial life by providing insight into how multiple lifelike characteristics can be combined into a single vesicle system.

these efforts is to develop components for use in protocells that will carry out specific metabolic activities. The intent of this work is to go beyond merely encapsulating proteins already found in nature within protocells. Instead, the scientists want to impart to protocells novel biochemical capabilities.

To accomplish this task, they need to develop methods that can generate novel proteins with metabolic properties extending beyond those found in nature. Scientists have already devised protocols that allow them to vary protein's amino acid sequences and to select variants with desirable properties. In addition, researchers have come up with a method to expand the genetic code (see chapter 4) and to manipulate the biochemical machinery that makes proteins, paving the way for creation of biomolecules with nonnatural amino acids.

What Szostak's group at Harvard University has achieved in less than a decade to further efforts to make artificial life—protocells—from the bottom up is widely praised as remarkable. Although many other researchers have also made significant strides, Szostak's lab has put together one of the most comprehensive programs in synthetic biology. As such it provides a representative sampling of what has been accomplished thus far.

Where We Go from Here

Synthetic biologists working from the bottom up may still be some distance from their ultimate destination, but the speed of the progress toward creating artificial life has been breathtaking. I wouldn't be surprised if Szostak or other scientists achieve this goal within the next decade. And when that happens, it will open up entire new vistas in biomedicine and biotechnology complementing those offered by the generation of artificial life-forms generated from the top down.

Both approaches raise deep questions about ethics and theology. If scientists can make life in the lab, what will their success mean? Isn't the creation of life God's domain? These questions become more acute in the context of the bottom-up approach to life, where scientists are literally piecing life together part by part as opposed to reengineering existing life-forms as in the top-down approach.

Is God Really Necessary?

While some scientists and others suggest the (anticipated) creation of artificial life makes the need for a Creator obsolete, I take the opposite view. As evidenced in both the top-down and bottom-up approaches, only by deliberate effort, inordinate ingenuity, and astonishing skill can synthetic biologists even begin the process of making artificial life. Their work empirically demonstrates that even the simplest life-form cannot arise without the involvement of an intelligent agent.

A few further details augment my argument. For example, vesicles do not automatically come together when fatty acids are added to water. Instead, Szostak and other investigators can coax vesicles to form only by judiciously selecting certain fatty acids. The length of the fatty acid molecule and its precise structure influence vesicle formation and robustness. The wrong choice results in fragile vesicles or may even render vesicle formation impossible.

Vesicle formation and stability also depend on vigilantly adjusting the concentration of the fatty acid in water and maintaining the solution conditions (pH and salt content). For some fatty acids, the water's temperature also determines whether vesicles form. Generally, the solution's temperature must be greater than the melting point of the pure fatty acid. In some instances, vesicle formation requires that researchers repeatedly freeze and thaw the solution. In other cases, extrusion through microscopic pores is required. The extrusion process also ensures that the vesicles are the desired size when they form.

In short, Szostak's team has been able to produce vesicles from fatty acids and to get them to grow and divide only by choosing to make them from a specific type of fatty acid (monounsaturated). Choosing the just-right type of fatty acid, in turn, depends on a comprehensive understanding of the relationship between amphiphile structure and the physical properties in the solution—understanding that stems from several decades of experimental and theoretical studies conducted by thousands of biochemists from around the world.

Biochemists have learned that they can encapsulate materials inside vesicles by including these substances in the solution used to form the vesicles. But as Szostak and his collaborators have discovered, this approach often poses further complications. The materials to be encapsulated can sometimes disrupt vesicle formation, and the procedures to make and size the vesicles can destroy the materials to be encapsulated. For example, RNA molecules with catalytic activity require magnesium and calcium ions, and yet encapsulating these biomolecules with the associated ions causes the fatty acids to precipitate from solution, completely destroying the vesicles. Szostak's team discovered that this destruction can be mitigated to some extent by carefully adding companion molecules (glycerol monoester) to the fatty acids when the vesicles form. Again, though, this step requires detailed understanding of the relationship between amphiphile structure and physical behavior and of how ions interact with these materials, not to mention exquisite manipulation.

Encapsulation also requires the added step of purifying the vesicles and their contents. Not all the material added to the solution becomes encapsulated. The leftover material must be removed from the solution. This removal is accomplished by passing the vesicles and free material through a column packed with porous materials. This porous matter allows the unencapsulated material to readily pass through while retarding the flow of the vesicles. The net effect is that the vesicles and their contents are separated from the free materials.

This purification process requires detailed understanding of the chemical and physical behavior of the vesicles, knowledge about the chemical and physical properties of the free material left in the solution, and insight into the chemical properties and behavior of the column packing material. This step also requires knowledge about the physical chemistry of the separation process.

The amount of intellectual effort to form vesicles and entrap materials—just two of the myriad steps necessary to assemble life—speaks of supreme wisdom, purpose, and power. And these efforts, conducted by some of the best scientific minds in the world, potentially challenge familiar visions of how life could originate through undirected natural processes. It seems more likely Szostak is emulating God's handiwork than making the Creator irrelevant.

The next chapter continues examining the quest to create artificial life from the bottom up by describing the efforts of synthetic biologists to create life as we *don't* know it.

6

A Scientist's Splendor

It was very different when the masters of science sought immortality and power; such views, although futile, were grand: but now the scene was changed. The ambition of the inquirer seemed to limit itself to the annihilation of those visions on which my interest in science was chiefly founded. I was required to exchange chimeras of boundless grandeur for realities of little worth.

Victor Frankenstein

Mary Shelley portrays Victor Frankenstein, the child, as an insatiable learner, particularly intrigued by the things of "heaven and earth" and the "mysterious soul of man." At thirteen, her character discovers the works of the ancient alchemists, men such as Cornelius Agrippa, Paracelsus, and Albertus Magnus. They too had been obsessed with discovering nature's secrets and with such insights had hoped to grab hold of the "philosopher's stone" and the "elixir of life."

As a student at the University of Ingolstadt, Frankenstein is chided by his professors for wasting time studying alchemy, unscientific teachings long replaced by the tenets of modern science. Victor superficially accepts this criticism and even agrees with it, but his yearning cannot be quelled.

Ultimately, the purview of modern science seems too limited to Frankenstein, who complains that scientists have "exchanged the discoveries of recent inquirers for the dreams of the forgotten alchymists." The desire of the ancients for immortality and power over nature—goals Frankenstein acknowledges as futile—finally drives him to abandon mundane research and discover the secret of bringing inanimate matter to life.

Perhaps synthetic biologists feel the same allure as the fictional Frankenstein. Unsatisfied with merely reengineering microbes from the top down or with assembling protocells from the bottom up, using mostly biomolecules and biochemical systems already found in nature, they long to make a life-form "as we don't know it." These scientists want to create artificial cells composed of chemical elements and molecules unlike anything known to exist on Earth.

Unlike the dreams of forgotten alchemists, however, this grand vision may not prove futile. Synthetic biologists have made some significant progress toward designing novel proteins—in a few instances from scratch—that can be used to impart protocells with nonnatural biochemical capabilities. A few dare to dream beyond this goal, hoping to generate totally new life-forms—creatures that rely on molecules *other* than DNA and RNA to store and transmit genetic information. Progress thus far indicates that one day synthetic biologists will

---

Poison in the Rocks

While in junior high, I never missed a chance to watch the original *Star Trek* series. In one of my favorite episodes, the crew of the *Enterprise* encounters a silicon-based life-form (a Horta) on the mining planet Janus VI. This idea intrigued me: could life be based on an element other than carbon?

Known life consists of carbon, hydrogen, oxygen, nitrogen, phosphorus, and sulfur (CHONPS). Carbon-based life requires a strict set of conditions for its existence. There are only a few places in our solar system (and perhaps beyond) that can conceivably support carbon-based life. But what if life could spring from other elements?

Starting with Silicon

This question isn't just a discussion topic among science-fiction buffs. It fuels attempts to make artificial life, discover the origin of life, and search for life on other planets. Perhaps life based on an element such as silicon could exist under more extreme conditions. In that case, life-habitable sites might abound throughout the universe.

Could life be structured around any other element besides carbon? What is so special about this element? Of the 112 known chemical elements, only carbon possesses sufficiently complex chemical behavior to sustain living systems as we understand them.[1] Carbon readily assembles into stable molecules comprised of individual and fused rings and linear and branched chains. It forms single, double, and triple bonds. Carbon also strongly bonds with itself as well as with oxygen, nitrogen, sulfur, and hydrogen.

possess the "elixir of life"—the capability to create life that's artificial in every sense of the word.

This chapter further amplifies efforts to create a new life-form from the bottom up, a research endeavor that has become increasingly expansive. A sampling of these efforts to make life from molecules—life unlike any found in nature—not only highlights fundamental questions about the very nature of life itself but also hints at unimaginable potential for biotechnology applications. (Readers who want a more expansive treatment can find resources in the references.[2])

Creating from Scratch

In this particular arena of synthetic biology, scientists literally rely on their imagination to create life. Unlike efforts to reconstitute life by piecing together existing biomolecules, this new endeavor strives to make life that is

Some astrobiologists think life could be based on silicon because it belongs to the same chemical group as carbon and therefore should display similar chemical properties. However, while silicon can form rings and chains, these structures lack the stability and range of complexity found in carbon-based compounds. Silicon-silicon bonds are much weaker than the corresponding carbon-carbon bonds, and unlike carbon-carbon bonds, silicon bonds are susceptible to oxidation.[3]

Maybe Some Arsenic Would Do

Phosphorus also plays a key role in forming important biomolecules, including DNA. Physicist and astrobiologist Paul Davies recently suggested that some unusual life-forms may use arsenic in place of phosphorus.[4] Arsenic appears below phosphorus in the same column of the periodic table and displays similar chemical behavior.

However, there are sound reasons to be skeptical of Davies's suggestion. Though arsenic and phosphorus share some chemical properties, the two elements also display significant chemical differences. Phosphorus is a nonmetal. Arsenic is a metalloid. Phosphorus reacts with oxygen to form phosphates, compounds that take part in the linkages that constitute the backbone of the DNA molecule. Arsenic also reacts with oxygen to form compounds called arsenates. Although phosphates and arsenates display some chemical similarities, the esters formed with arsenates are so unstable as to render these groups unusable in constructing the backbone of DNA (or its functional equivalent).

So far, as provocative as alternative possibilities may seem, life based on elements other than CHONPS must be considered science fiction.

completely new, utterly alien. (See "Poison in the Rocks," pp. 84–85.) This fresh approach intensifies philosophical and theological concerns. What will the creation of a completely new life-form mean for the future of life as we *do* know it? What will it mean for the creation-evolution controversy? Does it indicate that God is no longer necessary to explain life's origin? Are scientists actually "replacing God"?

Examining efforts to create artificial proteins and artificial DNA—key first steps to making life-forms unlike anything ever seen before—provides important insight.

Artificial Proteins: A Strategic Redesign

Virtually every activity in the cell requires proteins. (Again, readers unfamiliar with biochemistry may find the appendix helpful.) These molecules play an integral role in forming nearly all cellular and subcellular structures. Even the simplest life-forms need hundreds, if not thousands, of different types of proteins to function. When biochemists know which proteins constitute an organism's makeup and understand what each one does, they have a reasonably complete understanding of the fundamental biology of that organism.

Because of the importance of these biomolecules, biochemists expend a lot of energy trying to understand the structure and functional properties of proteins. One approach researchers use to decipher this relationship is to modify the amino acid sequence of proteins—and consequently their three-dimensional molecular architectures—to learn what effect structural changes have on the functional properties.

As biochemists become more adept at making architectural modifications, they've learned how to introduce such large-scale changes to protein structure that they can create novel, nonnatural biomolecules. These structurally altered proteins offer the opportunity for biochemists to develop fundamental understanding about how proteins work and to pave the way to use protein engineering for technology applications.

Ultimately, this type of work sets the stage for a generation of new life-forms. So of course synthetic biologists want to capitalize on the efforts of protein engineers. The idea is that once nonnatural proteins have been created, these novel biomolecules can be encapsulated within vesicles, thereby imparting protocells with functional capabilities unlike those possessed by any type of life on Earth.

Synthetic biologists working from the top down could also make use of artificial proteins. In this case, they would synthesize pieces of DNA containing the information to produce artificial proteins and introduce these artificial genes into any organism's genome. Once incorporated into the genome, the cell's machinery would produce these novel proteins as part of its normal metabolic processes. The end result would be a life-form with nonnatural biochemical capabilities created solely by human invention.

The creation of artificial proteins is a gateway to exciting new biotechnologies. At the same time, some researchers consider this work to provide ultimate proof for the evolutionary paradigm. They argue that the changes they make to protein structure and function somehow mimic the types of changes that occurred naturally throughout life's history.

But is this argument valid? A few representative studies in which biochemists have either reengineered new proteins starting with proteins found in nature or designed novel proteins from the ground up can help answer this question.

Making the Cut

Scientists from the Indian Institute of Science (Bangalore, India) performed experiments to understand the origin of one specific class of proteins called restriction endonucleases (see chapters 3 and 4, particularly the detailed discussion of these important enzymes in chapter 4).[5] Their aim was to develop a strategy for engineering novel, nonnatural restriction endonucleases for biotechnology applications.

To better understand their accomplishments, a little background information on proteins may be helpful. Even though a protein is a large molecule, only a small portion of its structure is immediately involved in molecular activities. The business portion is typically either a pocket or a crevice located on the three-dimensional surface of the folded protein chain. For proteins that catalyze (or assist) chemical reactions (enzymes), the pocket is the active site.

In some proteins, these active surface regions bind small molecules that elicit structural changes to the protein. Such changes trigger interactions between the protein and other cellular components, interactions that turn various biochemical pathways and processes on or off. Binding sites that are part of enzymes such as restriction endonucleases latch on to portions of large molecules, such as other proteins or DNA. The molecules (or regions of large molecules) that attach to active and binding sites are called substrates.

The chemical groups that form both active and binding sites arise from the amino acids that constitute the protein chain. Although these amino acids may be located in completely different regions of the protein chain, they are brought into appropriate juxtaposition when the protein chain folds into its three-dimensional shape.

Binding sites latch on to select molecules or select regions of proteins or DNA based on the precisely matched geometry of the substrate molecules, as well as the exacting molecular interactions that take place between the chemical groups found in the active or binding site and the substrates.

Evolutionary biologists propose that restriction endonucleases evolved from nonspecific endonucleases that cut DNA at random sequences instead

of at the highly selective sequences they normally operate on. This evolution could have occurred, they suggest, as a result of point mutations in the
region that identifies the DNA binding site on the protein surface. (Point
mutations cause the substitution of one amino acid for another in protein
molecules.) According to this model, once specificity was established, recombination and genetic shuffling of the DNA sequences that encode the
DNA recognition sites would have generated new restriction endonucleases
with different specificities.

To test this possibility, the research team attempted to engineer a highly
specific restriction endonuclease starting from one (R.KpnI) that indiscriminately binds to DNA sequences. But instead of passively allowing random
changes to the protein's amino acid sequence, the experimenters actively
engaged in a rational design strategy to determine which amino acids in the
R.KpnI protein they would alter. These workers made use of their detailed
understanding of the protein's structure and functional properties to develop
a redesign strategy.

After careful deliberations, the researchers concluded that replacing an
aspartic acid residue with an isoleucine moiety at amino acid position 163 in
the R.KpnI protein chain would likely alter this enzyme's specificity. When
they executed the plan, it worked. The team successfully modified R.KpnI to
generate a restriction endonuclease that precisely recognized and bonded to
a specific DNA sequence.

While this important work helps pave the way for strategic engineering of
novel, nonnatural restriction enzymes and thus expands the arsenal of tools
available to molecular biologists and biochemists, it also makes a point. It illustrates the in-depth knowledge and intense effort required to make a single
amino acid substitution that can alter the specificity of restriction endonucleases (and, by extension, other proteins as well).

Instead of providing evidence for natural-process change, this study empirically demonstrates that protein "evolution"—actually, protein redesign—
requires the insight and direct involvement of intelligent agents.

As an additional note, the researchers performing the experiment didn't
redesign the companion methylase protein (see chapter 4). This protein is
unnecessary for most biotechnology applications, but without its methylase
cohort in the cell, the reengineered restriction endonuclease wreaks havoc *in
vivo*, destroying the very DNA that comprises the bacterial genome.

One must consider the likelihood that a restriction endonuclease and its
partner methylase would simultaneously appear in any evolutionary scenario.
These events would require transformation in the restriction endonuclease
to take place at the exact same time as the corresponding changes in the
methylase. Such precise coordination again would reflect the influence of an
intelligent agent.[6]

Controlling the Chemistry

Another focus of intense interest to would-be creators is the power of small molecules inside the cell called allosteric effectors. These effectors, as their name suggests, impact the actions of proteins from a distance. As much as scientists want to design and engineer novel proteins, they also want to control these new proteins through allosteric interactions.

This remote-control capacity, called *allostery*, is particularly important to the creation of synthetic life because it provides the means to exert feedback and feedforward regulation of biochemical operations. The aim is to encapsulate proteins that can be influenced by allosteric regulation. This accomplishment would provide synthetic biologists with dynamic control over the activity of protocells, mimicking the ability of living organisms to respond to changes in the environment.

Recently a team of scientists succeeded in designing and producing a novel (nonnatural) allosteric enzyme that binds DNA when light shines on it.[7] This elegant work foreshadows the creation of novel proteins potentially useful in biotechnology and biomedicine and ultimately in the assembling of artificial life. Once again, this remarkable engineering achievement was interpreted by some as an insight into how evolution might have worked. But how appropriate is such an interpretation?

In addition to active and binding sites, many proteins harbor additional small-molecule binding sites on their surfaces. These surface locales are often far removed from the active and binding sites. When allosteric effectors bind to these allosteric sites, structural changes take place in the protein that translate through the entire molecule, thus modifying the structure of the active and functional binding sites.

Because of the fine-tuning of the interactions between substrates and protein active and binding sites, these structural changes—even if ever so slight—can affect substrate binding (and subsequent chemical changes to the substrate if the allosteric protein is an enzyme).

Allosteric effectors that shut down the protein's operation at the active or binding sites are called allosteric inhibitors. Those that increase activity are called allosteric activators. Evolutionary biologists propose that allosteric proteins evolved through genomic shuffling, the random recombination of regions of the protein-coding regions of an organism's genome.

To understand this proposal requires a little more detail about protein structure. (Readers concerned about getting bogged down in the details may wish to skip ahead to page 91.) When proteins fold, they form modular domains. The overall three-dimensional architecture of a protein can be thought of as the sum of these multiple structural modules or domains. Protein domains are stable, self-consistent regions that carry out specific functions, independent of the rest of the protein but contributing to the protein's overall activity.

Allosteric proteins consist of a domain(s) that binds allosteric compounds and other domains that contain active or binding sites. These modules connect to each other, usually through a structural junction that can transmit structural changes in the allosteric-binding domain to the proteins' functional region.

Evolutionary biologists think the regions of genes that encode protein domains can become shuffled through an assortment of biochemical mechanisms and, in the process, generate new proteins that are a mix and match of preexisting domains. In this way allosteric domains could have fused with functional protein domains to yield a new protein that is subject to allosteric regulation.

On the basis of this model, researchers from the University of Chicago developed a strategy to create a novel, nonnatural allosteric protein with two domains: one taken from the protein phototropin 1 and the other from the *trp* repressor, a DNA-binding protein.

The phototropin 1 domain absorbs light (in this case, the photon of light equates to a small molecule binding at an allosteric site) and thus undergoes a structural change. The DNA-binding domain of the *trp* repressor attaches to DNA in the presence of the small molecule tryptophan, thereby shutting down the genes that make this amino acid.

In contrast to the proposed evolutionary mechanism for the origin of allosteric proteins—again, a mechanism that requires protein domains to randomly combine and in the process happen to hit upon a novel protein with beneficial function for the cell—the biochemists who designed the artificial allosteric protein took painstaking care to marry the light-absorbing and DNA-binding domains. These efforts included:

- strategically choosing the best domains to combine;
- rationally selecting the juncture between the two domains; and
- fine-tuning the juncture by iteratively trying out amino acid compositions and sequences to find the exact structure that would provide an allosteric conduit between the two domains.

In other words, these researchers didn't just happen upon the protein they created, or even produce it with minimal effort. They invested enormous intellectual effort and labor-intensive diligence.

Perhaps their most impressive achievement was the selection of the junction between the two domains. Through careful reasoning, the scientists decided to use an alpha-helix to join them. (This conformation of the protein backbone resembles a spiral staircase.) The researchers noted that the bond angles between amino acids necessary to form an alpha-helix are highly restricted. This specificity means that any change in the bond angles of an alpha-helix caused by changes in the domains associated with them will unravel the helix. The unraveling process can then be used to transmit changes to another domain joined to the alpha-helix.

Scientists chose the light-absorbing domain of phototropin 1 and the DNA-binding domain of the *trp* repressor, in part, because both have terminal alpha-helical segments. Their reasoning was that these two alpha-helicies could be fused to form a juncture between the two domains that would transmit structural changes between them.

Once the researchers made this determination, they carefully designed the alpha-helix in a way that would allow the domains from the two proteins to maintain their natural three-dimensional structure once fused together. This fusion would then force a change in the DNA-binding domain when light impinged on the (added) phototropin 1 domain. This effort to create the right juncture between the two domains required a combination of rational design strategies with trial and error. And it succeeded.

Such significant achievements help biochemists gain some understanding as to how allosteric regulation works. They also provide a workable action plan for biochemists to design novel allosteric proteins that can be controlled by light. With the availability of this technology, the conceivable biotechnology and biomedical applications seem almost limitless. This work also helps set the stage for biochemists' success in creating artificial life in the lab.

When biochemists create such sophisticated artificial proteins, it may appear at first blush as if they are, at least in some ways, supplanting God. But is that actually the case?

The amount of effort required to design a single allosteric protein by joining together two domains of proteins that *already* exist in nature is truly enormous. The development and employment of an effective design strategy demanded a significant collaborative effort among some of the finest minds in the world. And these researchers relied on sophisticated laboratory technology to produce results.

If creating a single protein from already-existing parts takes this much effort and intellectual input, is it reasonable to think that undirected evolutionary processes could have accomplished this task through random genetic shuffling?

Do the Hustle

As part of their research endeavor, chemists often look for ways to speed up chemical reactions for practical reasons, if no other. They've discovered that the rate of many chemical reactions can be accelerated by using catalysts.

The use of catalysts is not confined to the laboratory. These compounds also feature prominently in living systems. Most of the chemical reactions necessary for life are accelerated by a special type of biological catalyst, enzymes. These biomolecules are proteins specifically structured to facilitate intracellular biochemical activities and operations. Enzymes can sometimes increase the rate of biochemical reactions by over a billion-fold! Without enzymes, life would be impossible because most of the chemical transformations necessary to sustain life proceed too slowly without some assistance.

Whenever possible, chemists and chemical engineers take advantage of the special properties of enzymes for industrial, commercial, food, and agricultural applications. Scientists and technologists find enzymes useful because these biomolecules accelerate chemical reactions with a high degree of chemical specificity. However, engineers have encountered numerous problems when attempting to use enzymes for large-scale applications. These biomolecules are unstable in organic solvents and at high temperatures. Enzymes also have a limited catalytic range because only a limited number of chemical reactions occur within living systems.

In response to these limitations, protein engineers are working to redesign enzymes found in nature. If they can stabilize enzymes under harsh conditions, they can extend enzymes' utility. These biotechnologists also look to produce enzymes from scratch that can catalyze novel, nonbiological reactions.

Recently a large team of collaborators published two papers reporting the creation, from scratch, of two enzymes capable of catalyzing nonbiological chemical transformations (the Kemp elimination and the retro-aldol reaction).[8]

As a reminder: even though enzymes are large molecules, only a small portion of their structure plays an immediate role in catalysis. Enzymes bind the chemical compounds (substrates) destined to react with each other in the active site. Once the chemical reaction is completed, the resulting products are released from the active site and more substrate molecules bind to it. This process allows an enzyme to catalyze round after round of chemical reactions.

Enzyme active sites can bind only select molecules. In other words, enzymes manifest a high chemical specificity. This selectivity stems from the ability of the enzyme's active site to precisely match the geometry of the substrate molecules. Another contributor is the set of exacting molecular interactions that occur between the chemical groups found in the active site and substrates.

Like other protein-binding sites, the active site is typically a pocket located on the folded protein chain's three-dimensional surface. The active site surface consists of a variety of precisely positioned chemical groups. As noted above, these chemical groups come from the amino acids that form the protein chain. The amino acids that contribute to the active site may be located in completely different regions of the protein chain, but they are brought into the appropriate location when the protein chain folds into a three-dimensional shape.

The spatial orientation of these chemical groups plays a critical role in the enzyme's ability to speed up chemical reactions. These chemical groups stabilize the transition state of the enzyme substrates when they react and shield the reactants from unwanted side reactions.

When molecules react, some chemical bonds are broken and others formed. Atoms within the molecule become redistributed. Chemical groups within and among the molecules temporarily associate and dissociate. These atomic-scale events proceed sequentially along a reaction coordinate. At specific points along the reaction coordinate, temporary molecular entities (transition states) exist. These molecular configurations are unstable and more energetic than either the original reactants or the final products. The less stable the transition state (or the higher its energy), the slower the reaction.

The chemical groups located within an enzyme's active site are oriented in such a way that they interact with the reactants as they advance along the reaction coordinate. These interactions stabilize the transition states, lowering their energy, and ultimately accelerate reactions.

Though conceptually simple, designing these two artificial enzymes was no trivial undertaking. The researchers' strategy involved:

1. Modeling the reaction mechanism and transition state;
2. Determining how to stabilize the transition state by placing chemical groups around the transition-state complex;
3. Designing an enzyme active site that yielded the proper placement of chemical groups;
4. Constructing the scaffolding of the protein chain to form and accommodate the active site;
5. Further fine-tuning of the resulting enzymes.

Executing this strategy required a large team of quantum and computational chemists, protein engineers, biochemists, and molecular biologists. The computations needed to design the active site and the initial enzyme architectures required hours of supercomputer time.

The primary reason so much effort went into designing the active site and protein scaffold was that the computational chemists and protein engineers weren't able to build enzymes from first principles. Instead, the researchers pieced together the enzymes from domains of about one hundred proteins of known structure, essentially mixing and matching protein regions to produce enzyme mosaics. Using this approach, lab workers then had to sort through combinations for about one hundred thousand different protein regions. Once a workable scaffold was created, the scientists optimized it using computational techniques. One of the target enzymes yielded fifty-eight candidates.

These candidate enzymes were synthesized and evaluated in the lab for their catalytic capabilities. Of the nearly five dozen possibilities, only eight performed well enough to go to the next stage. The structures of the best enzymes were then fine-tuned through a process known as *in vitro* evolution. For one created enzyme, the *in vitro* evolution step improved efficiency roughly two hundredfold.

Despite this enhancement, the enzyme operated with ten thousand to a billion times *less* efficiency than enzymes typically found in living systems. The study's authors admit, "Although our results demonstrate that novel enzyme activities can be designed from scratch and indicate the catalytic strategies that are most accessible to nascent enzymes, there is still a significant gap between the activities of our designed catalysts and those of naturally occurring enzymes."[9]

Still, this advance represents a landmark accomplishment, a towering intellectual achievement in every way. The ability to design enzymes that can catalyze novel, nonbiological chemical reactions will lead to a better understanding of protein structure and enzyme catalysis and will pave the way for protein engineers to design enzymes with industrial, agricultural, and biomedical utility.

Additionally, these efforts have bearing on the creation-evolution controversy. Given the effort required to design a single enzyme that, at best, compares unfavorably with any found in nature, the difference is astounding. Collaborative effort from a large number of brilliant minds was crucial to the results. These researchers relied on sophisticated mathematical algorithms and technology—supercomputers and laboratory instruments.

If it takes this much work and intellectual input to create a single enzyme from scratch, is it really reasonable to think undirected evolutionary processes routinely accomplished this task? And with far superior capability each time an enzyme emerged in nature?

Even the simplest known organism requires a few thousand proteins for its existence. How many coincidences must take place to account for the construction of the full range of enzymes necessary for life—all at once—let alone for the precise interactions life requires?

In addition to the questions these efforts raise about the origin of life, this new research provides direct experimental evidence that life's molecules (and therefore life) must originate from the work of an intelligent, intentional agent, one with far greater capacities and resources than an entire team of quantum and computational chemists, protein engineers, biochemists, and molecular biologists.

Artificial DNA: A Strategic Redesign

Scientists and laypeople alike equate DNA with life itself. This biomolecule—ideally suited to harbor genetic information—is so indispensable that many in the scientific community cannot imagine how any life-form could exist without it.

In recent years, however, a number of scientists have begun to wonder if there might be an alternative. These investigators speculate that life "as we don't know it" may exist elsewhere in the solar system or beyond and that perhaps these hypothetical organisms rely on something other than DNA. Such life might use a completely different type of molecule to store the information necessary for directing life's operations and for passing that information on to future generations.

This imaginative thinking has inspired some synthetic biologists to consider creating artificial life based on some genetic material other than DNA and RNA. As with the creation of nonnatural proteins, a huge amount of work has been invested in this area of synthetic biology. Here again, a sampling of research into the design of novel, nonnatural genetic material will suffice to show what's being accomplished in the lab.

As a first step toward this goal, most researchers are working to make variant DNA molecules with the hope that this accomplishment will lead to the development of genetic materials that have no structural relationship to DNA at all. As pointed out in the previous chapter, Jack Szostak and his colleagues are working to devise variant DNAs.[10] Thus far they've focused on two systems: glycerol nucleic acids (GNA) and phosphoramidate glycerol nucleic acids (pGNA). Instead of relying on ribose or deoxyribose as part of their backbone, as in RNA and DNA, respectively, these molecules use glycerol.

Szostak's team demonstrated that GNA can serve as a template to build a complementary DNA strand using DNA polymerase enzymes (proteins that make DNA by adding nucleotides, one by one, to a single strand of DNA), and conversely, DNA can function as a template to construct short GNA strands, again using certain types of DNA polymerases.

The scientist perhaps most closely associated with the creation of artificial DNA is Steven Benner, who recently formed the Foundation for Applied Molecular Evolution. Benner and his collaborators have designed DNA molecules that incorporate eight nonnatural nucleobases into their structure along with the four naturally occurring nucleobases (A, G, C, and T).[11] The artificial DNA molecules are referred to as AEGIS (artificially expanded genetic information systems).

These nonnatural nucleobases form base-pair partners just like A-T and G-C. Benner and his collaborators have shown that when nucleotides containing these nonnatural nucleobases are incorporated into DNA, they don't distort the DNA double helix.

What's more, the team demonstrated that DNA polymerases can use a DNA strand containing nonnatural nucleobases as a template to generate a complementary DNA strand. This result means that once researchers have synthetically made DNA containing nonnatural nucleobases, these molecules can replicate using DNA polymerases, just as does the natural form of DNA.

Researchers observe that these polymerases often make mistakes when assembling a DNA strand. Such mistakes alter the DNA sequence and, in effect, constitute mutations. Because of these mutations, the artificial DNA can evolve. In the future, Benner's group plans to subject their systems to "natural" selection, given that self-replication and evolvability are widely considered to be the two key properties of life.

This remarkable work sets the stage for more ambitious experiments that scientists hope will lead to the creation of artificial life-forms with novel, non-natural biochemistries. When researchers create artificial life-forms, many will likely triumphantly declare that God isn't necessary to explain life's origin.

When that time comes, perhaps a few scientists will be bold enough to counter that view. After all, this accomplishment will demonstrate empirically that if not for the involvement of creators, life could not have come about. Benner's work hints at this conclusion.

As a brief review, the preparation of artificial DNA molecules required careful laboratory manipulations on the part of highly skilled chemists. More importantly, to create artificial DNA molecules, Benner and his team had to develop well-thought-out design strategies. A significant amount of mental effort was expended to identify artificial nucleobases that would pair with each other in the DNA double helix without distorting it. The researchers also labored to identify nonnatural nucleobases that would be recognizable by DNA polymerases. Even though trial and error was part of this effort, the ingenuity of Benner and his team is evident throughout the experimental process.

One of the many hurdles Benner and his colleagues had to overcome was the incorporation of nonnatural nucleobases into DNA without distorting the double helix structure. To address this challenge, they changed the way nucleobases bind to sugars. (Instead of relying on an N-glycosidic linkage, found naturally in DNA, they had to use a nonnatural C-glycosidic linkage.) This success depended on the team's detailed understanding of DNA structure, not to mention their reliance on modeling studies that showed what would result from modifications based on the way the nucleobases bind to the sugar groups of DNA.

Given how much effort these scientists expended to make AEGIS, it seems unreasonable to think the highly optimized structure of DNA[12] originated via naturalistic evolutionary processes. This work argues that any type of life, known or not, must come from the work of a mind and a will coupled with resources and power.

Boundless Grandeur

The quest to make life in the lab is well underway. Protein engineers and synthetic biologists have made remarkable strides by producing nonnatural proteins using rational design principles. These researchers have also taken important steps toward creating nonnatural genetic materials by producing a variety of different types of artificial DNA.

Despite this success, the goal of making artificial life that is completely distinct from anything found in nature seems a long way off. One key hurdle is to find a biochemical process analogous to molecular biology's central dogma (see appendix, p. 203), a process that can decode the information stored in artificial genetic systems to produce functional molecules that carry out essential life-sustaining activities. The production of artificial life "as we don't know it" may be decades away. But this work will continue to capture headlines as researchers make important strides toward the final goal. Meanwhile, the theological implications will no doubt continue to generate debate in the creation-evolution discussion.

The synthetic biologists in the thick of this controversy aren't the first scientists to concern themselves with making life at the laboratory bench top. Origin-of-life researchers have been pursuing virtually this same goal for nearly six decades but for different reasons. They see creation of artificial, non-natural life-forms as a means to understanding how life originated on Earth, presumably with simple chemical compounds evolving first into protocellular entities and then into true cells.

To achieve this understanding, some researchers work to assemble life from the bottom up, hoping to recapitulate events thought to have occurred on early Earth as part of the origin-of-life process. This endeavor resembles the attempts of synthetic biologists to make protocells from the bottom up. Origin-of-life scientists want to discover ways to assemble increasingly sophisticated ensembles and aggregates of molecules with the hope that these entities will eventually operate as living systems. In doing so, they may learn the secrets of how life originated, or at least uncover clues about how this process took place.

Because of this parallel in the two endeavors, many origin-of-life investigators work in synthetic biology, and many synthetic biologists express interest in the origin-of-life question. In nearly all respects, these two areas of research intertwine.

And theological questions surround origin-of-life research just as they do work in synthetic biology. If life can emerge from nonliving systems through a chemical evolutionary process, then why did the first life-forms need a Creator?

The remainder of this book turns attention to bottom-up attempts to create life as part of the origin-of-life research program and discusses what this work means for the creation-evolution controversy. The exploration begins with an overview of the scientific models proposed to explain how life could have emerged on Earth through chemical evolutionary processes. Subsequent chapters examine the work of investigators whose work tests the different ideas proposed to explain life's origin.

7

The Particulars of Life's Formation

Sometimes I endeavoured to gain from Frankenstein the particulars
of his creature's formation: but on this point he was impenetrable.
  "Are you mad, my friend?" said he; "or whither does your sense-
less curiosity lead you?"

Robert Walton in *Frankenstein*

Through the fictional account of Victor Frankenstein, Mary Shelley explored the potency and peril of relying on science to address the most fundamental questions about life. The titular character represents those who would turn to "natural philosophy" to "unfold to the world the deepest mysteries of creation."

In some ways I identify with young Frankenstein, who decides to study chemistry as the means to gain understanding about the basic makeup of life and how it came to be. He progresses quickly in his studies at the University of Ingolstadt, gaining accolades for his accomplishments.

Yet Frankenstein's achievements lose importance to him after a lecture by one of his professors. The presentation stirs Frankenstein's intellectual curiosity, launching him on a quest to understand the "principle" that undergirds life. This curiosity about the nature of life (which I still hold) captivates Frankenstein to the point of an obsession. He begins spending long days and nights working in the lab in secret, driven to apprehend life's secrets and thus acquire godlike power.

Frankenstein's mentors consider such pursuits "off limits." As representatives of Shelley's culture, they consider the quest to comprehend the fundamental nature of life to be a waste of time, because such knowledge is "out of reach."

To his surprise, Frankenstein's devotion leads to success. He discovers "the cause of generation and life." In fact, he becomes "capable of bestowing animation on lifeless matter." Yet Frankenstein refuses to tell anyone about his breakthrough.

Sometimes the parallels between fact and fiction are startling. Stanley Miller was a young graduate student at the University of Chicago when he developed a keen interest in the "cause of generation and life" after hearing a lecture by Nobel Laureate Harold Urey. In his talk to faculty and students, Urey presented the current ideas about the early Earth's atmosphere and related them to the leading hypothesis of the day for life's origin, the Oparin-Haldane hypothesis.

For the first time, an approach seemed to provide a strictly mechanistic explanation for the generation of life. Although this idea had been proposed in the 1920s, no one had done any work to substantiate it for nearly three decades. But Miller's curiosity was piqued, and the idea soon became an obsession. Miller approached Urey and asked to join his lab expressly to pursue verification of the Oparin-Haldane hypothesis.

Urey initially discouraged Miller out of concern for the grad student's future, viewing that pursuit as too risky for a graduate student. Miller persisted, however, and Urey reluctantly agreed. But in the best interest of this PhD candidate, Urey set a time limit to show progress on the project. And, as the saying goes, the rest is history.

To everyone's surprise, Miller quickly generated amino acids and alpha hydroxy acids from a simple mixture of gases then thought to exist in the early Earth's atmosphere. He later determined the reaction pathway that produced these compounds. Miller provided experimental validation of the Oparin-Haldane hypothesis and in the process created the building blocks of proteins. Though Miller was far from "bestowing animation on lifeless matter," he appeared to be on the cusp of "unfolding to the world" one of "the deepest mysteries of creation"—the origin of life.

Unlike Frankenstein, real scientists are typically eager to communicate their accomplishments. And although standard academic practices call for research advisors to be listed as the primary author on papers generated within their lab, Urey selflessly insisted that Miller publish his work as the sole author. Though Urey's name rightfully belonged on the paper submitted to *Science*, Urey recognized the significance of Miller's work and wanted him to be the full beneficiary of the acclaim.

Both the *New York Herald Tribune* and *New York Times* wrote about Miller and his discovery on the same day his paper appeared in *Science*. A short time later, *Time*, *Newsweek*, and *Life* wrote about his work. Suddenly, at age twenty-three, Stanley Miller was propelled to worldwide fame.

Most graduate students are drawn to science by a fascination with nature and a deep desire to understand how it works. This allure provides the motivation to put in long, hard hours at the lab. Certainly this must have been true of Miller. Still, in the back of their minds, most young scientists hope their research will lead to a breakthrough so significant that it will propel them to global recognition. More often than not, this great expectation never materializes. But young Stanley Miller lived the dream.

Miller's impact on science has been profound. Because he was willing to tackle a question that many established scientists shied away from, his famous spark discharge experiments launched the origin-of-life research program as a formal scientific discipline. Miller's success inaugurated a series of similar experiments by other scientists.[1] Giddy with success, Miller and others believed they were only a few decades away from accounting for life's wholly spontaneous origin.[2]

Since then, hosts of scientists have performed countless experiments designed to reveal the particulars of life's origin from a naturalistic evolutionary standpoint. Researchers have attempted to identify:

- chemical routes that generate compounds such as amino acids, nucleobases, sugars, and fatty acids. These materials are the building blocks for more complex biomolecules, including proteins, nucleic acids, and cell membrane components (see appendix).
- reactions that will cause these building blocks to assemble into more complex biomolecules.
- physicochemical routes that culminate in the emergence of metabolic networks.
- processes that cause complex biomolecules and protometabolic pathways to aggregate into precellular entities that, in turn, evolve to yield bona fide life-forms.

Fitting Partners

In their quest to understand life's genesis, origin-of-life researchers have much in common with synthetic biologists. Some of the most prominent figures in origin-of-life research even cross over to investigate questions in synthetic biology. Synthetic biologists want to create nonnatural life in the laboratory by reengineering life from the top down *or* by piecing together molecules from the bottom up. Origin-of-life researchers want to understand how life emerged from inanimate matter on early Earth via undirected evolutionary processes from the bottom up.

These two activities frequently overlap. To understand the origin of life, investigators go into the lab and manipulate chemicals in an attempt to identify chemical reactions and physical mechanisms that can generate life's building blocks from simple compounds likely present on early Earth. In turn, the researchers conduct experiments to learn how these building-block materials could assemble themselves into more complex molecules that aggregate and evolve to eventually form living systems.

Origin-of-life researchers do essentially the same thing as synthetic biologists. The only difference is their emphasis. Origin-of-life researchers' attempts to re-create life are constrained by the conditions and resources available on primordial Earth. Synthetic biologists use whatever means available to generate life from scratch.

Many origin-of-life researchers see attempts to create artificial life in the lab as providing important clues for how life originated. As synthetic biologists figure out how to assemble molecules into increasingly complex entities that ever so closely resemble life, the laboratory pathways they develop may well mirror events that took place on early Earth during life's chemical evolution. As synthetic biologists get closer and closer to creating life in the lab, their work encourages the belief that life could have emerged on early Earth through similar chemical processes.

At the same time, many origin-of-life investigators have begun to apply what they've learned in studying origin-of-life questions to tasks facing synthetic biologists. For example, as scientists discover chemical routes that yield life's building blocks and lead to the assembly of these materials into more complex materials, they can apply this knowledge to jump-start efforts to create artificial life. Because the disciplines are now so intertwined, exploring how life may have originated provides useful insights for creating life in the lab.

The Particulars of Formation

Victor Frankenstein adamantly refuses to tell anyone how he created his monster for fear someone may repeat his "mistake." Origin-of-life researchers seem far less reticent.

Scientists enthusiastically proffer numerous ideas to explain life's beginnings. Some are well-grounded in evidential support and others highly speculative. These ideas—prolific in number and complexity—at times appear to have no relationship to each other. Yet most origin-of-life scenarios actually share key features. The critical components common to these models include:

- synthesis of prebiotic molecules;
- concentration of prebiotic molecules;
- formation of life's building blocks;

- assembly of life's building-block molecules into complex biomolecules;
- development of self-replication;
- emergence of metabolism;
- aggregation of biomolecules to form protocells;
- evolution of protocells into true cells.

Interestingly, synthetic biologists follow this exact sequence in their attempts to create life from the bottom up.

An overview of the widely recognized "textbook" description for life's origin makes a good starting point for exploring the features so central to all evolutionary origin-of-life descriptions. This widely recognized textbook model has been strongly influenced by the Oparin-Haldane hypothesis of the early twentieth century, as are all credible origin-of-life explanations. A review of various evolutionary approaches to the origin-of-life question provides important background for understanding the quest to create life in the lab.

By the Book

The textbook scenario for life's origin begins shortly after Earth's formation (see Figure 7.1).[3] Early Earth's conditions differed markedly from conditions today. So evolutionary biologists have postulated that gases such as water vapor, ammonia, methane, carbon monoxide, carbon dioxide, and nitrogen made up primordial Earth's atmosphere.

Of crucial importance to this scenario is the likely lack of atmospheric oxygen. This type of "reducing atmosphere" can sustain the formation of small prebiotic molecules (such as hydrogen cyanide, formaldehyde, etc.) under high-energy conditions. Over the years, origin-of-life researchers have suggested numerous high-energy sources as catalysts for the formation of prebiotic

FIGURE 7.1

"Textbook" Description of Life's Origin

Early Earth's Atmosphere → **Simple Prebiotic Molecules** (aq) → **Prebiotic Soup**
Energy   *Energy*

Prebiotic Molecules → **Biomolecules** → **Protocells**
Condensation Reactions   *Aggregation*

Protocells → **Simple Cells** → **LUCA***
Time   *Time*

*Last Universal Common Ancestor

molecules. The list of potential energy sources includes lightning, ultraviolet radiation, solar and volcanic heat, cosmic rays, and ionizing radiation from radioactive elements in the Earth's crust.

Once formed, according to the textbooks, these prebiotic molecules accumulated in Earth's oceans over vast periods of time to form the legendary primordial or prebiotic soup.[4] Within this chemical soup, the prebiotic molecules reacted over the eons to form more complex molecules such as amino acids, sugars, fatty acids, purines, and pyrimidines. These molecules, in turn, functioned as building blocks for more complex molecules that eventually led to the biomolecules—DNA, RNA, and proteins—found in modern cells.

According to this description, a self-replicating molecule at long last came together, and the increasing concentration of complex molecules in the soup prompted their aggregation into protocells. These entities supposedly possessed partial cellular properties and became predecessors of the first true cells. Undirected chemical and physical events are credited with transferring their self-replicating ability to the protocells. The scenario goes that over time, evolutionary processes (e.g. chemical and natural selection) gradually transformed the protocells, increasing their capacity to self-replicate and to carry out various metabolic processes. As these changes occurred, the protocells gained greater complexity.

Ultimately, these protocells are said to have yielded an organism, referred to as the last universal common ancestor (LUCA). LUCA presumably resembled modern-day prokaryotes, such as bacteria and archaea (archaebacteria). Prokaryotes are single-celled organisms, about 1 micron across, that lack a nucleus and other internal cell structures. LUCA, seen as the root of the evolutionary tree of life, then evolved to yield life's three major domains.

Current Origin-of-Life Scenarios

Today, the origin-of-life research community has progressed beyond the Oparin-Haldane hypothesis, beyond the familiar textbook description for life's beginning still taught in most schools.[5] Both new discoveries and recognized problems with the Oparin-Haldane explanation (to be discussed in chapter 9) have prompted this movement. Figure 7.2 highlights the various origin-of-life scenarios currently under consideration and reveals some of the complex relationships among these models.[6]

Finding the Right Place

The textbook description for life's origin focuses exclusively on a terrestrial location. While most researchers attempt to explain life's beginning as an

FIGURE 7.2

Current Explanations for Life's Origin

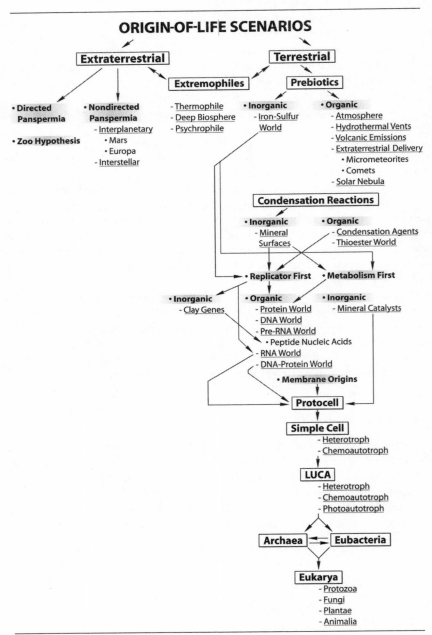

event on Earth, a number of investigators look elsewhere in our solar system or beyond for life's origin, or at least for the origin of prebiotic molecules. For these scientists, life's origin on Earth equates to its arrival, or the arrival of its building blocks, from an extraterrestrial location.

Much of the research emphasis for extraterrestrial origin-of-life models, called *panspermia models*, centers on identification and characterization of life transport mechanisms between planetary bodies and stellar systems. Nevertheless, extraterrestrial explanations must, at some point, account for life's initial emergence. Because these extraterrestrial scenarios rely on, and overlap with, models that attempt to explain life's start on Earth, a focus on terrestrial origin-of-life models seems sufficient for our purposes. (See my book *Origins of Life*, coauthored with astronomer Hugh Ross, for a detailed discussion of panspermia models.[7])

Finding the Source of the Soup

All origin-of-life scenarios require a source of prebiotic compounds. The Oparin-Haldane hypothesis considered reactions in Earth's atmosphere as the chief means to generate these compounds. Some researchers still pursue atmospheric reactions as their source.[8] Others, propelled by recent discoveries about life-thwarting conditions in early Earth's atmosphere, explore other mechanisms for prebiotic molecule production.

A few origin-of-life researchers speculate that early Earth's volcanoes functioned as a source.[9] In their hypotheses, the gases emitted by volcanoes take the place of atmospheric gases. They postulate that reducing gases made up the volcanic emissions on early Earth and energy sources such as volcanic lightning provided the spark that catalyzed reactions within the volcanic gases to produce prebiotic compounds.

Perhaps the most popular alternative location for prebiotic synthesis in current origin-of-life thought is deep-sea hydrothermal vents.[10] Presumably, the gases released at these vents reacted, with the assistance of metal ions and sulfide, to produce prebiotic compounds. The discovery of microbes inhabiting these environments—organisms considered some of the oldest on Earth—further bolsters this line of thought.[11]

Closely related to the notion of hydrothermal vent production of prebiotics is the iron-sulfur world model proposed and advocated almost exclusively by German patent lawyer and chemist Günter Wächtershäuser.[12] Wächtershäuser asserts that pyrite (FeS_2) played a central role not only in producing the first prebiotic compounds but also in forming the earliest metabolic pathways. According to his scenario, pyrites accumulated at the edge of deep-sea hydrothermal vents when iron(2) sulfide reacted with hydrogen sulfide. The energy released from pyrite formation and the catalytic activity of pyrite surfaces drove the formation of prebiotic molecules from the carbon monoxide and hydrogen gas emitted by the seafloor vents.

Rivaling the deep-sea hydrothermal vent models in popularity today are models that propose comets, micrometeorites, and interplanetary dust particles as extraterrestrial delivery vehicles bringing prebiotic compounds to Earth.[13] Advocates of these models point to the detection and recovery of a wide class of organic compounds in meteorites as supporting evidence.

Alternatively, some scientists maintain that prebiotic materials were already present in the gaseous nebula that condensed to form the solar system. Support for the idea that prebiotic materials are endogenous to the solar system, and perhaps the early Earth, comes from the detection of biologically interesting compounds in nebulae and forming solar systems.

Condensing the Soup

Once prebiotic compounds (such as amino acids, sugars, and nucleotide bases) supposedly formed and accumulated sufficiently to generate either global or localized primordial soups, the next phase of chemical evolution kicks in. In this step, the building-block materials are said to react with one another to form more complex molecules. As subunit molecules link together to form chainlike structures, they eventually yield compounds such as nucleic acids (RNA and DNA), proteins, and other essential biomolecules.

One challenge to this scenario is that when condensation reactions take place, water molecules form. For example, when two glycine molecules (amino acids) condense, the product is diglycine and a water molecule. Because water is a by-product, condensation reactions are thermodynamically prohibited in an aqueous environment, such as a prebiotic soup.

Most origin-of-life scenarios respond to this challenge by relying on a localized evaporation of the prebiotic soup, such as deposition of prebiotic compounds through tidal actions onto the shores of volcanic islands, for example. Under dehydrating conditions, condensation reactions become energetically feasible. However, condensation reactions still require assistance. So some origin-of-life explanations include the speculation that the reactions responsible for generating prebiotic molecules also yielded condensing agents.[14]

These compounds participate in chemical reactions by removing a water molecule from the reactants and adding the water molecule to their (the condensing agents') structural makeup. Thus, condensing agents drive condensation reactions. Origin-of-life investigators maintain that if the prebiotic soup contained condensing agents and codeposited them along with other prebiotic compounds in locations where the prebiotic soup evaporated, these compounds could have, in principle, facilitated the formation of more complex biomolecules.

Support for such scenarios comes from lab experiments demonstrating the ready production of condensing agents (for example, cyanamide, cyanogen, cyanoformamide, cyanate, diaminomaleonitrite, trimetaphosphate, and pyrophosphates) under conditions that may conceivably simulate early Earth's environment. Other experiments show that these condensing agents promote the initial steps of protein formation from amino acids and nucleic acid (DNA and RNA) formation from sugars and nucleotide bases.

While the appeal to condensing agents finds its way into more traditional origin-of-life scenarios, more current explanations rely on mineral surfaces as the catalyst for condensation reactions.[15] Mineral surfaces have (1) chemical characteristics that allow them to bind organic molecules, including prebiotic compounds; and (2) properties that make them ideally suited to assist chemical reactions.

Origin-of-life researchers theorize that mineral-assisted formation of complex biomolecules from prebiotic precursors could have occurred either at locations where the prebiotic soup evaporated or within the aqueous environment of the prebiotic soup. Since prebiotic compounds can adsorb (bind to the surface) to mineral surfaces, minerals found on the early Earth may have bound and sequestered prebiotic compounds and promoted iterative condensation reactions before the complex biomolecules desorbed from the mineral surface. In support of this idea, origin-of-life researchers have used clays (kaolinite, montmorillonite) to drive the condensation of amino acids to form protein precursors (peptides) and short RNA chains from activated nucleotides.[16]

Nobel Laureate Christian de Duve points to another possible mechanism to account for the formation of complex biomolecules. He calls this explanation the thioester world model.[17] Thioesters are sulfur-containing compounds that possess high-energy sulfur-carbon chemical bonds. The cell uses high-energy thioesters to store and provide the chemical energy needed to form fatty acids.

Presumably, thioesters could have formed in sulfur-rich environments such as hydrothermal vents. Thioester derivatives of prebiotic compounds, such as amino acids, readily react with other amino acids to form condensation products because of the chemical instability of the high-energy thioester bond. This reaction could possibly have occurred under either arid or aqueous conditions.

A Difference of Opinion

Regardless of where prebiotic compounds came from or how they condensed to form more complex biomolecules, naturalistic origin-of-life scenarios must next identify self-organization pathways capable of generating two of life's key biochemical features: self-replication and metabolism. From a molecular standpoint, self-replication describes the capacity of a complex molecule to guide its own reproduction, typically by acting as a template that directs the assembly of chemical constituents into molecules identical to the original.

Metabolism defines the entire set of chemical pathways in the cell. The foremost of these are pathways that lead to the chemical transformation of relatively small molecules. Some of these pathways generate chemical energy through the controlled breakdown of fuel molecules such as sugars and fats. Other pathways produce, in a stepwise fashion, the building blocks for the assembly of proteins, DNA, and RNA, as well as cell-membrane and cell-wall components.

Life's metabolic pathways often share multiple molecules. So the cell's metabolic routes interconnect to form complex, reticulated webs of chemical interactions.

As part of an intramural debate, one group of origin-of-life researchers argues that self-organization started with metabolism (the metabolism-first model), while the other insists that life emerged from self-replicators (the replicator-first model).

Proponents of the *metabolism-first model* maintain that mineral surfaces catalyzed the formation of a diverse collection of small molecules that, over time, evolved to form an interconnected series of chemical reactions. Once in place, the proponents say, these interrelated chemical reactions formed the basis for the cell's metabolic systems, and eventually these chemical networks became encapsulated to form protocells replete with a form of protometabolism.[18] Some metabolism-first scenarios, such as the iron-sulfur world, even suggest that pyrite or other minerals became encapsulated along with the protometabolic networks and thereby became life's first catalysts. According to the metabolism-first idea, once protometabolic systems were established, they gave rise to self-replicating molecules.

Enthusiasts of the *replicator-first model* propose that a naked replicator emerged and later became encapsulated along with the precursor molecules needed to sustain its activity. Metabolism subsequently developed, according to this view, as a means to support the production and turnover of the replicator's building blocks and ultimately its self-replicating activity. Early efforts to determine the original replicator's identity led to a debate over which came first, DNA or proteins. This controversy brought light to a proverbial "chicken-and-egg" problem.[19]

Scientists have long known that proteins and DNA totally depend on one another when it comes to their synthesis and biochemical roles in the cell. DNA stores all the information the cell needs to function. DNA replication produces duplicate copies of this information and transmits it to the next generation as part of the reproductive process. However, even though scientists refer to DNA as a self-replicating molecule, its synthesis (and hence replication) requires a suite of proteins. In other words, proteins replicate DNA.

Yet without DNA, the cell can't produce the very proteins needed for practically every cell function. DNA contains the information used by the cell's machinery to synthesize proteins. Because of their complete interdependence, DNA and proteins would have had to emerge simultaneously—an event origin-of-life researchers are hard-pressed to explain.

Exploring the RNA World

Many origin-of-life researchers look to RNA as a potential resolution to the chicken-and-egg problem. A chainlike molecule that shares many structural similarities with DNA, RNA plays the role of an intermediary in protein formation. As you recall, it conveys the information stored in DNA to the cell's protein-making systems.

Many origin-of-life investigators think RNA was the earliest replicator, predating both DNA and proteins.[20] According to the RNA world hypothesis, RNA took on the contemporary biochemical functions of both DNA and proteins, operating as a self-replicator that catalyzed its own synthesis. Supposedly, numerous RNA molecules that possessed a wide range of catalytic activity emerged over time. RNA world biochemistry centered exclusively on RNA.

With time, the RNA world is thought to have transitioned first to an RNA-protein world, then, with the addition of DNA to the cell's arsenal, to contemporary biochemistry. As the RNA world transitioned to the DNA-protein world, RNA's original function would have become partitioned between proteins and DNA, with RNA assuming its current intermediary role. The RNA ancestral molecules presumably disappeared without leaving a trace of their primordial existence.

The RNA world model had its roots in the late 1960s, based on ideas advanced by Francis Crick, Leslie Orgel, and Carl Woese. These three posited a primitive cellular system based on RNA.[21] In the mid-1980s, the discovery of RNA molecules with enzymatic activity (ribozymes) propelled the RNA world hypothesis to prominence, and there it remains.[22] Perhaps most exciting for its proponents is the recent recognition that the ribosome (the subcellular structure that directs protein synthesis) is, in essence, a ribozyme.[23]

Since that discovery, several researchers have produced a number of ribozymes that engage in a range of potential biological activity.[24] Included in this list are RNA molecules that have been engineered to self-replicate.[25] For many origin-of-life researchers, this success adds further credibility to the RNA world scenario.

Given the predominance of the RNA world hypothesis, much of the origin-of-life research that takes place in the lab focuses on identifying chemical routes toward the production of both the prebiotic compounds and the condensation reactions that could lead to RNA. Meanwhile, these efforts also fuel attempts to create artificial life in the lab and have been used by Szostak's group in their quest to make protocells (see chapter 5).

Searching for Alternatives

Despite the popularity of RNA, some origin-of-life researchers are looking beyond RNA for the first replicator. Making RNA building blocks is difficult enough that some scientists are revisiting the possibility that either DNA or proteins functioned as the first replicators. New studies that demonstrate DNA's capacity to catalyze chemical reactions (to a limited degree) and proteins' ability to self-replicate revitalize the DNA and protein world scenarios.[26]

Other origin-of-life investigators have incorporated an additional, earlier stage to the RNA world pathway. These pre-RNA world scenarios promote the idea of self-replicating molecules structurally simpler and more stable than RNA. One chief candidate for the first replicator is a class of compounds called peptide nucleic acids (PNA).[27] This type of molecule is a protein-DNA hybrid. Its backbone resembles that of a protein, and its side groups are the same as those found in DNA and RNA. In principle, PNA may possess the characteristics necessary to self-replicate.

A Missing Step

One of life's defining features, as discussed in chapter 2, is the presence of a membrane that surrounds the cell and segregates its contents from the external environment. In addition to defining life's boundaries and forming internal cell compartments, cell membranes play a central role in energy production and support a variety of biochemical processes. For example, cell membranes regulate the transport of materials into and out of the cell.

The formation of (presumably) primitive cell membranes and their subsequent evolution into contemporary membranes represent key stages in the emergence of the first protocells. Yet, over the years, researchers have given only limited attention to cell membrane origins. Scientists simply have assumed that once the components that form cell membranes were present, they readily and spontaneously self-assembled and self-organized in the presence of water.[28]

Origin-of-life researchers also maintain that, once formed, primitive cell membranes readily encapsulated self-replicators and protometabolic pathways through dehydration-hydration cycles that occurred either when the prebiotic soup experienced localized evaporation or when tidal action occurred along the shoreline of volcanic islands.

For origin-of-life researchers, then, a crucial question must be answered in their attempt to account for cell membranes and consequently the emergence of the first protocell: what was the source of the self-assembling prebiotic compounds that formed primitive cell membranes? Some origin-of-life researchers posit their production on early Earth and others suggest extraterrestrial delivery made these compounds available.[29]

Tracing a Common Ancestor

Origin-of-life researchers maintain that once protocells arose, natural selection took over to transform them into simple cellular entities. Cellular evolution supposedly occurred as random chemical and physical changes generated modified protocells with increased metabolic efficiency and improved reproductive efficacy.

Some scientists assert that the first cells were heterotrophs, organisms that presumably consumed preexisting organic compounds from the prebiotic soup to gain the energy and raw materials necessary for sustaining their primitive cellular activities. The chief difficulty with a heterotroph-first model, however, would be overconsumption of the organic foodstuff. Without a means to replenish the raw materials needed to sustain their heterotrophic lifestyle, these organisms would have self-exterminated.

Other origin-of-life investigators posit that the first cells were autotrophs. These organisms possess the capability to generate energy and biomolecules from simple inorganic materials in the environment. Two known types of autotrophs are photoautotrophs and chemoautotrophs. Photoautotrophs capture solar energy, whereas chemoautotrophs harvest chemical energy from materials in their environments.

Because of the added metabolic complexity photoautotrophs would have required, most origin-of-life researchers have abandoned them as good candidates for the first cells. More scientists lean toward considering chemoautotrophic pathways as the ones that emerged along with the protocells' other biochemical systems. The chemoautotroph-first model alleviates the overconsumption problem; however, it places a significant *additional* demand on the origin-of-life scenario—an explanation for the emergence and evolution of complex chemoautotrophic pathways.

After simple cells took hold, origin-of-life researchers maintain, those cells evolved to produce the last universal common ancestor (LUCA). Some scientists see LUCA as a single cellular entity; others view LUCA as a community of cells that coevolved and coalesced to root the evolutionary tree of life.[30]

Once established, LUCA supposedly diversified to yield life's major domains. According to the standard textbook model, LUCA cleanly evolved into Eubacteria and Archaea domains. These two domains consist of morphologically indistinguishable prokaryotes that differ fundamentally at a biochemical level. The standard model has undergone revision as origin-of-life investigators have discovered what seems to be the rampant transfer of large amounts of genetic material between bacteria and archaea after their divergence from LUCA.[31] This exchange of genetic material would demand that the base of the evolutionary tree of life take on a complex, highly reticulated pattern.

This overview merely highlights some of the particulars of life's formation. The details of how life actually originated have yet to be fleshed out. Though origin-of-life researchers claim promising experimental and observational support for chemical evolution, careful reflection on lab efforts strongly suggests otherwise. The next chapter lays out a general framework to help assess the significance of prebiotic experiments. It sets the stage for chapters 9 through 13, which provide a closer look at some of the key stages thought to have occurred in the origin-of-life process.

8

Conquering the Challenges

The materials at present within my command hardly appeared adequate to so arduous an undertaking; but I doubted not that I should ultimately succeed. I prepared myself for a multitude of reverses; my operations might be incessantly baffled, and at last my work be imperfect: yet, when I considered the improvement which every day takes place in science and mechanics, I was encouraged to hope my present attempts would at least lay the foundations of future success.

Victor Frankenstein

On the cliffs of an icy mountain, the fictional Victor Frankenstein finally comes face-to-face with the monster he has created. Disgusted by what he sees, Frankenstein overflows with contempt for the beast. The creature's demand turns Frankenstein's revulsion to horror. The monster desires a suitable mate, a female to love and who can share in the creature's life.

After hearing the brute's humble and woeful tale of self-discovery and rejection by humans, Frankenstein nearly relents. Summoning all the rage and loathing he can muster, Victor refuses the creature's request. He fears the havoc *two* monsters might wreak on unsuspecting humans. And what if the creatures reproduce? Frankenstein is afraid to compound his mistake.

Unlike Shelley's fictional "creator," origin-of-life researchers eagerly anticipate the development of self-replicating entities in the lab. For many, this goal represents the holy grail not only of synthetic biology but also of origin-of-life research. The ability to self-replicate is perhaps one of life's most important features. Many scientists express confidence that the ability to account for life's beginning will arise from the discovery of chemical evolutionary pathways that can yield information-rich molecules capable of directing their own replication with a high degree of fidelity.

During the winter of 2009, it appeared that researchers were close to reaching this goal. Science news headlines announced "Self-Replicating Chemicals Evolve into Lifelike Ecosystem."[1] Written for popular consumption, this article (and others) described work by scientists from the Scripps Research Institute in La Jolla, California. Lab workers had produced an RNA molecule that could replicate. Then they went one step further and forced this molecule to evolve by mutating it so that over time the molecule generated a population of self-replicators with varying capacities for reproduction. These molecules continued to evolve as they reproduced from generation to generation, giving rise to an ecosystem of self-replicators that competed against each other for "survival" with the most efficient reproducers dominating the molecular population. Those of lesser abilities simply disappeared from the system.

On the surface, it appears as if this lab work provides important insight into the origin-of-life question and implies that life (or at least one of its key properties) can emerge all on its own. It looks as if the Scripps scientists accomplished what Frankenstein dared not contemplate.

This type of work is often cited by proponents of chemical evolution. But how firmly does it support their case? Careful examination of these lab efforts reveals strategic and tactical involvement by researchers to produce self-replicators and guide their evolution. So great was their effort that this scientific intervention prompts genuine questions as to whether these types of self-replicating entities realistically could have arisen through undirected processes on early Earth or anywhere else in the universe (see chapter 11).

Laying the Foundation for Success

Herein lies the difficulty with origin-of-life research. These scientists are laboring to understand how undirected chemical and physical processes could have transformed simple chemical compounds into life. But investigators can't go back in time and directly observe the chemical evolution that presumably took place. Though the ancient geochemical record can be probed for clues, these efforts permit only a small glimpse of what might have happened. Studying Earth's oldest rocks has provided key insights into the available chemical resources on early Earth and the likely geochemical and biochemical activities, but the picture is incomplete and often muddled.[2]

As a result, origin-of-life researchers have no choice but to go into the lab and perform experiments with the overarching objective of recapitulating the origin of life. And if they can't achieve that goal, at least their experiments might provide some understanding as to how life could have emerged on Earth.

Unfortunately, however, when scientists do laboratory experiments, they are no longer passive observers of undirected processes. Instead, these researchers become active participants,

1. Designing the protocol;
2. Assembling the apparatus;
3. Supplying the media and reagents for the experiment;
4. Adjusting the initial conditions and regulating them throughout the study;
5. Monitoring the course of chemical and physical changes, usually by withdrawing material from the apparatus.

In other words, human beings interject themselves into the experiment's design, ironically, to demonstrate that life can emerge all on its own without purposeful intervention. In large measure, the scientists from the Scripps Research Institute exemplified this irony when they worked intensively to create an ecosystem of self-replicators.

This intellectual and hands-on involvement runs the risk of making the experiment artificial, no longer reflecting the actual evolutionary events thought to have occurred on early Earth. Instead, these efforts reflect what's possible when a researcher—an intelligent agent—orchestrates physicochemical processes. From an evolutionary standpoint, human involvement is undesirable because the physicochemical processes thought to spawn life would have proceeded without any outside intervention.

Herein lies a conundrum. Lab experiments designed to evaluate various origin-of-life models may not be relevant if the workers conducting research overextend their reach in the design and execution of the protocol. Still, some researcher involvement in origin-of-life experiments is unavoidable. Researchers have no choice but to assemble equipment, add reagents, manipulate initial conditions, and monitor the experimental outputs. Without these actions, there would be no experiment.

This dilemma raises some questions: At what point does researcher involvement render results illegitimate? When does the experiment transition from one providing important insight into the key steps in chemical evolution to one with questionable relevance?

This concern makes a critical assessment of researcher involvement essential.[3] Remarkably, such considerations are seldom mentioned when scientists reflect on the success (or failure) of their experiments. In fact, more often than not, any impact the investigators had on the outcome of their experiment is ignored. As a consequence of this oversight, origin-of-life researchers often appear closer to accounting for life's start than they really are.

Chapters 9 through 13 look more closely at the key stages proposed by origin-of-life investigators for life's genesis (summarized in the previous chapter). Can these stages proceed on their own accord, or do they require the work of a Creator? That's the key question. Central to answering it is a realistic appraisal of the necessity of researchers' involvement in obtaining positive results from origin-of-life experiments. If scientists' involvement is not critical, then support for chemical evolution grows. But if it is necessary for success, then support for the idea that life's start required a Creator grows.

Unfortunately, the way to judge the impact of researcher involvement on experimental outcome is somewhat unclear. There are no hard-and-fast criteria by which to evaluate. So there is much room for debate. For example, is it "tampering" to control the pH and temperature of a chemical reaction once the initial conditions have been established? How much "control" is acceptable, and in what circumstances?

Perhaps the most important factor to consider when assessing the legitimacy of researcher involvement is the *purpose* or *goal* of the experiment. That consideration can help determine when it's acceptable for researchers to be extensively involved in the execution of the study and when it's not.

A New Hope

As origin-of-life researchers work to understand how life came from nonlife, they conduct at least three different categories of experiments, each designed to address specific kinds of questions, and each with its own set of goals.

Proof-of-Principle Experiments

Initial proof-of-principle experiments are undertaken simply to determine if physicochemical processes that could support different stages in the pathway to life's origin even exist. The goal of these experiments is to address questions such as the following:

- Is it possible for reactions among simple gaseous molecules and other inorganic materials to generate life's building blocks, including amino acids, nucleobases, sugars, and fatty acids?
- Is it conceivable that these building-block materials could combine to form more complex biomolecules such as DNA, RNA, and proteins?
- Is there any way homochirality can arise from racemic mixtures?
- Can RNA molecules carry out a range of catalytic activities? Can they self-replicate?
- Is there any process that will allow primitive cell membranes to assemble from fatty acids and other simple amphiphilic compounds?

From a scientific vantage point, researcher intervention is irrelevant when it comes to these proof-of-principle experiments because the goal of this work is simply to determine if certain physical and chemical outcomes are even possible—*in principle*. Researchers doing these types of studies aren't immediately concerned with how *realistic* the experimental conditions are with respect to the early Earth. They're merely trying to understand what is physically and chemically permissible to even consider.

Because researchers often don't know at the outset whether a physical or chemical process is possible, they must try different experimental protocols, carefully controlling and manipulating variables to make a determination. If a particular experiment fails, it doesn't necessarily mean the process in question is impossible from an evolutionary standpoint; it may mean that the researchers haven't discovered the specific conditions required to support the process. On the other hand, if the experiment is successful, scientists haven't necessarily explained a particular stage in the origin of life; they've shown only that the physicochemical process is possible. Any conclusions must then be tested further.

Mechanistic Studies

Once researchers have established that a particular physicochemical process is feasible, they then work to understand its mechanistic basis. The goal of this second class of studies is to ferret out the chemical and physical factors that dictate the outcome of the process. Mechanistic studies also identify the physical and chemical intermediates that link the starting materials to the end products. These experiments address questions such as:

- How does the specific process proceed from start to finish?
- What intermediate structures form in the process?
- What is the temperature and pressure dependence of the process?
- How do solution conditions, including pH and salinity, affect the process? Is the process sensitive to these factors? If so, why?
- Do the concentration and ratio of starting materials influence the process? If so, why?

When it comes to mechanistic studies, researchers' influence on the outcome can't be avoided. In fact, the more the researchers are involved, the better. This may seem counterintuitive, since the goal of origin-of-life research is to explain how life could have emerged via unguided processes. And, typically, the more researchers involve themselves in the design and execution of an experiment, the more artificial and unrealistic the results become. However, only by the elaborate design and deliberate manipulation of experimental conditions can scientists tease out the critical mechanistic features of the process under investigation.

As with proof-of-principle experiments, researcher intervention is irrelevant in evaluating mechanistic studies. When researchers perform these types of investigations, they aren't immediately concerned with the likely conditions and available resources on the early Earth and how they relate to the process. Rather, they are trying to develop a detailed understanding of the physics and chemistry of the processes. Ironically, these efforts, with limited regard to the conditions of the early Earth, are ultimately critical for assessing whether the proposed physicochemical pathway to the origin of life has relevance to early Earth's conditions and supports the notion of chemical evolution.

Geochemical Simulation Experiments

Simulation experiments are perhaps more important than all others for testing the validity of naturalistic origin-of-life models. Researchers conduct these tests to determine whether the different steps in putative origin-of-life pathways realistically could have taken place under the conditions thought to exist on early Earth. Although lab workers can show that a particular physicochemical process is possible in principle and can dissect its mechanism, it's still incumbent upon them to demonstrate that it could have operated on early Earth.

As with nearly everything in science, executing geochemical simulation experiments is less than straightforward. Several factors complicate these investigations. The first arises from the lack of full knowledge as to what resources were available on early Earth. While planetary scientists and geologists are slowly reaching some consensus on primordial Earth's conditions, these researchers still debate significant issues. For example, uncertainties remain about the:

1. Exact composition of Earth's atmosphere;
2. Length of time the planet remained in a molten state;
3. Timing of the formation of Earth's crust;
4. Time frame over which oceans became a permanent feature;
5. Chemistry and composition of early Earth's oceans;
6. Temperature conditions on early Earth.

These uncertainties mean that scientists attempting simulation experiments are often "shooting at a moving target." Work done today in conditions thought to emulate those of early Earth may be meaningless tomorrow if new advances overturn prevailing assumptions about those conditions.

Another problem has to do with the immense complexity of early Earth's environment. The number of chemical species and local variation in the physical milieu of early Earth was likely extreme. There's no adequate way to model this physicochemical diversity in the laboratory—short of combining a bewildering array of chemicals into a single apparatus. Scientists describe these types of studies as synthesis-in-the-whole or Beilstein experiments.

The problem with a synthesis-in-the-whole approach is that the number of potential interactions among compounds in the experiment becomes so copious as to render impossible any real understanding about what happened during the experiment and why. Even though this type of experiment most closely approximates reality, it holds limited value for advancing our understanding of chemical evolution.

Another problem facing geochemical simulations is how to replicate the immense timescale available for chemical evolution on early Earth. Traditionally, origin-of-life researchers have posited that chemical evolution took place over hundreds of millions, if not a billion, years. More recent assessments allow only about ten million years for life's origin to take place.[4] In either case, investigators have no way to reproduce this timescale in the laboratory. The protracted time available for the operation of some physical and chemical processes on early Earth may have been critical for the origin of life. Yet these slow processes may never occur discernibly in a laboratory experiment's timescale. Thus it's impossible to evaluate directly their contribution to life's start.

To get around these difficulties, origin-of-life researchers have no choice but to simplify and alter geochemical simulation experiments. For example, instead of adding thousands of chemicals to a laboratory flask, lab workers might add only a few select compounds for the sake of probing a single physicochemical interaction (among the thousands) that might have taken place on early Earth. By doing enough of these experiments, researchers hope to piece together the network of interactions most likely to have occurred and also establish plausible sequences of events over longer geological timescales. Though admittedly artificial, this type of work can be meaningful if researchers do everything possible to ensure that all other experimental parameters mimic the geochemical conditions of early Earth.

To accelerate slow processes, investigators may raise the temperature of the experiment, alter the energy sources that spark various processes, modify the chemicals to react more quickly, or add catalysts. Again, as much as possible, scientists strive to make sure all other parameters closely match what they know of early Earth's geochemical conditions.

These deviations from geochemical reality often represent a frustrating trade-off for origin-of-life investigators. As helpful and necessary as modifications might be, they certainly run the risk of making simulations unrealistic and therefore irrelevant. And once again, modifications raise questions about whether these physicochemical processes actually could have taken place and produced life on early Earth apart from the involvement of an intelligent agent to direct them toward a specific outcome.

Achieving the Goal

For experiments to validate chemical evolution, researchers must also pay careful attention to these factors in particular:

- *Energy sources.* Researchers must use appropriate sources of energy. The outcome of a simulation can be easily influenced by varying the type and characteristics of energy input.
- *Solution conditions.* As mentioned previously, scientists must ensure that the reaction media have realistic pH values and salinity levels. Both variables can significantly alter physicochemical processes.
- *The concentration and ratios of starting materials.* As already noted, researchers can control the outcome of a chemical reaction by varying these parameters. For the geochemical simulation to be meaningful, concentrations and ratios of starting materials can't deviate too far from the absolute and relative levels thought to exist on early Earth.
- *Interferents.* Scientists must also make sure their experimental design takes into account materials that can interfere with the process under investigation. Ideally, these materials should be added to the apparatus at levels closely resembling those thought to have existed on early Earth.

Reality demands that at some point origin-of-life researchers must bring their simulation experiments to a stop. And yet they need to let the experiments run long enough to assess what changes are most likely to occur *after* the end products have formed. For example, these newly formed materials may, in turn, react to form new compounds that would frustrate a step in the chemical evolutionary pathway. End products may also break down once formed. Ironically, the same conditions needed to induce compounds to react often will cause the end products of the reaction to decompose. If researchers prematurely end an experiment, they may compromise the experiment's geochemical relevance.

Overlooking or minimizing these effects can produce a false sense of success. And so can the researchers' essential monitoring activities, which include the withdrawal of samples from the experiment. If too much material is removed from the experimental system, the removal can actually drive the process toward greater completion than might otherwise be the case. Again, this effort runs the risk of generating inaccurate results.

Origin-of-life researchers have no choice but to go into the lab to perform experiments with the overarching goal of recapitulating life's start. But when scientists direct experiments, they become active participants and are no longer passive observers of undirected processes. To some extent, this involvement runs the risk of making the experiment artificial, no longer reflecting the actual evolutionary events thought to have occurred. Instead, it reflects what's possible when an intelligent agent controls physicochemical processes.

Though the intent of origin-of-life investigators is to avoid influencing the outcome of geochemical simulations, such avoidance is easier said than done. And unfortunately, to judge the impact of a researcher's involvement on the outcome of such studies is far from easy. Often the degree of a scientist's influence on the experimental outcome is legitimately debatable.

Nevertheless, an assessment of researcher involvement is essential in considering whether or not a particular experimental result supports chemical evolution. The next several chapters discuss why that's the case, beginning with an evaluation of studies designed to demonstrate how prebiotic materials could have formed on early Earth.

9

Promised Impossibilities

> The ancient teachers of this science . . . promised impossibili-
> ties, and performed nothing. The modern masters promise very
> little; they know that metals cannot be transmuted, and that the
> elixir of life is a chimera. But these philosophers, whose hands
> seem only made to dabble in dirt, and their eyes to pore over the
> microscope or crucible, have indeed performed miracles. They
> penetrate into the recesses of nature, and show how she works
> in her hiding places.
>
> M. Waldman in *Frankenstein*

On the eve of the release of their twelfth studio album (*No Line on the Horizon*), U2's guitarist The Edge told *Rolling Stone*'s Brian Hiatt that despite more than two and a half decades and eleven straight successful albums, "We were fighting for our relevance," this time around.[1] For rock musicians, one of the worst things that can happen to them is to lose relevance. It's one of the worst things that can happen to a scientist too.

I witnessed this painful loss firsthand in Oaxaca, Mexico, at the 2002 meeting of the International Society for the Study of the Origin of Life (ISSOL '02).

Stanley Miller had been like royalty at ISSOL '99 in San Diego, where I saw him for the first time. During a poster session, I observed him moving from one presentation to another, engaged in vigorous discussion with presenters and fellow participants. What a thrill to be in the presence of such a legendary figure.

And what a difference three years can make. At ISSOL '02 I felt a strong sense of sorrow and compassion for Stanley Miller. He appeared to be in the last years of his life, and indeed he was. Miller died in the late spring of 2007.[2] Confined to a wheelchair and severely debilitated, at times he seemed all but forgotten. While other conferees made their way to the hotel veranda to enjoy a coffee break between sessions, eager to discuss the papers just presented, Miller often remained behind in the lecture hall waiting for his caretaker to show up and help him along.

One particularly heartrending moment came during a session on prebiotic chemistry. With Miller seated at the front of the room in the place reserved for his wheelchair, the conference chairman pointed out in his introductory remarks that Miller's work could no longer be considered relevant. Although quick to extend respect to Miller and qualify his assessment by emphasizing the historical value of Miller's work, the harm had been done. The painful reality was that Stanley Miller had devoted his life to understanding how life had originated, and now as he neared his life's end, his great contribution was deemed insignificant and irrelevant to answering the question.

Miller's work was cast aside because scientists in Miller's day held an incorrect understanding of the composition of early Earth's atmosphere. And this incorrect view influenced the design of Miller's experiments. As new understanding emerged, his geochemical simulation experiments modeling chemical events thought to have occurred in Earth's primordial atmosphere were shown to be unrealistic—and thus irrelevant.

The problem that rendered Miller's work meaningless looms large for origin-of-life researchers as they try to understand the genesis of prebiotic materials. How realistic are the laboratory experiments designed to validate this key stage in the origin of life? Do they adequately resemble the physicochemical conditions on the early Earth? Origin-of-life investigators have devoted several decades to gain some insight as to how prebiotic materials formed. Some scientists have followed in Miller's footsteps, studying the atmospheric chemistry of the early Earth in the hope of finding a way to make this particular scenario viable. Others have pursued the possibility of alternative locations for production of prebiotic materials, places such as volcanoes and deep-sea hydrothermal vents. Some have even contemplated the possibility that prebiotic materials originated elsewhere and were delivered to the early Earth from extraterrestrial sources.

The question before us is which of these approaches, if any, is irrelevant? Can they, like Miller's initial efforts, be ruled out because they incorrectly model the environment and conditions of the early Earth? Or have origin-of-life researchers truly found a way to explain the genesis of prebiotic materials?

Up in the Air

Under the traditional origin-of-life scenarios, Earth's earliest atmosphere was thought to consist of reducing gases (gases rich in hydrogen, such as molecular hydrogen, methane, ammonia, and water vapor). Lab experiments like the one performed by Stanley Miller demonstrate that under these conditions some biologically interesting prebiotic compounds do come together.

Miller's initial experiments were both geochemical simulations and proof-of-principle studies. He successfully demonstrated that simple gaseous molecules can react to form amino acids and other biologically significant compounds. Miller also conducted mechanistic studies, determining the reaction mechanism responsible for the production of amino acids. It turns out that the spark discharge through the gas mixture produced amino acids indirectly. The discharge generated hydrogen cyanide and formaldehyde. These compounds readily react with ammonia to form glycine, the simplest amino acid, via the so-called Strecker reaction.[3] And once glycine forms, it can react with hydrogen cyanide and formaldehyde to generate amino acids of higher molecular weight. More complex amino acids could also form if hydrogen cyanide and ammonia reacted with higher molecular weight aldehydes, such as acetaldehyde generated from a spark discharge through a reducing atmosphere.

At that time, Miller's experiments seemed to have had some geochemical relevance, but advances now indicate that Earth's earliest atmosphere was not reducing but neutral—consisting of nitrogen, carbon dioxide, carbon monoxide, and water vapor.[4] Although a mixture of reducing gases may have been present in early Earth's atmosphere, it wouldn't have lasted long. Ultraviolet radiation impinging on that atmosphere would have readily broken down ammonia and methane. And molecular hydrogen would have been lost to outer space because of its low molecular weight. Additionally, asteroid and comet collisions with early Earth would have stripped away the planet's primeval atmosphere. The secondary atmosphere that replaced the original appears to have been neutral.

Miller and colleagues then explored the production of organic materials in neutral atmospheres. As current findings stand, a neutral atmosphere could not have sustained the production of prebiotic molecules.[5] In other words, under more geochemically relevant conditions, organic materials do not form. Miller and his collaborators did discover, however, that prebiotic molecules can be made in a neutral atmosphere *if* high levels of hydrogen gas are included.[6] But, again, because molecular hydrogen evaporates into outer space so readily, it most likely escaped early Earth's atmosphere rapidly and would not have been available to assist in the origin of life.[7]

One recent study, however, has revived some hope that atmospheric chemistry can contribute to prebiotic compound production under neutral conditions.[8] A team of researchers from the US and Canada claims that even though the atmosphere was neutral, it had high levels of molecular hydrogen (perhaps up to 30 percent). Based on their geophysical modeling of early Earth, researchers conclude that the escape efficiency of hydrogen from the atmosphere was not as great as previously thought. When coupled with the outgassing of hydrogen from the crustal materials of early Earth, this escape inefficiency would allow hydrogen levels in the atmosphere to remain relatively high. And these high levels would promote the production of organic materials even under neutral conditions. However, the results are not universally accepted.

One researcher has challenged the study's conclusion by noting that the model used by the US and Canadian scientists didn't take into account *all* the relevant geophysical factors. And when the full range of parameters is considered, the escape of hydrogen from the atmosphere is as efficient as traditionally thought. In other words, early Earth's atmosphere was more likely hydrogen poor.[9] Additionally, the escape efficiency of hydrogen from the early Earth's atmosphere would be irrelevant because giant impactors striking Earth shortly after its formation would have stripped away the primeval atmosphere and, with it, most of the hydrogen, ammonia, and methane.

A few years before his death, Stanley Miller and several collaborators assessed atmospheres consisting of carbon monoxide as a possible matrix for the production of prebiotic materials.[10] According to this alternative scenario, carbon monoxide, rather than carbon dioxide, was present in the primordial atmosphere. Miller and his team maintain that such would have been the case if the early Earth's crust was in a more reduced state than it is today and if cool temperatures were prevalent on the planet's surface. These researchers see support for this scenario in the fact that comets may have delivered carbon monoxide to early Earth.

Miller's team showed that gas mixtures comprised of carbon monoxide, nitrogen, and water can produce organic compounds (including amino acids) when bombarded with high-energy protons (a component of cosmic rays). On the surface, this finding seems to indicate that if carbon monoxide had been present in the primordial atmosphere, cosmic rays could have stimulated the production of primordial soup ingredients.

Additional factors spoil the relevance of this scenario for the production of prebiotic compounds. It remains uncertain that carbon monoxide was ever present in the primitive atmosphere. Even if this gas had been introduced through cometary delivery or through the outgassing of the crust, its duration in the atmosphere would have been brief. Carbon monoxide readily reacts with photochemical products of water to produce carbon dioxide. In other words, water vapor in Earth's atmosphere effectively removes carbon monoxide. Further, because the chemical bond between carbon and oxygen is so stable, only the high-energy components of cosmic rays can break it apart—a necessary step to start the process along the chemical routes to prebiotic materials. But the calculated flux of cosmic radiation is too low to produce a sufficient quantity of prebiotic materials to keep up with their subsequent chemical decomposition in the primordial soup.

Though carbon monoxide atmospheres could have potentially generated prebiotic compounds, the yield of these compounds would have been too low to be meaningful because of the stability of the carbon-oxygen bond and the requirement of highly specific atmospheric conditions and compositions. Although Miller and his co-workers eloquently demonstrated the conditions necessary for carbon monoxide to play a role in the generation of prebiotic materials, they failed to show that these conditions would be relevant to the early Earth.

Killer Oxygen

Another factor that complicates evolutionary scenarios centers on the oxygen content in the primeval atmosphere. Oxygen shuts down atmospheric prebiotic chemistry pathways. Even minute amounts of oxygen inhibit the production of organic materials.[11] Miller was careful to exclude oxygen from his experiment, assuming this gas was not present on early Earth. But in recent years this assumption has been questioned. It now appears there may well have been low, but significant, levels of molecular oxygen present in early Earth's atmosphere.

Ultraviolet radiation impinging on atmospheric water generates oxygen. This radiation causes water molecules to break down, initiating a sequence of reactions that culminates in the production of molecular oxygen. And yet no one is certain, thus far, how important this process was early on in Earth's history or how much photolytically generated oxygen may have been present in the primeval atmosphere.[12] Recent work by Romanian physicist Ivan Draganić identifies another potential source of oxygen. This scientist points out that between three and four billion years ago the intensity of radiation from the decay of uranium, thorium, and potassium-40 must have been much greater than it is today.[13] This radiation, when passing through pockets of water, converts water into molecular oxygen and reactive oxygen species such as hydrogen peroxide and the short-lived superoxide and hydroxyl free radicals. These compounds are highly reactive and destroy organic molecules. The presence of radiation means the continual production of oxygen and reactive oxygen species in any body or layer of Earth's water. Undoubtedly some of that oxygen remained dissolved in the water. The rest must have escaped to accumulate in the atmosphere.

Ironically, the absence of oxygen would have also frustrated prebiotic chemistry. Oxygen interacts with ultraviolet radiation to produce ozone. This compound shields the Earth's surface from the harmful effects of ultraviolet radiation that can cleave the chemical bonds of organic materials. These effects explain why so many people today are concerned about the Earth's ozone layer. It's also why origin-of-life researchers are concerned about the lack of oxygen in early Earth's atmosphere. Without oxygen and, hence, ozone in early Earth's atmosphere, prebiotic compounds would be destroyed shortly after formation.[14] Scientists refer to this no-win situation as the oxygen-ultraviolet paradox. If present, oxygen inhibits prebiotic chemical reactions. If absent, no ozone is generated and prebiotic materials are rapidly destroyed after they form.

In the late 1990s, Stanley Miller and collaborator James Cleaves proposed one way out of this conundrum.[15] They maintained that materials dissolved in the Earth's oceans could operate as a sort of prebiotic sunscreen, protecting organic molecules within the primordial soup. Miller and Cleaves identified several candidates. For example, they suggested that tholins (high-molecular-weight materials produced in Miller-Urey–type experiments) and the hydrogen cyanide polymer (a high-molecular-weight compound formed when hydrogen cyanide repeatedly reacts with itself) could have afforded this protection. These materials could have formed on early Earth as a result of chemical reactions taking place in the atmosphere, provided that the atmosphere consisted of reducing gases. Both types of high-molecular-weight materials strongly absorb ultraviolet radiation. This proposal has validity, however, only if the Earth's atmosphere consisted of reducing gases. Yet if it did, questions remain about the levels of tholins and hydrogen cyanide polymers present in early Earth's ocean. Unless these materials are available at a high enough concentration, they will afford very little protection from ultraviolet radiation.

Miller and Cleaves went on to speculate that elemental sulfur produced by the photolytic breakdown of hydrogen sulfide might also be able to provide a shield from ultraviolet radiation. Elemental sulfur strongly absorbs ultraviolet radiation. The problem with this proposal centers on the insolubility of elemental sulfur. Unless sufficient amounts are dissolved in the oceans, then sulfur will offer little protection.

Carl Sagan and Christopher Chyba suggested another solution to the oxygen-ultraviolet paradox.[16] These two scientists speculated that the shield against this harmful radiation resided in the atmosphere rather than in the ocean. Based on mathematical models of atmospheric chemistry, they concluded that the photolytic breakdown of methane would have generated higher-molecular-weight materials that would, in turn, form an organic haze. And this haze could have protected ammonia from being destroyed by ultraviolet radiation. As Sagan and Chyba noted, however, this possibility depends on the accuracy of mathematical models for the atmosphere and on how realistic the input values for different atmospheric parameters are. If either proves incorrect (a distinct possibility given how little we know about early Earth's conditions), it would indicate that the ultraviolet shield generated from methane breakdown products may not have existed or may have been inadequate. Whatever the case, concern about the mathematical model and inputs may be considered moot. Impact events taking place on early Earth would have stripped away the initial atmospheric methane and ammonia. It is highly unlikely the secondary atmosphere replacing the original one would have included methane and hence an ultraviolet shield.

The Energy Crisis

Other issues confronting scenarios that appeal to atmospheric chemistry as the generator of prebiotic materials relate to possible energy sources available to drive the reactions. Many simulation experiments designed to mimic reactions taking place in the primeval atmosphere have utilized electrical discharges such as sparks, arcs, and semicoronas.[17] Origin-of-life researchers have focused on these energy sources because they presumably model the effects of lightning as it passes through the Earth's atmosphere. Another reason they look to these forms of energy is that they produce the biggest yield of prebiotic compounds in the laboratory.

These large yields help origin-of-life researchers develop a better understanding of what atmospheric chemistry can contribute to life's genesis, but the high yields actually represent an experimental artifact, for several reasons. For one, electrical discharges (i.e., lightning) were not the primary source of energy on early Earth. The most abundant form of energy would have been ultraviolet radiation from the Sun. Unfortunately, simulation experiments have demonstrated that the yield of prebiotic materials is vanishingly small when ultraviolet radiation is used as the energy source.[18] This result explains why origin-of-life researchers gravitate toward using electrical discharges in their experiments. They want to obtain the largest yields possible to gain the best possible understanding of the chemical reactions that could have taken place in the primordial atmosphere. But, when the most realistic energy sources are used, even for reducing gas compositions, the production of prebiotic materials is negligible.

Another concern has to do with the energies of the electrical discharges used in geochemical simulations. It turns out that they are typically a couple of orders of magnitude greater than the electrical discharge could have been on early Earth. This reduced energy would have dramatically compromised the yield of prebiotic materials. According to astrobiologist Horst Rauchfuss:

> [Chyba and Sagan] suggest that the values assumed by Miller and Urey in 1959 for lightning and corona discharges were too high by a factor between 20 and 100! Thus, the estimates for the rates of the prebiotic synthesis of biomolecules also need a drastic downward correction; the hypothetical "primeval soup" then becomes much thinner![19]

Another problem arises from the destructive effects of electrical discharges. Even though these discharges are needed to drive chemical reactions in gas mixtures, they also destroy prebiotic compounds if the materials are exposed continuously to the influence of the electrical discharges. To avoid these destructive effects, origin-of-life workers usually design their experiments in such a way as to protect the chemical products once they form.[20] Although this protection is necessary to gain an understanding of the outcome of the electrical discharge experiments, it creates an unrealistic scenario. The protective removal of prebiotic materials would not have been available on early Earth.

While origin-of-life researchers have shown, in principle, that under the right conditions and chemical compositions, atmospheric chemistry can generate biologically interesting compounds—providing a potential jump-start of chemical evolution—and have gained a good understanding of the chemical mechanisms undergirding this type of chemistry, they have failed to demonstrate the geochemical relevance of their findings. Experiments said to model conditions of early Earth actually do not. When more realistic conditions are employed in simulations, experiments fail to provide validation. It appears as if the atmosphere of the early Earth could not have supported the chemistry needed to form prebiotic compounds.

Many origin-of-life researchers readily acknowledge this concern. In May 2003, Jeffrey Bada and Antonio Lazcano, longtime associates of Miller, wrote an essay for *Science* commemorating the fiftieth anniversary of the publication of Miller's initial results. They echoed what I heard at ISSOL '02—that the Miller-Urey experiment carries historical significance but not scientific importance in contemporary origin-of-life thought. Bada and Lazcano wrote:

> Is the "prebiotic soup" theory a reasonable explanation for the emergence of life? Contemporary geoscientists tend to doubt that the primitive atmosphere had the highly reducing composition used by Miller in 1953.[21]

In his book *Biogenesis*, origin-of-life researcher Noam Lahav passes similar judgment:

> The prebiotic conditions assumed by Miller and Urey were essentially those of a highly reducing atmosphere. Under slightly reducing conditions, the Miller-Urey reaction does not produce amino acids, nor does it produce the chemicals that may serve as the predecessors of other important biopolymer building blocks. Thus, by challenging the assumption of a reducing atmosphere, we challenge the very existence of the "prebiotic soup," with its richness of biologically important organic compounds.[22]

I would go so far as to maintain that origin-of-life researchers failed to establish atmospheric chemistry as a realistic source of prebiotic materials, but they have also unwittingly demonstrated that this chemistry requires the input of an intelligent agent to successfully produce organic materials. Mechanistic studies highlight the need for careful adjustment of the gas composition and concentrations, selection of the right type of energy source, and implementation of special features to isolate and protect the prebiotic products from their energy source once they have formed. In other words, apart from the experimenters' handiwork, gas phase reactions would never produce organic compounds.

Given the inability of atmospheric chemistry on early Earth to support prebiotic molecule production, some origin-of-life investigators suggest other geological mechanisms for production of life's building blocks. Perhaps prebiotic molecules spewed forth from volcanoes.

An Idea That's About to Explode

What if volatile compounds released from Earth's mantle through volcanic emissions provided the reducing gas mixtures needed to form prebiotic compounds?[23] Volcanic eruptions emit large quantities of gas and ash. The gases could reasonably serve as the raw materials to make prebiotic compounds, with ash providing a catalytic surface to assist the reactions. Energy to drive the generation of prebiotic materials could presumably come from volcanic lightning and the intense heat released during eruptions. Origin-of-life researchers point out that the frequency of volcanic eruptions was much higher on early Earth than it is today, making this source of prebiotic materials even more significant, theoretically.

Geochemical simulation experiments seemed to have provided further support for this idea.[24] For example, by heating a gas stream consisting of methane, ammonia, and water to temperatures of 1,120 K, researchers were able to detect the production of a handful of amino acids. In another study, scientists produced low levels of amino acids and other interesting compounds by passing an electrical discharge through a gas mixture of carbon dioxide, nitrogen, and ammonia heated to 800 K, with volcanic ash as a catalyst.

The key focus in evaluating these studies centers on the composition of volcanic gases emitted on early Earth. The two geochemical simulation studies conducted to date made use of reducing gas mixtures. But today the Earth's crust exists in an oxidized state. As a result, gas exhalations from volcanoes consist primarily of water, carbon dioxide, nitrogen, and sulfur dioxide. This oxidizing gas mixture cannot support prebiotic molecule synthesis, as shown by a recent study conducted by a team from Mexico. The researchers used a hot plasma (to simulate volcanic lightning) as an energy source to probe the reactivity of a gas mixture that consisted of water, carbon dioxide, carbon monoxide, nitrogen, and hydrogen. (This gas combination presumably mimics the emissions of Hawaiian volcanoes.) Though they made nitrogen monoxide, they failed to generate any organic materials.[25]

The challenge is to determine, and then replicate, the composition of volcanic emissions in ancient times. Using chromium minerals as markers, studies of some of the oldest known volcanic materials indicate that volatiles released from Earth's mantle 3.6 billion years ago were identical to today's volcanic emissions—oxidizing, not reducing.[26] In other words, evidence indicates that the gases emitted during volcanic eruptions on early Earth were no more

Miller-Urey Redux?

I'm always amazed by what turns up when I clean out our garage: forgotten stuff that brings back memories and, occasionally, old things that still have value.

And this is exactly what some former students and associates of the late origin-of-life researcher Stanley Miller discovered when they cleaned out his lab after his death. Old vials left over from experiments brought back memories of his famous spark discharge experiment. What's more, these old vials may actually shed valuable new light on how prebiotic materials could have formed on the early Earth. They may even give new importance to the famous Miller-Urey experiment.

Miller actually performed three versions of the spark discharge experiment. All three permutations yielded amino acids and other organic compounds. Miller decided to focus his efforts on the version that now appears in biology textbooks. He chose the one he figured most closely modeled the atmosphere of early Earth.

Still, Miller held onto cases of vials containing materials from the other two variations of the spark discharge experiment. He also kept the notebooks in which he carefully documented the experimental work he performed.

Wondering whether they might find treasure in this trash, Miller's former students and colleagues decided to reanalyze the vials using state-of-the-art analytical methods unavailable to Miller fifty years ago.[27]

To their surprise, Miller's successors discovered that the "textbook" version of the Miller-Urey experiment was not the most successful. The most productive synthesis was one that introduced water into the headspace as a fine mist using an aspirator. This particular experimental rig produced more amino acids with a greater chemical diversity than did the textbook experiment.

The design of this forgotten experiment intrigued researchers because it models volcanic emissions that could have occurred on early Earth. Accordingly, volcanic lightning could have served, they reasoned, as the energy source that generated prebiotic compounds as it passed through volcanic gases and steam—again assuming the volcanic emissions on early Earth consisted of reducing gases.

Miller's cohorts have argued that this rediscovery gives new relevance to Miller's classic experiment. They suggest that the source of prebiotic materials on early Earth may have been volcanic emissions, not chemical reactions in the atmosphere. However, as noted (page 132), the geochemical relevance of "volcanic" experiments is as questionable as Miller's "atmospheric" experiments, given studies of ancient volcanic emissions.

capable than emissions today of supporting the production of prebiotic compounds. This finding renders ancient volcanic chemistry largely irrelevant to the origin of life.

Once again, researchers have successfully provided proof of principle that volcanic emissions in the presence of volcanic ash and a suitable energy source (such as intense heat or electrical discharges) can yield prebiotic materials. But they have also shown that the composition of the gas mixture is critical and, as a consequence, that the required gases most likely would not have been emitted during volcanic eruptions on early Earth.

Under the right conditions, volcanic emissions can generate biologically interesting compounds for chemical evolution, but research has failed to demonstrate geochemical relevance. Despite efforts to model the conditions of early Earth, experiments thus far miss that mark. When more realistic conditions are employed in simulations, they fail to provide validation. It appears that volcanic emissions on the early Earth could not have been the source of prebiotic compounds.

Under the Sea

Currently, one of the most popular ways for origin-of-life researchers to account for prebiotic materials on early Earth is to appeal to deep-sea hydrothermal vents. These scenarios take on increasing importance as origin-of-life researchers come to grips with findings that the early Earth's atmosphere could not have supported production of prebiotic materials. Researchers propose that gases released at these vents reacted, with the assistance of metal ions and sulfide, to produce prebiotic compounds. Laboratory experiments simulating a hot, chemically harsh environment modeled after deep-sea hydrothermal vents indicate that amino acids, peptides, and other biomolecules can form under such conditions. Such results lend powerful support to this set of models.[28]

Here again the question must be raised: how relevant are these geochemical simulation experiments to the origin of life? One concern relates to the unintended influence of the investigators on the outcome of hydrothermal vent simulations. It is no easy task to mimic hydrothermal vent conditions in the laboratory, in part because these environments are characterized by extremely high water temperatures (up to 400°C) and the high pressures at the ocean floor created by 6,000 to 15,000 feet of water. Reactions in the lab must be carried out in specially designed stainless steel vessels that can withstand high pressures and intense heat. These vessels typically have quartz inserts where the reactions take place and a variety of ports for (1) introducing gases and liquids into the vessel, (2) withdrawing samples, (3) monitoring the temperature, and (4) releasing the pressure from the system.

Researchers at the State University of New York (SUNY), Stony Brook, have expressed concern that the hydrothermal vent simulations conducted in these systems may be unduly influenced by the vessel material, quartz inserts, and sample tubing.[29] They pointed out the possibility that contamination could be introduced into the experiment from the tubing used to plumb the reaction vessel, and they noted that the vessel and insert materials could take part in the reaction as catalysts.

To address these concerns, the researchers heated pure water to 200°C under 400 psi (atmospheric pressure is 14.7 psi) in vessels made up of stainless steel and titanium and in tubing made up of various polymers, stainless steel, and titanium. In doing so, they discovered that vessels and tubing made from titanium gave clean results, but the tubing made from polymers gave off organic compounds. Formate, acetate, and propionate appeared in the system, presumably extracted from the tubing material. They also discovered that both the stainless steel vessel and the tubing facilitated decomposition of these organic compounds into a variety of other compounds that could, in turn, react to produce a diversity of chemical species.

This outcome indicates that at least some of the results of hydrothermal vent simulations must be considered artifactual. The formate, acetate, propionate, and similar compounds produced at low levels in simulation studies— intriguing because they are part of intermediary metabolic pathways and can further react to generate other important biological materials—may well originate from contamination in the reaction apparatus. They may have no bearing at all on the type of chemistry that's possible at hydrothermal vents.

It would be inaccurate to conclude that the results of all hydrothermal vent experiments are untrustworthy based on the study by the SUNY researchers. And yet their work reveals the difficulty of conducting geochemical simulation studies and how easily even the best scientists can be fooled into thinking a result is authentic despite their extreme care to mimic conditions thought to exist on early Earth.

Perhaps the most significant problem facing hydrothermal vent models for production of prebiotic materials is the chemical instability of these compounds once they form. To illustrate the magnitude of this problem, years ago a team led by Stanley Miller found that at 350°C the amino acid half-life in a water environment is only a few minutes (in other words, half the concentration of amino acids decompose in just a few minutes). At 250°C the half-life of sugars measures in seconds. For a nucleobase to function as a building block for DNA or RNA, it must be joined to a sugar. For peptides (chains of amino acids linked together with much lower molecular weight than proteins), the half-life is anywhere from a few minutes to a few hours, depending on the identity of the peptide and environmental conditions. RNA molecules hydrolyze within minutes at 250°C and within just seconds at 350°C. These results led Miller and his team to conclude that the same vent conditions that can produce amino acids and/or nucleotides also destroy them.[30] In other words, molecular decomposition most likely outstrips chemical synthesis at hydrothermal vents. To get around this problem in geochemical simulations, researchers stop the reactions before this decomposition takes place, creating false success.

It is possible for some biomolecules to survive after assembly in deep-sea hydrothermal vents. A fraction of those produced in the superheated water would surely make their way to cold water in the neighborhood of the vents within a few seconds after leaving the vents' chimney. However, origin-of-life researchers James Cleaves and John Chalmers observe that this fact doesn't help the scenario.[31] Escape of prebiotic molecules from hydrothermal vents into the open ocean results in a loss of concentration. Many reactions that scientists acknowledge as critical to the origin of life require relatively high concentrations of reactants. The dilution of materials away from hydrothermal vents would only frustrate the origin of life, even if it did help prebiotic compounds survive.

As Miller's team pointed out, the density of hydrothermal vents on the Earth today is such that all the water in the oceans circulates through the vents over the course of 10 million years. But when life originated on Earth 3.8 billion years ago, the density of hydrothermal vents was much higher, reducing the circulation time. Any possible success in the assembly of life molecules anywhere in Earth's oceans would have been largely lost as those molecules circulated through the vents, given how rapidly biologically important compounds break down under high temperature conditions.

Researchers at Penn State and SUNY, Stony Brook, identified yet another problem with prebiotic formation at deep-sea hydrothermal vents: lack of ammonia.[32] For prebiotic molecules to be synthesized at deep-sea hydrothermal vents, ammonia must be present. Ammonia serves as a key starting material in the synthesis of amino acids and other biologically important nitrogen-containing compounds. But ammonia did not exist at appreciable levels on early Earth. For prebiotic synthesis to occur at hydrothermal vents, ammonia must form there. Laboratory experiments demonstrate that, in principle, ammonia *could* form there from nitrogen via a route that involves hydrogen sulfide or another route involving iron(2) sulfide. However, these same studies show that the hydrogen sulfide–mediated route yields too low a level of ammonia to sustain prebiotic compound formation, and the iron(2) sulfide reaction proceeds too slowly.

Like volcanoes, Earth's early atmosphere, and other suggested sources, deep-sea vents appear inadequate to generate prebiotic materials on early Earth. Laboratory experiments illustrate that, in principle, under the right conditions and chemical compositions, hydrothermal vents may be able to generate biologically interesting compounds that could have played a role in chemical evolution. Researchers, however, have failed to demonstrate the geochemical relevance of their results.

Production of Prebiotic Materials under Acidic, Alkaline, and High Saline Conditions

One reason origin-of-life researchers postulate that prebiotic materials were generated at deep-sea hydrothermal vents is the existence of thriving microbial communities at these locales today. The reasoning goes like this: because life exists at hydrothermal vents, it could have originated there. And the first step in this life-assembly process would be the synthesis of prebiotic compounds there.

Following this same line of thinking, some scientists speculate that life arose under highly acidic, highly alkaline, or highly saline conditions given that life currently exists in these environments. However, as origin-of-life investigators James Cleaves and John Chalmers point out, acidic, alkaline, and saline conditions typically frustrate chemical pathways associated with the origin of life.[33] As a case in point, highly acidic conditions inhibit the production of amino acids (by shutting down the Strecker reaction), the reaction of hydrogen cyanide with itself (a key step in the generation of nucleobases), and the formation of sugar molecules.

Highly alkaline conditions also retard the formation of sugars. And highly saline systems prevent primitive cell membranes from assembling. In short, this speculation leads nowhere.

Again, I would even maintain that origin-of-life investigators have unwittingly demonstrated that the input of an intelligent agent is required to successfully produce organic materials, whether at hydrothermal vents or elsewhere. In other words, apart from the experimenter's handiwork, it is unlikely that hydrothermal-vent chemistry could ever produce organic compounds.

No Soup for You!

The struggle origin-of-life researchers experience in attempting to identify a viable source of prebiotic materials raises questions about whether a primordial soup ever existed on early Earth. It's intriguing to note that no evidence for a primordial soup has ever been recovered from the geochemical record. If a prebiotic soup had indeed existed on early Earth, then it's reasonable to expect researchers would have found residue of this complex chemical mixture in the oldest rock formations on Earth. Yet as origin-of-life researcher Noam Lahav notes:

So far, no geochemical evidence for the existence of a prebiotic soup has been published. Indeed, a number of scientists have challenged the prebiotic soup concept, noting that even if it existed, the concentration of organic building blocks in it would have been too small to be meaningful for prebiotic evolution.[34]

In the face of the mounting difficulties associated with generating prebiotic materials on early Earth, it has become increasingly vogue for origin-of-life researchers to explore the possibility that these compounds (or the starting materials needed to make life's building blocks) originated in an extraterrestrial location and were then transported to Earth. The evidence to support these ideas doesn't come from laboratory experiments. Instead, it's based on astronomical observations and chemical and spectroscopic analyses of interstellar dust clouds, solar nebula, comets, asteroids, meteorites, micrometeorites, and interplanetary dust particles. It is beyond the scope of this book to address the problems with these scenarios. Instead, I would refer curious readers to the book I coauthored with astronomer Hugh Ross, *Origins of Life*, where these difficulties are discussed in detail.[35]

Research over the last fifty years has failed to identify a viable source of prebiotic materials. Yes, researchers have successfully demonstrated in the laboratory that—in principle—numerous pathways exist that are capable of yielding prebiotic compounds. What's more, they have developed a good mechanistic understanding of the chemistry. But these insights combined with new information about the conditions of the early Earth indicate that chemical reactions needed to generate prebiotic materials would have been frustrated on the primordial Earth. In many cases, the mechanistic studies have revealed that the proposed prebiotic chemical reactions are insufficiently robust to operate on early Earth. Given enough expertise and exacting experimental conditions, chemists can make virtually any organic compound. But geochemical simulations unduly rely on researchers' expertise and on highly selective experimental conditions that never would have existed on early Earth more than 3.8 billion years ago. In other words, the success of geochemical simulation experiments rests on researcher involvement. And this involvement provides empirical evidence that apart from the work of an intelligent agent, the first steps in the origin-of-life process cannot take place.

So we move on to the next question: if prebiotic materials are taken as a given, can the next steps in the origin-of-life pathway occur via chemical evolutionary mechanisms apart from the work of a mind?

10

The Agony of Reflections

I cannot describe to you the agony that these reflections inflicted upon me: I tried to dispel them, but sorrow only increased with knowledge.

Frankenstein's monster in *Frankenstein*

My teenage daughters spend a lot of time in front of the mirror. I used to do the same when I was their age, but not as much as my girls. I marvel at the ritual they go through each time they look at their reflection— checking hair, makeup, expressions, and more. What they do in front of a mirror is a little science and a little art. For most teenagers, life without a mirror is unimaginable.

Frankenstein's monster, on the other hand, abhors his reflection. It reveals a figure he comes to recognize as "hideously deformed and loathsome." This awareness grows in him slowly over the course of several months while he hides near a cabin in the woods, secretly watching its occupants. The meager dwelling is home to an impoverished family rich in love. The way they care for each other touches something inside him and sparks a yearning. As he learns about them, he also learns about himself. And then one day the epiphany comes—the realization why people run from him in terror whenever he encounters them. He is not the same "nature as man." There is no one like him. He is a grotesque monster.

Origin-of-life researchers are a bit like my daughters and a bit like the monster: drawn to the mirror but disturbed by it too. These scientists are concerned with explaining why life's molecules reflect one mirror image (a condition called *homochirality*), a defining and necessary feature of life. In a very real sense, life without this mirror is unimaginable.

To adequately explain the spontaneous emergence of life, origin-of-life researchers must account for the origin of homochirality. This task has been truly agonizing. For the last half century, researchers have labored with little success to understand how this property of life came about. While numerous proposals to explain the genesis of homochirality have been advanced, none seems compelling and most are riddled with problems. So scientists slog on in pursuit of viable mechanisms that can generate this life-essential characteristic. What does their work mean for explanations that appeal either to natural processes or to a Creator to account for life's beginnings?

Defining Homochirality

One of the most intriguing features of chemical systems is the fact that some molecules are mirror images of each other. These molecular mirror images appear in organic compounds when four different chemical constituents bind to a central carbon atom. (The central carbon atom is called the chiral carbon.) For example, the compound alanine (an amino acid) includes one hydrogen atom plus amino, carboxy, and methyl groups, all bound to a central carbon atom. But these four groups joined to a central carbon atom can be arranged in two different ways, each mirroring the other, and still be called alanine.

The mirror images are a consequence of the fact that the four different chemical groups linked to the chiral carbon can be spatially oriented in one of two possible arrangements. These arrangements turn out to be reflections of each other, and as mirror images, they cannot be overlaid on one another in a way that all the chemical groups coincide. Because they can't be superposed, molecular mirror images (called *enantiomers*) are distinct chemical entities.

Sometimes chemists refer to the enantiomers as being either left- or right-handed. Scientists use this imagery because chirality can be illustrated by the hands, which align (like mirror images) with the palms together, but not when placed on top of each other with both palms facing down. The configuration of chemical groups around the chiral carbon has an orientation that can be viewed as either right-handed or left-handed. Each is distinct from the other. When facing the same way, the corresponding "fingers" don't line up.

Life's Handedness

Some of the compounds that play a key role as life's building blocks, such as amino acids (protein constituents) and the sugars deoxyribose and ribose (which build DNA and RNA, respectively), are chiral compounds.

FIGURE 10.1

Chiral Molecules

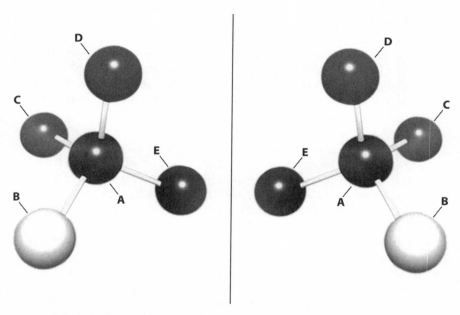

In this example, the amino acid has two mirror image configurations. In life molecules the building blocks must all be of only one configuration—either all right-handed or all left.

It turns out the amino acids that comprise proteins and the sugars that form the backbones of DNA and RNA have uniform chirality. Biochemists call this condition homochirality (*homo*=same; *chirality*=handedness). The amino acids in proteins have the same chirality, a left-handed configuration. And the sugars in DNA and RNA have identical chirality, a right-handed configuration.

Homochirality is a strict requirement for life. Chirality dictates the three-dimensional positioning of a molecule's chemical groups. And the spatial location of the chemical moieties plays an essential role in the interactions that stabilize the three-dimensional structure of proteins. (Remember that a protein's structure determines its function.) For some proteins, the incorporation of even one amino acid of the opposite chirality into its backbone will disrupt the protein's structure and hence its function. The two complementary strands of DNA cannot bind with each other to form the crucial double helix structure unless all the nucleotides are of the same handedness. Moreover, without homochirality, genetic material cannot copy itself.[1] Additionally, laboratory experiments demonstrate that the "wrong" enantiomeric form of a nucleotide inhibits the assembly of DNA and RNA.[2]

Homochirality and Life's Origin

In order to adequately explain the spontaneous emergence of life, researchers must somehow account for the origin of homochirality. The strict structural requirements of molecules such as proteins, DNA, and RNA mean that the origin of homochirality must *precede* the origin of these biomolecules. In other words, without preexisting reservoirs of exclusively left-handed amino acids and exclusively right-handed sugars, the naturalistic assembly of proteins, DNA, and RNA is prohibited. (The exact reverse—reservoirs of exclusively right-handed amino acids and exclusively left-handed sugars—could also provide the building blocks for proteins, DNA, and RNA.)

The difficulty in accounting for the origin of homochirality stems from the fact that chemical reactions that generate chiral compounds from achiral starting materials typically produce a 50:50 mixture of the two mirror images. (This type of mixture is called *racemic*.) In other words, chemical processes, as a rule of thumb, yield racemic rather than homochiral products—unless a chiral excess already exists at the outset for one of the reactants, or unless the reaction catalyst displays chirality.

This inconvenient truth has led many origin-of-life scientists to explore physical and astronomical mechanisms to explain the genesis of homochirality. Meanwhile, a minority of researchers remains convinced that chemical solutions to the problem will be found, and they diligently pursue this line of investigation. Either way, some mechanism must exist to generate homochirality because slight chiral excesses have been detected among amino acids in carbonaceous chondrite meteorites.

Amino Acids in Meteorites

On September 28, 1969, a meteorite fell on Murchison, Australia.[3] Numerous fragments were collected, and the largest piece, weighing about seven kilograms, has been dubbed the Murchison meteorite.

Within months of the meteorite's fall, chemist Keith Kvenvolden conducted the first analysis of its composition and identified extraterrestrial amino acids within it.[4] At least seventy-four different amino acids were recovered from the meteorite, some of which are found in biological systems and some of which are not.[5] Excitement about this find was tempered by concern that some of the amino acids and other organic materials found in the meteorite represented contamination from terrestrial sources. The Earth's environment is loaded with compounds derived from living organisms. Once meteorites make contact with Earth's environment, these compounds easily become infused into the meteorite by a variety of mechanisms. Even though the Murchison meteorite was recovered shortly after it fell, contamination remains a legitimate concern.

Because of this concern, Kvenvolden performed a reanalysis of the Murchison.[6] In particular, he compared the amino acid abundances near the exterior of the samples with the abundances at the interior. The exterior samples had higher concentrations of amino acids. He also noted that the exterior samples revealed excesses of left-handed amino acids. The elevated amino acid levels and chiral excess can readily be accounted for if at least some of these amino acids were derived from living organisms and penetrated the meteorite after it reached Earth. Kvenvolden issued a point of caution: "These results indicate that the outside of the meteorite had been exposed to significant terrestrial contamination and serve as a warning that samples of the Murchison meteorite can be affected to varying degrees by terrestrial influences."[7]

Still, some of the amino acids (and other organic compounds) are endogenous to the Murchison. A number of nonbiological amino acids in this meteorite do not come from living entities on Earth. One way to know is that nearly all the amino acids in the Murchison consist of racemic mixtures of left- and right-handed forms. If the amino acids were derived from life on Earth, there would be an excess of the left-handed enantiomer. And finally, the isotopic composition of the amino acids—rich in carbon-13 and deuterium—indicates these materials come from an extraterrestrial source.[8]

One discovery associated with the Murchison's amino acids that caused considerable excitement was the detection of slight chiral excesses in some of the nonbiological amino acids. Researchers found a 7 to 10 percent excess of the left-handed enantiomer in α-methylalloisoleucine, α-methylisoleucine, α-methylvaline, and an 18 percent elevation of the left-handed enantiomer in isovaline.[9] This result is not unique to the Murchison. Researchers detected a chiral excess of amino acids in other carbonaceous chondrites as well, including some with minimal exposure to contaminants. For example, recent work identified a 12 to 14 percent chiral excess for isoleucine and alloisoleucine in the GRA 95229 meteorite recovered in Antarctica. Researchers believe this meteorite is exceptionally pristine.[10] A chiral excess of about 15 percent for isovaline has also been noted in the carbonaceous chondrite Orgueil.[11] If these chiral excesses were detected in biologically occurring amino acids, the results could be dismissed as terrestrial contamination. But because the chiral excess shows up in nonbiological materials, some process must have taken place in the meteorite either before or during the solar system's formation.

These findings raise crucial questions about the origin of homochirality. Apparently some naturally occurring physicochemical processes account for some degree of homochirality. Discovering them is critical for chemical evolutionary models. To gain some clues, origin-of-life researchers have turned their attention to the laboratory.

The Origin of Homochirality: Possible Chemical Mechanisms

Though fundamental chemical problems remain, recent progress has been made to identify possible chemical mechanisms that can generate homochirality. As mentioned above, chemical reactions that yield products with chiral carbons typically produce racemic mixtures of the enantiomers. However, some highly unusual reactions can produce a chiral excess of one enantiomer relative to its counterpart. And other less esoteric chemical processes have been identified as possible contributors to the genesis of homochirality. One such process is oligomerization.

Oligomerization

Processes that combine smaller molecules (referred to as subunits, or monomers) into larger molecules are called oligomerization reactions. The term *monomer* refers to a single molecular unit (*mono*=one, *mer*=unit), and an oligomer is a compound composed of several molecular units (*oligo*=few; *mer*=unit). The oligomerization processes join molecular units (monomers) together in a head-to-tail fashion, usually. At a certain size, the oligomer becomes a polymer, an extremely large molecule made by linking together subunits (*poly*=many; *mer*=unit). DNA, RNA, and proteins are polymers with nucleotides and amino acids, respectively, as the monomers.

Some lab studies have shown that oligomerization reactions are inhibited when a racemic mixture of monomers supplies the reaction. More specifically, researchers have observed that if they add the opposite enantiomeric form of a nucleotide to the mix during DNA and RNA oligomerization reactions, the addition frustrates assembly of these biomolecules.[12] Some consider this inhibition a form of chemical "natural selection." In their view, this chemical selectivity means only homochiral RNA oligomers will assemble (and hence be "fit to survive"). Those that can't form, by definition, aren't available for chemical evolution and the subsequent origin of life. These researchers maintain that homochirality emerged through some type of chemical selection.

The chief problem with this model resides in the probability of assembling sufficiently long RNA (or protein) oligomers to be meaningful in the origin of life. For RNA molecules (or proteins) to adopt higher-order three-dimensional structures capable of biological activity (or proto-bioactivity), these compounds need to consist (minimally) of about fifty subunits. If the incorporation of homochiral subunits into the growing chain is 50 percent, the probability of assembling an RNA (or protein) chain that is fifty subunits in length is 2^{50} (about 10^{15}), and the probability of assembling one that is one hundred subunits long is 2^{100} (about 10^{30}). These probabilities seem too remote to support the idea that homochirality could emerge via this chemical selection mechanism.

Some scientists have suggested that perhaps another type of chemical selection can rescue the scenario from these staggering improbabilities. What if, they ask, enantiomers with the same handedness react preferentially to form the oligomer chain? Perhaps once an enantiomer is incorporated into a growing chain, it preferentially extends the chain by reacting with the same mirror image from the racemic mixture that is feeding the oligomerization. This hypothetical selectivity would increase the probability of generating a homochiral oligomer. But no such selectivity has been observed thus far in laboratory experiments.

To adequately explain the origin of homochirality via chemical evolution requires discovery of some means to produce a homochiral pool of monomers. Theoretical work conducted in the early 1950s by chemist F. C. Frank—about the same time Stanley Miller performed his famous spark discharge experiment—suggests a possible way for this pool to be generated by a chemical reaction. Frank's idea depends on a highly unusual chemical process called asymmetric autocatalysis.[13]

Asymmetric Autocatalysis

A chemical reaction in which one or more of the products of the transformation serve as a catalyst is called autocatalysis. As products are generated, they catalyze the reaction, exponentially speeding up the process. In asymmetric autocatalysis, the enantiomeric products selectively exert their catalytic activity, driving the production of more compounds of the same molecular handedness.

In exact racemic mixtures, asymmetric autocatalysis would lead to no chiral excess, no increase of one enantiomeric form over the other. Strictly speaking, however, the enantiomeric products of chemical reactions are never an exact 50:50 mixture. Statistical fluctuations cause a nearly imperceptible imbalance of enantiomers, with one chiral form slightly outnumbering the other. In reactions that manifest asymmetric autocatalysis, this slight excess—created by statistical effects—is amplified. The enantiomer in excess preferentially catalyzes the production of more of the same chiral form. After a period of time, the initial chiral imbalance would become amplified and the products of the reaction would eventually become dominated by one chiral form exclusively.

According to Frank, this mechanism could have produced homochirality if there were some way to generate biologically significant compounds on the early Earth through a reaction that adhered to asymmetric autocatalytic behavior. This idea, a theoretical construct for nearly forty years, gained momentum in the mid-1990s when the Japanese chemist Kenso Soai discovered the first real case of asymmetric autocatalysis (now dubbed the Soai reaction).[14]

The Soai reaction involves the alkylation of pyrimidyl aldehydes by dialkylzincs. The product of this reaction is a pyrimidyl alcohol that can exist in left- and right-handed configurations. It turns out the alcohol products catalyze this transformation.

As the pyrimidyl alcohol products form, statistical fluctuations cause these compounds to display a slight excess of one of the enantiomers over the other. This minor imbalance sets up asymmetric autocatalysis. The more abundant enantiomer selectively catalyzes the production of its corresponding chiral configuration. Over time, chiral excesses on the order of nearly 99 percent are achieved.

Although this discovery may seem a possible breakthrough in explaining the origin of homochirality, significant problems remain. First, the Soai reaction is the only real-life example of asymmetric autocatalysis discovered to date, making it a scientific oddity, not a widespread phenomenon. Added to this concern is the fact that the Soai reaction has no biological relevance whatsoever. None of the reactants or products are materials found in biological systems.

Another problem associated with asymmetric autocatalysis as a mechanism to generate homochirality is its transient nature. Theoretical studies indicate that the chiral excess generated by this type of reaction is short-lived. Once the system achieves homochirality, it rapidly decays from near a 99 percent chiral enrichment to about 50 percent. This decay is caused by the activity of the "other" enantiomer. This compound also operates as an autocatalyst, competing with its mirror image. The loss of homochirality occurs as a consequence of this competition. Once homochirality is achieved for one enantiomer, the activity of the opposite-handed molecule increases, restoring the balance.

What's surprising is that this decay doesn't happen in the Soai reaction. It turns out that the loss of homochirality is prevented in the Soai reaction by a highly unusual effect. The enantiomer that achieves an excess not only operates as an autocatalyst but also functions as an anticatalyst, inhibiting the production of the other enantiomeric form. The one enantiomer stops its counterpart's autocatalytic activity, preventing the competition between them.

Researchers have shown via theoretical study and laboratory work that *in principle* asymmetric autocatalysis can produce homochiral pools of compounds. But in reality this process represents an anomaly, depending on a highly unusual chemical mechanism. The success of the Soai reaction depends on Soai's brilliant insight in selecting the reactants and deciphering the specific mechanisms of his reaction and then carefully designing and executing the experiment. No chemists like Soai would have been present on early Earth to assist in the generation of homochirality. Asymmetric autocatalysis lacks geochemical relevance.

Other chemists and astrobiologists have developed what seems a more geochemically relevant scenario. Instead of relying on an autocatalytic mechanism to generate chiral excess, their hypothesis points to the slight enantiomeric excess of amino acids found in carbonaceous chondrites as the source of homochirality. In this scenario, certain amino acids in the meteorites generate chiral excess by functioning as asymmetric catalysts in prebiotic reactions.

Chemists and astrobiologists Sandra Pizzarello and Arthur Weber have shown that the amino acids isovaline and alanine—compounds that display chiral enrichment in the Murchison meteorite—can catalyze the formose reaction (a potential prebiotic route; see pages 159–160) and, as a consequence, influence the chiral distribution of the reaction products.[15] The formose reaction, which produces sugars, is considered an important prebiotic reaction, generating compounds that are part of the structural makeup of DNA and RNA.

When amino acids that catalyze the formose reaction harbor a chiral excess, the sugar products generated by this process also display a chiral excess. The amino acids are able to transfer the chiral excess to the sugars. Researchers observed that when the amino acid catalysts were enantiomerically pure, the sugar products displayed a chiral enrichment up to 10 percent. But as the enantiomeric purity of the amino acid catalysts decreased, the chiral excess of the sugar products also dropped proportionally. The excess became imperceptible when the enantiomeric imbalance of the amino acid catalyst hit 10 percent, the level observed in the Murchison.

The two researchers also noted a chiral enrichment when homochiral dipeptides were used as the catalysts.[16] (A *dipeptide* is a complex formed by joining together two amino acids.) In some cases, the dipeptide catalysts yielded an 80 percent chiral enrichment. Origin-of-life researchers think dipeptides could have formed on early Earth, but it remains unclear in what quantity. Fairly high concentrations of dipeptides were required in the laboratory experiment to generate the chiral enhancement.

These results gave rise to the notion that the slight chiral enrichment observed for amino acids in carbonaceous chondrites could have generated enantiomeric excesses in sugars that may have eventually led to homochirality in biochemical systems. As intriguing as this idea may be, it stretches credulity. First, the extent of the chiral enrichment generated in sugars by the asymmetric catalysis with amino acids is limited, at best, even when the amino acids possess 100 percent enantiomeric purity. The level of chiral enrichment is a far cry from the 100 percent needed for biochemical systems. This problem seems to be sidestepped by the use of dipeptides. But again, while these compounds may have been present on early Earth, it remains extremely unlikely that the levels of these materials would have been sufficient to generate high levels of chiral excess. The same can be said for the reactions catalyzed by amino acids. The levels required are geochemically unrealistic. Further, the amino acid- and dipeptide-catalyzed reactions require exacting laboratory conditions dependent upon carefully controlled pH and temperature.

Apart from the direct involvement of an intelligent agent, it is debatable that either asymmetric autocatalysis or asymmetric catalysis with amino acids could possibly generate homochirality. The laboratory work to date simply does not have much relevance to the conditions of early Earth. A chemical process that *does* have geochemical relevance creates a further problem for chemical evolutionary explanations of homochirality.

Racemization

While certain chemical reactions can generate temporary homochiral excess, others destroy it. The reason is that enantiomeric compounds naturally undergo a special type of reaction called *racemization*. This process causes enantiomerically pure compounds to transform over time into a racemic mixture through a structural inversion that "flips" one molecular image into its counterpart. Based on laboratory studies, researchers estimate that a set of homochiral amino acids becomes completely racemic in one thousand years at 50°C and in one million years at 0°C under dry conditions.[17] (The presence of water speeds up the racemization process.[18])

The consequences of racemization are troubling for chemical evolutionary scenarios. Even if mechanisms (whether chemical, physical, or astronomical) exist to generate a homochiral pool of monomers on early Earth, that condition would be relatively short-lived on geological timescales. Most laboratory studies that identify processes able to yield chiral enrichment fail to let those experiments continue long enough for racemization reactions to take place. Because researchers stop their experiment as soon as they achieve some enrichment, they unwittingly create a false sense of success. Realistic chemical evolutionary scenarios must counterbalance the chiral buildup processes with destructive processes. Tackling this problem head-on, one research team has recently suggested that racemization reactions at hydrothermal vents may actually help explain the genesis of homochirality.

Hydrothermal Vents

As discussed in the last chapter, many in the origin-of-life community think life could have emerged at deep-sea hydrothermal vents on the early Earth. A team of Japanese researchers extended this idea, proposing that these environments not only generated prebiotic materials but also spawned the seeds of homochirality.[19] In their simulation studies designed to mimic the hydrothermal vent environment, these investigators noticed that both left-handed and right-handed versions of the amino acid alanine undergo racemization from a pure state at 230°C in a matter of thirty to forty minutes. To their surprise, however, the left-handed enantiomer is racemized to a slightly lesser degree than the right-handed form. They noted that this effect was concentration dependent, occurring at higher levels of alanine. These findings led to the claim that this differential process produced a chiral excess of amino acids

Peptide Nucleic Acids and Homochirality

Several years ago, Stanley Miller formally acknowledged the intractability of the problem of homochirality's origin. Consequently, he proposed that the first self-replicating molecules were achiral peptide nucleic acids (PNA).[20] He was attracted to PNA molecules because they contain no sugars or phosphates and because they can form base pairs and helical structures just as DNA can.

The nucleobases of PNA are joined together through a molecule of acetic acid and a nonnaturally occurring achiral amino acid, 2-aminoethyl glycine (AEG). For a PNA origin-of-life option to be viable, an abundant prelife source of nucleobases, acetic acid, and AEG must be found. So far, a source has been identified for only the simplest of these molecules (acetic acid). AEG has not been detected either in extraterrestrial sites or in the terrestrial realm.

Stanley Miller's team has made AEG in the laboratory, but the conditions hold questionable relevance for early Earth.[21] A source of PNA (either on Earth or in outer space) at the time of life's origin, or a naturalistic pathway for adequate PNA production, must be demonstrated. Perhaps most troubling: once assembled, PNA molecules are stable—too stable. Highly reluctant to let go of the daughter molecules they may have duplicated, PNA would have reproduced extremely slowly, if at all. Also, scientists have yet to demonstrate that PNAs can perform the variety of enzymatic activities that would drive evolution from a PNA world to an RNA world.

on early Earth and could have seeded other processes that ultimately led to our homochiral biochemistry.

Yet again, though interesting, the claim defies the realities of early Earth. It is hard to escape the fact that racemization happens rapidly under hydrothermal vent conditions, destroying enantiomerical purity. And the chiral excess generated is extremely small, nowhere near the 100 percent required by living systems. The dependence of the differential racemization on high levels of alanine is also troubling and makes the results of the study seem artificial. If not for researchers' careful adjustments to the initial conditions of the reaction, no chiral excess, however slight, would have been generated. And if the concentration of amino acids in the oceans of early Earth were less than the minimum amount needed for the reaction to take place, the differential racemization would be irrelevant to the origin of life.

The Origin of Homochirality: Possible Physical Mechanisms

Because of the barriers scientists face in their attempts to explain the genesis of homochirality via chemical processes, most have turned their attention to the possibility of physical mechanisms. Some of the first proposals relied on parity violations of the electroweak force. However, more recent models appeal to (1) preferential interactions between enantiomers and mineral surfaces; and (2) differential crystallization of enantiomers. As with chemical explanations, these approaches have met with marginal success, at best.

Parity Violations

It's not just chemical compounds that can be mirror images of each other. So can physical phenomena. In physics, the parity principal states that physical processes that display symmetry about a central plane operate as mirror images. According to this principle, nature shows no preference for either right- or left-handedness. In the 1950s, however, physicists discovered an exception to this rule, referring to this anomaly as a parity violation. Two Chinese scientists, who later won the Nobel Prize for their work, demonstrated that the electroweak force (which controls radioactive decay) prefers the left-hand configuration. When an unstable nucleus in an atom undergoes radioactive decay, it emits polarized radiation with a slightly left-handed orientation.[22] Some physicists and chemists have suggested that the parity violation of the electroweak force can impact chemical reactions and may have given rise to homochirality.[23]

Further research into this mechanism reveals that the parity violation of the electroweak force has minimal impact on chemical reactions. In his book *Chemical Evolution and the Origin of Life*, astrobiologist Horst Rauchfuss points out that the energy difference between the left- and right-handed forms of amino acids is extremely small (10^{-14} Joule per mole of material) and would "thus have either no influence on chemical reactions or only a very limited effect on chemical reactions."[24] Origin-of-life researcher Robert Hazen echoes this conclusion: "One problem with these asymmetric processes is that they seem to yield only the slightest excess of one handedness over the other—generally less than a miniscule fraction of one percent. Such minute effects hardly seem sufficient to tip the global balance toward L-amino acids or D-sugars."[25]

Mineral Surfaces

Some origin-of-life investigators suggest that mineral surfaces can generate homochirality.[26] This proposal (gaining in popularity) asserts that mineral surfaces with specific spatial orientations selectively adsorbed either left-handed or right-handed amino acids (or some other compounds) on the early Earth and thus prompted the emergence of homochirality. Researchers have explored this idea using quartz and calcite minerals. When crystals are exposed to dilute solutions of amino acids in the laboratory, scientists have observed, based on the handedness of the amino acid and the crystal surface, that the two amino acid enantiomers will differentially adsorb to these surfaces, generating a chiral excess.[27]

It's crucial to note that for the differential adsorption to occur, the mineral surfaces must be scrupulously clean. (The protocol involved two cycles of successive washings in this order: deionized water, ultrapure methanol, methylene chloride, methanol, deionized water.) Any contaminants from the laboratory or from handling by researchers—even an unintended fingerprint—prevent the selective adsorption of enantiomers.[28] One must consider, then, the likelihood that mineral surfaces on early Earth would have been spotlessly free of contaminants. Arguably, the washing represents unwarranted researcher intervention. But perhaps the larger problem with this concept is the limited chiral enrichment (about 10 percent or less) that occurs on such surfaces.[29] It seems singularly unimpressive given the strict homochirality life requires. Furthermore, opposite-handed crystal surfaces occur with equal frequency in nature, so chiral buildup could take place only in microscopically limited environments, not everywhere on Earth. These two factors prohibit the natural development of homochiral reservoirs of amino acids or sugars.[30]

Crystallization

Louis Pasteur conducted some of the first studies on chirality. As part of his work, he observed that when a racemic mixture of tartaric acid crystallized from solution as the water evaporated, crystals formed that consisted purely of either the left-handed or the right-handed enantiomers. This separation occurs because the solely left-handed or right-handed version of tartaric acid fits together more snugly in crystals than do mixtures of left- and right-handed forms. This preference for the same mirror image leads to the formation of enantiomerically pure crystals.

This phenomenon has prompted some origin-of-life researchers to suggest that maybe differential crystallization of prebiotic materials on early Earth led to homochirality in living systems. For example, when evaporated to dryness in the presence of a porous material, aspartic acid and glutamic acid will form crystals that are enantiomerically pure.[31] The researcher who made this observation pointed out that this chiral separation represents an anomalous situation. Normally when precipitated from solution, amino acids form racemic crystals. The presence of porous materials allowed the formation of supersaturated solutions during evaporation. This condition allowed enantiomerically pure crystals to form. While it's conceivable that evaporation of water in the presence of porous materials could have taken place on early Earth, it is important to note how dependent this process is on special laboratory conditions.

A research team from Columbia University headed up by Ronald Breslow suggests that the material left behind in the solution when amino acids crystallize is what accounts for the homochirality. These investigators have demonstrated for the amino acid phenylalanine that a slight chiral excess becomes amplified when this amino acid crystallizes out of solution.[32] While the ensuing crystal possesses a 50:50 mixture of the two enantiomers, the liquid phase becomes enriched with the enantiomer that initially showed a slight excess. They found that a chiral excess of only about 1 percent can become amplified to about 90 percent after just two rounds of crystallization. This enrichment stems from the reduced solubility of amino acid complexes formed when left-handed and right-handed versions combine as compared with that of complexes formed from left-handed and left-handed forms (or right-handed and right-handed forms). This difference in solubility causes the crystal to exclude the enantiomer that is initially in excess.

Based on discovery of this behavior, the team from Columbia University proposes the following scenario to explain how homochirality originated: First, they note meteorites like Murchison show a slight chiral excess in certain amino acids. So meteorites delivering amino acids to the early Earth might have seeded the oceans with amino acids containing a slight chiral excess. Then, as the ocean waters washed onto ancient shorelines and water evaporated, amino acid crystals formed, leaving behind a greater chiral excess in the waters that returned to the oceans. Eventually, the amino acids in the oceans would have been populated with nearly 100 percent of one enantiomer at the expense of the other. The end result, they claim, as this chiral excess gets transferred to molecules taking part in the origin-of-life process, is the birth of homochirality.[33]

At first glance this scenario may seem reasonable. Closer examination, however, exposes a fundamental flaw: rather than promoting homochirality in life molecules, chiral excess in Earth's oceans would, in fact, detract from it.

Consider the reactions by which peptides (small protein chains) are made. Amino acids will not react with each other in water to form peptides. (In water, the reverse reaction, in which peptides break down into the constitutive amino acids, is favored.) Origin-of-life researchers posit that this difficulty can be overcome. They suggest that amino acids deposited onto ancient shorelines begin to react as the water that carried them there evaporates, and the minerals on the shore can serve as catalysts, promoting the reaction process.

Herein lies the difficulty: according to the mechanism proposed by the chemists from Columbia University, the amino acids deposited on the shore would be a racemic mixture, displaying little if any chiral excess. The chirally enriched amino acids remain highly diluted in ocean waters, where they're unable to react to form peptides. In other words, the mechanism proposed as the generator of homochirality would actually inhibit it, not promote it.

The Origin of Homochirality: Possible Astronomical Mechanisms

Researchers have noted in laboratory studies that circularly polarized radiation can generate a chiral excess of amino acids by selectively destroying one enantiomer.[34] Circularly polarized light in the ultraviolet region of the spectrum will preferentially interact with enantiomers that have a handedness that matches the direction of the circularly polarized radiation (called *magnetochiral anisotropy*).[35] Based on these results, a number of astrobiologists and origin-of-life researchers have proposed that interactions between prebiotic materials and circularly polarized radiation set the stage for the emergence of homochirality.

Discussion of this astronomical mechanism to generate homochirality is beyond the scope of this book. A detailed assessment of this proposal appears in *Origins of Life*, a book I coauthored with astronomer Hugh Ross. Suffice it to say, researchers have demonstrated—in principle—that circularly polarized ultraviolet radiation can generate a modest chiral excess from a racemic mixture. They have also shown that, in the laboratory, the success of this process depends upon researchers removing the radiation source at the right time to allow the maximum production of chiral excess, while also minimizing the overall destruction of the prebiotic material. If the prebiotic material is continuously exposed to radiation, total destruction of the prebiotic material will ensue. Researchers have struggled to identify realistic astronomical sources of circularly polarized radiation. Failure to do so renders the laboratory observations of chiral excess being generated by circularly polarized light astronomically unrealistic and irrelevant to chemical evolution and the origin of life.

The Agony of Reflections

To explain the spontaneous emergence of life, researchers must find a way to account for homochirality. A number of proposals have been advanced, each relying on some chemical, physical, or astronomical mechanisms, but none seems anywhere near adequate and most are riddled with intractable problems, as this chapter illustrates. It's true that researchers have been able, in laboratory conditions, to identify a number of processes that can generate chiral excess. Scientists have also developed a good mechanistic understanding of how chiral excess is generated for many of the processes they have identified and studied. But with the exception of asymmetric autocatalysis, none of these processes produces an imbalance of more than about 20 percent. The discovery of amino acids that display chiral enrichment in carbonaceous chondrite meteorites suggests that some of these processes are at work in nature. And yet this limited excess is essentially meaningless because living systems demand strict homochirality.

Many of the mechanisms that generate enantiomeric excess in the lab have questionable geochemical (and astronomical) relevance. They require careful selection of the appropriate chemicals, careful adjustment of the experimental conditions, and a relatively high concentration of reactants. Researchers must then stop the experiment at the precise moment before degradation and racemization take over. So it is debatable whether any chiral excess would result at all in natural conditions. The combination of artificial conditions and careful manipulation by researchers required to cause even the slightest movement toward homochirality indicates that apart from the work of intelligent agents, homochirality would never arise.

But what if ample pools of homochiral prebiotic compounds somehow did come to exist on early Earth? What if some yet-to-be discovered pathways could yield chirally pure prebiotic materials poised to evolve chemically into metabolic pathways and information-rich molecules? The next chapter offers a glimpse into the likelihood that these prebiotic compounds (a hypothetical prebiotic soup) could have generated information-rich molecules capable of self-replication and other essential biological functions.

11

United by No Link

> Like Adam, I was apparently united by no link to any other being
> in existence; but his state was far different from mine in every other
> respect. He had come forth from the hands of God a perfect crea-
> ture, happy and prosperous, guarded by the especial care of his
> Creator; he was allowed to converse with, and acquire knowledge
> from, beings of a superior nature: but I was wretched, helpless,
> and alone. Many times I considered Satan as the fitter emblem of
> my condition; for often, like him, when I viewed the bliss of my
> protectors, the bitter gall of envy rose within me.
>
> Frankenstein's monster in *Frankenstein*

Many interesting comparisons can be made between Mary Shelley's *Frankenstein* and the biblical account of human origins found in Genesis 2. Yahweh made the first human from the dust of the ground and animated him with his divine breath. Frankenstein gave his monster life by animating tissue he cobbled together. The Creator made human beings for a relationship with him and sacrificed himself to restore that relationship once it was broken. Frankenstein abandons his creation, repulsed by what he has made and sickened by the disfigured beast. Both Adam and the monster went through a process of self-discovery—the first man in the Garden of Eden under the guidance of his Maker; the man-beast in the woods by his own devices. Both Adam and the monster come to the realization that it is not good to be alone. Yahweh gave Adam a suitable helpmate, Eve. Frankenstein denies the beast the companionship he so desperately desires. Yet both creatures rebel against their creator, desiring the role of master for themselves. Perhaps Frankenstein's monster is justified, but Adam and his companion, Eve, were not.

In a sense, Victor Frankenstein represents the fruit of human rebellion. Like a god, he aspires to attain the capability "of bestowing animation upon lifeless matter," and then he uses this knowledge to make a man-like wretch, with disastrous consequences. One question raised by Mary Shelley's story involves the appropriate boundaries of science. According to the worldview of many people, the creation of, manipulation of, and control over life—particularly human life—belong exclusively to God.

Perhaps this view explains why many people respond to origin-of-life researchers with a measure of suspicion. They see these scientists as undermining God's position, replacing him with physicochemical processes. It's true many in the origin-of-life community maintain that life's origin needs no Creator.

Yet despite their nontheistic stance, ironic parallels exist between the efforts of some origin-of-life researchers and the biblical narrative of the Creator's activities. For example, some researchers see minerals and clays as playing an integral role in the genesis of life. They'd say that life came from "the dust of the Earth"—just as Adam did.

One of the first scientists to propose a scientific model for the role of clays in the origin of life was Graham Cairns-Smith. In the 1970s, this University of Glasgow chemist advanced the idea that life was originally clay-based.[1] Cairns-Smith thought the mineral crystals in clays could have served as the first genetic material.[2] According to his model, "genetic" information would have been harbored in the rows of mineral that comprise the crystal. Information stored in the crystals could have been copied when new crystal layers formed on the clay surfaces. The preexisting layers would have functioned as templates, dictating the patterning and composition of newly assembled crystal layers.

In Cairns-Smith's model, organic materials present on early Earth could have bound to the mineral crystals in the clays. Then the clay template would have aligned and organized the organic materials. The ordering of the organic material would have also represented information. As a by-product of this ordering, the clay minerals would have transferred their information content to the organic compounds. Over time, the organic materials would have taken over harboring genetic information through this transfer mechanism.

Most origin-of-life researchers reject Cairns-Smith's ideas. They simply don't agree that clay minerals can harbor enough information to operate as genetic material.[3] Still, a key part of this model lives on and plays a prominent role today in many origin-of-life scenarios: the idea that mineral and clay surfaces assist the chemical processes needed to organize building-block materials into metabolic pathways and information-rich molecules, such as RNA.

A number of origin-of-life researchers have pursued this line of investigation. But if there's one scientist who has championed the importance of clays in chemical evolution, it's James Ferris.[4] Over the last couple of decades, he has focused intensely on the catalytic role of clays in assembling RNA molecules from chemically activated nucleotides, RNA's building blocks. Ferris and his co-workers have produced a prodigious amount of data showing how clays facilitate the assembly of molecules critical to the RNA world hypothesis.[5]

I had the pleasure of attending Ferris's opening lecture for ISSOL '02 in Oaxaca, Mexico.[6] He gave a summary of his lab's extensive research, describing how he thought clays could catalyze a key step in the RNA world hypothesis and thus in the origin of life. I was deeply impressed with the amount of work his group had done and the way they had systematically studied various clay-assisted reactions.

After delivering his presentation, Ferris entertained questions, as is customary at scientific meetings. Typically queries are intended to gain clarification of a point or to garner a bit more information. Sometimes questioners will challenge the interpretation of an experiment or observation or criticize some aspect of the study itself. Though public challenges to one's work can be a bit uncomfortable, they are usually issued—and handled—in a professional manner. Everyone present understands that it's all part of the process of science. No offense is intended. But what followed Ferris's talk was completely unexpected.

During the question-and-answer session, Robert Shapiro, a well-known origin-of-life researcher in his own right, raised his hand. When Ferris acknowledged him, Shapiro stunned everyone by issuing an objection to Ferris's entire body of work. Instead of detailing scientific issues related to experimental protocols or interpretation of the data, Shapiro summarily dismissed decades of work, asserting that Ferris's research efforts offered little insight into chemical evolution. Instead, Shapiro announced, Ferris had provided elegant proof for intelligent design.

Shapiro's comments were about as unwelcome as someone cursing out loud at a church service. Many in the origin-of-life community hold a contemptuous view of intelligent design (ID). These scientists don't appreciate creationists' repeated challenges to the evolutionary paradigm. Most scientists regard ID as a threat to science and an irritating thorn in their side. As soon as the initial shock of Shapiro's comment wore off, a murmur rippled through the audience. Ferris's face reddened as the scholar fought to contain his anger. And to his credit, he did.

Despite my horror at Shapiro's breach of decorum, a realization dawned. Shapiro had raised a valid issue, regardless of how scientists at the presentation reacted. I had to agree with Shapiro. Ferris's efforts *do* amount to a powerful case for life as the work of a Creator.

In the preceding two chapters, I covered a range of ideas that the origin-of-life community has been exploring in attempts to account for the generation of prebiotic materials and the emergence of homochirality on early Earth. I argue that researchers have successfully identified a number of physico-chemical processes that in principle could produce, at least temporarily, en-antiomerically enriched prebiotic materials. Through painstaking laboratory efforts, researchers have developed a good understanding of the mechanisms associated with these processes. But investigators have yet to demonstrate that these processes could either (1) work sufficiently well or (2) operate unencumbered under the geochemical constraints of early Earth. In other words, these processes appear to lack geochemical relevance. As I mentioned, if researchers hadn't carefully selected the appropriate chemicals, carefully adjusted the experimental conditions and the concentration of reactants, and precisely stopped the experiment before degradation began, then it is debatable that physicochemical processes could have produced any supply of homochiral building blocks. The artificial conditions and careful manipula-tion by researchers indicate that apart from the work of intelligent agents, the generation of the right types of prebiotics and the origin of homochirality could never have taken place.

For now, however, let's sidestep this apparent roadblock. Let's assume the right building blocks are in place. Let's move on to examine what some origin-of-life researchers think is the next stage in chemical evolution: the organization of building-block materials into information-rich molecules. As discussed in chapter 7, this idea is generally referred to as the replicator-first scenario. According to advocates of this view, the key event in life's history was the emergence of a naked replicator that later became encap-sulated along with the precursor molecules needed to sustain the replica-tor's activity. Metabolism subsequently emerged as a means to support the production and turnover of the replicator's building blocks and ultimately its self-replicating activity.

The most important idea within the replicator-first scenarios is called the RNA world hypothesis (see chapter 7). According to this view, RNA simul-taneously took on the biochemical functions of both DNA and proteins by operating as a self-replicator that catalyzed its own synthesis. According to the RNA world hypothesis, numerous RNA molecules manifesting a wide range of catalytic activity emerged over time. Eventually, the RNA world transitioned to an RNA-protein world, then gave way to contemporary biochemistry with the addition of DNA to the cell's arsenal. As the RNA world transitioned to the DNA-protein world, RNA's original function became partitioned between proteins and DNA, with RNA assuming its current intermediary role. In other words, the RNA ancestral molecules presumably disappeared without leaving a trace of their primordial existence.

Specifically focusing on the RNA world hypothesis, one must ask how successful origin-of-life researchers have been in explaining the origin of information-harboring molecules. Are their approaches geochemically relevant to the conditions of the early Earth? And what does this work mean for the argument that a Creator most likely accounts for life's beginnings?

Making the Case for the RNA World

As the late origin-of-life investigator Leslie Orgel noted, "It may be claimed, without too much exaggeration, that the problem of the origin of life is the problem of the origin of the RNA World."[7]

RNA is a large complex molecule chemists describe as a polymer. Its subunits or monomers are called *ribonucleotides*. RNA can be considered a molecular chain. The links of the chain are the ribonucleotides, joined together in a head-to-tail fashion. Each ribonucleotide is made up of three components: a ribose sugar, a phosphate group, and a nucleobase. Four different nucleobases are used to form RNA: the two pyrimidines, cytosine and uracil; and the two purines, adenine and guanine. The nucleobases are ringed compounds. Pyrimidines consist of a single ring, and the purines are formed by the fusion of two rings.

Ribonucleotides are complex molecules. A ribose sugar serves as the centerpiece of this subunit molecule. Attached to the ribose are both a nucleobase and a phosphate group. RNA forms when the phosphate group of one nucleotide binds to the ribose of another. When several ribonucleotides link up in this way, the net result is a chain-like structure. The backbone of the chain consists of alternating ribose sugars and phosphate groups. Extending from the chain are nucleobases. Because four different nucleobases can be used to build a ribonucleotide, the sequence of the side groups extending from the backbone can vary. The sequence of nucleobases comprises the information content of the RNA molecule. The sequence of the nucleobase side groups also dictates the way the RNA molecule folds into its three-dimensional shape. And its three-dimensional architecture determines its functional capabilities.

"To solve the problem of the RNA world," researchers must establish the validity of several processes. These include:

- reasonable prebiotic chemical routes that will generate the building blocks (nucleobases, ribose, and phosphate) of RNA;
- reasonable prebiotic routes that will assemble these building blocks into ribonucleotides;
- a realistic reaction scheme that will chemically activate the ribonucleotides;
- reasonable prebiotic routes that will assemble RNA from its building blocks into molecular chains long enough to form ribozymes;
- capacity of ribozymes to carry out a range of catalytic activities necessary to sustain an RNA-based biochemistry;
- emergence of an RNA self-replicator.

Making the Building Blocks of RNA

How have researchers fared thus far in their efforts to identify geochemically relevant processes for the production of the components of RNA?

Nucleobases

Chemists have discovered two possible pathways toward production of cytosine. One route involves a reaction between cyanoacetylene and cyanate, and the other begins with a reaction between cyanoacetaldehyde and urea.[8] These four compounds could have been present in early Earth's supposed prebiotic soup. Once cytosine forms, it can convert into uracil fairly easily.

As Shapiro has demonstrated, however, the two chemical routes have questionable geochemical relevance.[9] He points out that cyanoacetylene, cyanate, cyanoacetaldehyde, and urea would have existed at insufficient levels on primordial Earth to effect the production of cytosine. Even if they had been present at appropriate levels, interfering chemical reactions would have quickly consumed these compounds before cytosine could form. Cyanoacetylene rapidly reacts with ammonia, amines, thiols, and hydrogen cyanide. Cyanate undergoes rapid reaction with water. In the presence of water, cyanoacetaldehyde decomposes into acetonitrile and formate. When cytosine does form, it rapidly decomposes. At room temperature and with a neutral pH, cytosine breaks down, losing half its molecules in 340 years. At 0°C, its half-life is 17,000 years, still too short a time for cytosine to be part of the supposed first self-replicator.[10]

To date, scientists have been unable to produce cytosine in spark discharge experiments. They have also failed to recover cytosine from meteorites or extraterrestrial sources.[11] Since meteorites (and other extraterrestrial materials) serve as a proxy for early Earth's chemistry, the absence of cytosine in these sources would seem to affirm Shapiro's conclusion.

In the early 1960s, shortly after Miller's famed spark discharge experiment, chemist Juan Oro showed that adenine could be generated by heating a concentrated solution of ammonia and hydrogen cyanide for several days. Adding formaldehyde to the reaction increases the amount of adenine generated by the reaction.[12] A variant of this reaction can lead to the production of guanine.

As with the prebiotic synthesis of cytosine, problems abound for the production of adenine and guanine. In his analysis of prebiotic simulation experiments that produced adenine, Shapiro showed that adenine formation on early Earth is as unrealistic as formation of cytosine for many of the same reasons.[13]

Many materials in the early Earth's environment would interfere with the generation of both adenine and guanine by reacting with key intermediates, siphoning them away from the desired reaction pathway. Also of concern is the hydrolysis of hydrogen cyanide by water to form formamide and ammonium formate. This reaction occurs much more efficiently than the reactions that generate adenine and guanine. Another problem has to do with the unrealistically high levels of hydrogen cyanide and ammonia needed for the production of purines. Such concentrations could have existed only in early Earth's polar regions where ice was abundant. In the presence of ice, high concentrations of reactants accumulate in so-called eutectic phases of liquid water associated with the ice. Laboratory experiments show that adenine and guanine form in frozen water held for several months between -10°C and -30°C. Purines and pyrimidines would have required mutually incompatible environmental conditions on early Earth for their formation. Purines would have needed extremely cold temperatures. Pyrimidines would have required much higher temperatures, well above 0°C.

Recent work by James Cleaves and Stanley Miller has uncovered an additional problem.[14] Nucleobases readily react with formaldehyde and acetaldehyde, compounds most certainly present on early Earth, to form both small molecule derivatives and large intractable molecules. Even under mild conditions, these reactions take place so rapidly that they would preferentially occur at the expense of reactions that could lead to RNA. Thus, if nucleobases could form, competing reactions would likely consume them. Ironically, the compounds that consume the nucleobases once they form are the ones that could have assisted in the production of adenine and guanine.

Ribose

The only known plausible prebiotic route to ribose (and all sugars) is called the Butlerow reaction (also known as the formose reaction).[15] This reaction begins with the one-carbon compound formaldehyde, which readily forms in spark discharge experiments. In the presence of an inorganic catalyst (calcium hydroxide, calcium oxide, alumina, and clays, for example), formaldehyde reacts with itself and resultant products to generate two, three, four, five, six, or more carbon sugars.

Though this route to ribose and other sugars exists, most researchers question its applicability to the origin-of-life scenario.[16] Multiple competing reactions would likely have prevented sugar production. Unless a special type of compound called an initiator is present, the Butlerow reaction won't occur. Instead, the formaldehyde will undergo the Cannizzaro reaction, in which formaldehyde reacts with itself to form methanol and formic acid.[17]

Numerous side reactions dominate formose chemistry. As a consequence, this one reaction yields over forty different sugar species with ribose as a minor component. If this reaction were in operation on early Earth, it could never have yielded enough ribose to support an RNA world.[18] Laboratory formose reactions are free of contaminants that would likely be present on early Earth. Ammonia, amines, and amino acids, for example, react with formaldehyde and the products of the formose reaction.[19] These side reactions would have consumed key reactants and frustrated the formation of ribose and other sugars.

As with cytosine, decomposition negatively affects ribose formation. Sugars decompose under both alkaline and acidic conditions and are susceptible to oxidation. Even within a neutral pH range, sugars decompose.[20] At 100°C, under neutral conditions, ribose's half-life is seventy-three minutes. At 0°C, ribose has a half-life of forty-four years. Deoxyribose, the sugar component of DNA, likewise has limited stability even under neutral conditions.

The instability of sugars is reflected by their virtual absence from meteorites. The only sugar that has yet been recovered from a meteorite is dihydroxyacetone (a three-carbon sugar), and this compound was found in extremely low abundance.[21] The other compounds discovered in meteorites (sugar alcohols and sugar acids) are structurally distinct from sugars and irrelevant to the origin of life.

Recently, three independent teams of origin-of-life investigators have suggested ways that ribose could have been stabilized and preferentially selected from a complex sugar mixture on early Earth. Steve Benner and colleagues have shown that ribose can form complexes with borate and that these complexes inhibit ribose decomposition. They also discovered that the Butlerow reaction could have taken place in the presence of borate and borate-containing minerals, again avoiding ribose destruction.[22] These researchers argue that borate minerals present on early Earth would have prevented the decomposition of ribose and other sugars. But it is doubtful that the distribution and levels of borate minerals on early Earth would have been sufficient to impact chemical evolution in this dramatic way.

Another team of researchers showed that glycolaldehyde phosphate could react in a modified Butlerow reaction to form just a handful of sugar products, one being ribose phosphate.[23] (Glycolaldehyde forms when two formaldehyde molecules combine with each other.) The difficulty with this proposal arises from the extremely high pH needed for the reaction to take place, not to mention the high levels of gylcolaldehyde phosphate it requires. Also, it is unclear if a source of phosphate would have been present on early Earth to form glycolaldehyde phosphate from glycolaldehyde in the first place.

Jack Szostak's group has discovered that ribose selectively partitions into vesicles made up of materials thought to constitute primitive cell membranes. Accordingly, these vesicles serve as models for protocells (see chapter 13).[24] Szostak's team argues that this partitioning isolated ribose from other sugars that would have been formed by the formose reaction on early Earth. The problem with this suggestion is that the vesicles used in these experiments were formed with materials (and under conditions) that would not have existed on early Earth.

High-Energy Phosphate Compounds

For phosphate groups to be added to ribose, they must exist in a high-energy form. Among the most likely high-energy forms are polyphosphates. The breakage of these high-energy phosphate bonds releases energy that can drive the attachment of the phosphate group to the ribose sugar.

Researchers propose several possible prebiotic chemical routes to polyphosphates.[25] The most common include (1) the heating of apatite (a phosphate-containing mineral); (2) the high-temperature heating (from 392 to 1,112°F, 200 to 600°C) of dihydrogen phosphates; and (3) the phosphates' reaction with high-energy organic compounds.

Although several plausible routes to polyphosphates exist, researchers wonder if these chemical pathways have any relevance to early Earth.[26] For instance, to produce polyphosphates from apatite and dihydrogen phosphate, water must be completely driven from the system—an impossibility for phosphate minerals confined in rocks. Furthermore, the high temperatures needed to form polyphosphates would, in turn, destroy any organic products.

The suggested production of polyphosphates from high-energy chemicals (allegedly formed in spark discharge reactions on early Earth) lacks chemical robustness. These reactions require unrealistically high abundances of starting materials and produce low yields. Laboratory spark discharge experiments performed under a wide range of chemical conditions failed to yield polyphosphates when phosphates were included in the reaction vessel.

Even if a means existed on primordial Earth to form polyphosphates, their availability for prebiotic reactions is unlikely since calcium ions drive polyphosphates to precipitate out of solutions. These ions would have been everywhere on early Earth.[27] Given the extreme rarity (or nonexistence) of polyphosphate minerals on Earth today, the conclusion that prebiotic polyphosphate synthesis took place on early Earth seems unjustified.

Studies on possible prebiotic production of nucleobases, ribose, and polyphosphates demonstrate that even though researchers have identified chemical pathways to these compounds, the lack of available starting materials, as well as chemical interference by other environmental materials and the rapid decomposition of reactants and end products, would have largely precluded their *formation*. In other words, no viable chemical routes to these key life molecules have been found.

I appreciate the origin-of-life community, not only for its remarkable achievements but also for its integrity in widely acknowledging problems with the prebiotic production of nucleobases, ribose, and polyphosphates. In fact, in the opening plenary lecture of ISSOL '02, distinguished scholar Leslie Orgel had the courage to say, "It would be a miracle if a strand of RNA ever appeared on the primitive Earth."[28] As a preface to this comment, Orgel remarked, "I hope no creationists are in the audience." Laughter erupted throughout the room.

The late Leslie Orgel was not advocating a supernatural explanation for life's origin. Rather, he was simply acknowledging the intractable problem of accounting for its emergence through natural processes. He was aware that if it wasn't for chemists carefully controlling the amounts and purity of the chemical components added to the reaction mixtures, adjusting the reaction conditions, and stopping the reactions before the desired products decomposed, the building-block materials would never form. If anything, these research efforts provide direct, empirical evidence that apart from the work of an intelligent agent, this prebiotic chemistry could not occur in a way that leads to the origin of life.

Making Ribonucleotides

From Orgel's perspective, "The synthesis of nucleosides from ribose and the nucleobases is the weakest link in the chain of prebiotic reactions leading to oligonucleotides."[29] For decades chemists have struggled to discover a way to make ribonucleotides by directly reacting ribose with the pyrimidine nucleobases (uracil and cytosine). Researchers have succeeded in making ribonucleotides using purines by heating these compounds with ribose and certain salts, such as magnesium chloride. But these reactions are highly inefficient, generating a complex mixture of products with low yields of purine nucleotides, about 2 to 5 percent of the total product mixture.

A team of chemists has discovered a possible way around this obstacle. Instead of dividing prebiotic reactions into those that lead to sugars and those that yield nucleobases and then trying to find a way for the sugars to combine with the nucleobases to eventually form ribonucleotides, chemists from the University of Manchester took a different tack. They looked for a way to get the two prebiotic routes to intermingle.

This novel approach led to a breakthrough. It turns out that activated ribonucleotides could readily form in the laboratory in a few simple steps.[30] Key to this prebiotic sequence is the reaction of cyanamide and glycolaldehyde to form 2-amino-oxazole. (Cyanamide is a material traditionally viewed as part of the chemical pathways to some of the nucleobases, and glycolaldehyde is the first product in the formose reaction.) This compound, in turn, reacts with glyceraldehyde (formed when glycolaldehyde reacts with formaldehyde) to form a sugar derivative, pentose amino-oxazoline. This derivative reacts with cyanoacetylene (one of the starting materials in the prebiotic synthesis of cytosine) to generate anhydroarabinonucleoside. This compound can react with pyrophosphate and urea to form an activated ribonucleotide, a compound poised to react with other activated ribonucleotides to form RNA chains.

As promising as this chemistry may seem, the researchers encountered a serious problem. In unbuffered reactions (in which the pH isn't controlled), a variety of products result at each step in the pathway. As a consequence, the essential one, 2-amino-oxazole, is present in the system only at low levels. Meanwhile, multiple unwanted products interfere with the remainder of the pathway, frustrating the generation of activated ribonucleotides.

To address this problem, the researchers included phosphate in the reaction mixtures. Phosphate functions as both a catalyst and a buffer, controlling the pH of the reaction mixture, eliminating many of the unwanted by-products. In other words, one of the key reactants in the last stage of the chemical route plays a role in earlier reactions, facilitating the production of ribonucleotides. The researchers also discovered that exposing the final reaction mixture to UV radiation selectively destroyed unwanted by-products as well, helping to increase the relative amount of ribonucleotides in the final mixture.

Using chemical compounds likely to be present on early Earth, the University of Manchester team found a plausible prebiotic route for the production of ribonucleotides. Instead of thinking about sugar and nucleobase chemistries separately, these scientists allowed the two chemistries to work together. This conceptual breakthrough allowed them to discover a very simple chemical route to produce activated ribonucleotides, chemically complex materials. In addition, these researchers allowed reactants from the final steps of the chemical pathway to interact with reactants in the early stages of the process. This too represents a conceptual advance in origin-of-life studies and provides a reasonable way to "clean up" unwanted side reactions that otherwise would interfere with the production of the ribonucleotides. The use of UV radiation to "purify" the final product also makes sense. UV radiation would have been present on early Earth.

Without question, these chemists have made an important contribution to the evolutionary paradigm. Their work paves the way for others to approach problems of prebiotic chemistry in an unconventional way that may lead to other key advances. But have they really rescued the RNA world hypothesis?

Not yet. The first concern is that no route has been found toward production of two of the four ribonucleotides needed to make RNA molecules. The reaction scheme works only for ribonucleotides that consist of pyrimidines. So the breakthrough takes us only partway to finding the source of activated ribonucleotides. Second, although the researchers examined some ways the proposed prebiotic routes could intermingle, they still didn't take into account all the possible side reactions that could frustrate the reaction sequence. For example, they ignored all the reactions that would competitively destroy cyanoacetylene and cyanoacetaldehyde, two key components in this pathway. The researchers conducted their laboratory experiments using purified chemicals, carefully controlling the compounds added to the reactions. This level of control would not have been present on early Earth, again raising concerns about the geochemical relevance of their work.

A third problem has to do with the use of UV radiation to clean up unwanted by-products of the reaction in the last step of the sequence. While exposure to UV radiation may have helped the last step of the reaction by selectively destroying contaminants, it also would have indiscriminately destroyed all of the reactants in the earlier steps of the chemical route. This type of selectivity wouldn't have been available on the early Earth. The Sun's UV radiation would have continuously bathed the planet.

A fourth concern relates to the reactivity of chemically activated ribonucleotides. RNA chains can't assemble without them, but these compounds are so highly reactive that they would have quickly been consumed by materials present in early Earth's environment. Their high reactivity means it's unlikely these materials would have existed in sufficient abundance to help the RNA world scenario. It's a no-win situation.

Perhaps the most significant problem with the proposed process is the dependence on phosphate. In the laboratory experiments, high levels of phosphate were essential to the efficient operation of the pathway. And these levels simply wouldn't have been present on early Earth, for reasons previously described.

The chemists from the University of Manchester accomplished much. They did a masterful job of identifying, in principle, a chemical route that could have generated two of the four ribonucleotides, and they also went a long way toward deciphering the chemical mechanisms that dictate the reaction sequence. However, they have yet to demonstrate that this chemical pathway has geochemical relevance. The conditions required to make this reaction sequence work simply wouldn't have been present on early Earth.

Once again, these researchers have inadvertently provided direct, empirical evidence that apart from the work of an intelligent agent, this prebiotic chemistry could not take place in a productive way for the origin of life. If it weren't for chemists carefully controlling the amounts and purity of the chemical components added to the reaction mixtures, adjusting the reaction conditions (which included adding the appropriate level of phosphate), and selectively exposing the final reaction products to UV radiation as a way to get rid of unwanted by-products, the generation of activated ribonucleotides would not have occurred.

Commenting on this work, Shapiro said, "The flaw with this kind of research is not in the chemistry. The flaw is in the logic—that this experimental control by researchers in a modern laboratory could have been available on the early Earth."[31]

Assembling RNA Molecules

Another key step in the RNA world scenario for life's emergence is the assembly of RNA molecules from the ribonucleotide building blocks. This stage of the model suffers from as many problems as do the earlier steps.

Researchers noted early on that ribonucleotides won't react in water to form oligonucleotides of RNA. By evaporating solutions with an acidic pH and then heating them, lab workers can produce very short-chain oligonucleotides in the presence of activating reagents. The links between the building blocks include those that occur naturally in biological systems (3′–5′ linkages) and those that do not (2′–5′ linkages).[32]

To improve the chances of generating RNA oligonucleotides in the laboratory, origin-of-life investigators have turned their attention to chemically activated ribonucleotides. To activate the ribonucleotides, chemists add chemical groups to these molecules that make them more likely to react with other ribonucleotides to form RNA chains. As part of the reaction sequence, the activating groups dissociate from the ribonucleotides and don't appear in the final product. Researchers have had little success in using biologically relevant polyphosphates as activators. The nucleoside-5′-polyphosphates react way too slowly in the lab.[33]

Further experimentation shows that phosphorimidazolides do a better job of activating ribonucleotides for oligomerization. These compounds can be generated by reacting nucleoside-5′-polyphosphates with amines or compounds called imidazoles. In water, these compounds react more rapidly than nucleoside-5′-polyphosphates but yield complex mixtures of short-chain RNA oligonucleotides and cyclic complexes.[34]

In the mid-1990s, James Ferris and his research team stirred excitement within the scientific community by assembling lengthy RNA molecules. Ferris used clays as a catalyst so that ribonucleotides activated with phosphorimidazolides would react to produce RNA oligomers. This assembly was accomplished by washing solutions of the reactants over clay surfaces, then allowing the solutions to evaporate.[35] Commentators heralded this work as a key demonstration that prebiotic conditions on Earth could have produced self-replicators.[36]

Closer evaluation of this effort, however, prompts a different conclusion. First, apart from the unlikelihood that activated ribonucleotides would have formed under the prevailing conditions of early Earth, even if they had formed, they would have been so reactive as to combine with all sorts of compounds in the environment, thereby frustrating the generation of RNA molecules.[37]

As Shapiro points out, Ferris's teams conducted these experiments under selective conditions that excluded potential chemical interferents, ignoring what Shapiro has dubbed the homopolymer problem (see "The Homopolymer Problem," page 168).[38] Shapiro also highlights another concern. The clay used by Ferris's teams is a variety known as montmorillonite. This clay is widely distributed throughout the Earth, but not all montmorillonite clays are equal. The success of clays as catalysts depends on the location it comes from. Ferris and his collaborators found that clay provided specifically by the

American Colloid Company, which sources its clays from Wyoming, had the best likelihood of generating RNA molecules.[39] This particular clay, Volclay, is processed before it is delivered to the customer. Presumably this processing plays a critical role in the catalysis.

Equally problematic is the need to pretreat the clay before it's used as a catalyst. If this preparation doesn't happen, the oligomerization reactions don't occur. Copper, iron, and zinc ions, normally associated with the clays in nature, interfere with RNA assembly. These materials must be removed by a special procedure called a titration, which replaces the offending metals with benign sodium.[40]

Orgel's teams identified another problem. Though mineral surfaces may promote RNA formation, they also catalyze RNA decomposition.[41] The breakdown occurs on surfaces of both lead- and calcium-containing minerals. These workers also discovered that the amino acids glutamate and histidine stimulate the disassembly of RNA in a solution. Japanese researchers demonstrated that rare Earth elements (such as cerium) present in the primordial oceans would have catalyzed the breakdown of the RNA backbone linkage.[42] Although proteins can prevent the dismantling of RNA, the inhibition of this cleavage would require an unrealistically high level of proteins in the early oceans.

Another challenge for mineral-assisted RNA formation is the irreversible attachment of RNA to mineral surfaces once the molecular chain grows to a certain length. This attachment would prevent an RNA molecule from being available for the origin-of-life process if it should happen to form on a clay surface.

Orgel and his colleagues demonstrated in the laboratory that once an RNA chain exists, it can serve as a template assisting the assembly of another RNA chain. These experiments made use of activated ribonucleotide phosphorimidazolides, while others used condensing agents to promote the reaction between ribonucleotides.[43] These RNA-building reactions can take place in fairly dilute solutions, but could they have occurred in the context of the early Earth's environment? Most likely chemical interferents would have interrupted chain formation, and the presence of racemic mixtures of ribonucleotides would have frustrated chain assembly (see chapter 10). As Orgel's team demonstrated, the incorporation of opposite-handed nucleotides proves fatally disruptive to template-assisted formation of RNA chains.[44]

Another challenge comes from the inherent instability of the RNA chain. As individual building block molecules are added to the chain (extending its length), water molecules react with the RNA (a process called *hydrolysis*) to break apart the chain. In other words, competing reactions of growth and degradation would have prevented the chains from attaining the requisite length to generate a ribozyme.

A team of Italian biochemists recently found a possible way around the degradation problem.[45] In laboratory experiments, short RNA molecules reacted with themselves in water to produce longer RNA molecules, some two and four times the length of the original RNA starting compounds. This dramatic capacity to at least double in length would seem to allow prebiotic RNA molecules to progressively increase in size as their growth outpaced their breakdown.

The reaction between RNA pieces in water was unexpected because watery environments typically promote breakdown, not growth, of the RNA chains. So what happened? Upon close investigation, it appears as if the RNA chains pair in solution to form duplexes and quadraplexes in which the two RNA chains align. These configurations bring chemical groups on the ends of the RNA molecules into close proximity where they readily react with each other to extend the chain length. This pairing of the RNA molecules creates a local environment for the reactive chemical groups distinctly different from what they experience when free in solution.

While the researchers demonstrated that, in principle, chemical pathways to extend the chain length of RNA molecules do exist, once again their work bumps into reality. When the specifics of this new research are carefully considered, no one can envision how this type of chemistry could happen under the conditions of the early Earth. It turns out the doubling and quadrupling of RNA fragments is a fastidious process, highly dependent upon temperature, pH, the size and the sequence of the RNA fragments, and the presence of co-reactants. In particular, the research team showed that formation of the duplexes and quadraplexes (needed to bring the appropriate chemical groups into sufficient proximity to react) required low temperatures and acidic or neutral pH values. At higher temperatures and alkaline pH, the RNA complexes did not form.

Nor will the RNA duplexes and quadraplexes form from shorter RNA fragments. RNA chain lengths of ten subunits or longer are required for the RNA fragments to couple. The research team also discovered that RNA fragments of unequal length form less-stable aggregates and are consequently less likely to combine. The investigators further found that the efficiency of the reaction could be improved by adding cofactors, small molecules with structures closely related to the structure of the subunits of the RNA fragments. It appears the cofactors help stabilize the RNA complexes.

In other words, if not for the careful design and execution of the reactions under laboratory conditions—carefully managed by researchers—the RNA fragments won't couple. So it's unlikely the coupling happened naturally on early Earth. Biochemists also observed that the degradation of the RNA fragments took place simultaneously with the coupling. This observation means any conditions that deviate from the "laboratory" optimal will not

The Homopolymer Problem

Given the challenges to the RNA world hypothesis, some scientists have suggested that a molecule other than RNA may have been the first self-replicator. They propose molecules such as peptide nucleic acids (see chapter 10) to play the part.

Regardless of their specific chemical identity, candidates for the first self-replicating molecule must possess common chemical features. Such molecules must be made up of smaller chemical subunits that link to form chains. The side groups that extend from the self-replicator's backbone must be chemically and physically varied to provide the physicochemical information essential to the self-replication process, but the self-replicator's backbone must consist of a repetitious structure.

To function as a self-replicator, a molecule needs a template to direct the assembly of subunit molecules into an identical copy of itself. Self-templating (and therefore self-replication) is possible only if the backbone's structure repeats with little if any interruption or variation.[46] Therefore, the subunit molecules comprising the self-replicator must all consist of the same chemical class.

Chemists call these chainlike molecules with structurally repetitive backbones *homopolymers* (*homo*=same; *poly*=many; *mer*=units). DNA, RNA, proteins, and the proposed pre–RNA world self-replicators (such as the peptide nucleic acids) are all homopolymers and satisfy the chemical requirements to function as self-replicators.

While undirected chemical processes can produce homopolymers under carefully controlled laboratory conditions, early Earth's state was anything but pristine.[47] The chemical compounds found in the complex chemical mixture that researchers say existed on early Earth would have interfered with homopolymer formation. If these mixtures yielded anything, they would have produced polymers with highly heterogeneous backbone structures—molecular entities that cannot function as self-replicators. Shapiro has shown this interference to be the case specifically for proteins, RNA, and peptide nucleic acids. The likely chemical components of any prebiotic soup would have not only interrupted the structural regularity of the self-replicator's backbone but also prematurely terminated its formation or introduced branch sites.

The homopolymer problem effectively devastates the replicator-first hypothesis for the origin of life. For Shapiro, the only possible alternative is a metabolism-first model (discussed in the following chapter).

While undirected natural processes cannot generate homopolymers under the conditions of primordial Earth, the biochemical processes within the cell can. The cell makes homopolymers with efficiency because of the high degree of specificity possessed by its biochemical machinery. This specificity overcomes the thermodynamic tendency of random chemical processes to produce polymers with a haphazard backbone composition.

only hamper the efficiency of the coupling reactions but also bring about a net breakdown of the RNA fragments.

When it comes to assembling RNA oligonucleotides from ribonucleotide building blocks, the bottom line is this: laboratory simulation experiments that synthesize RNA on mineral surfaces differ substantially from early Earth's conditions. When scientists consider more realistic scenarios, they quickly discover that RNA assembly could not have occurred in the natural prebiotic realm to any appreciable extent. If not for intelligent agents activating the ribonucleotides with the optimal chemical groups, carefully selecting the right type of clay, and pretreating it to remove inhibiting metal ions, RNA oligonucleotides would not assemble at all.

Generating Self-Replicating RNA Molecules

A critical stage in the RNA world scenario involves the emergence of a self-replicating RNA molecule along with the evolution of a full ensemble of RNA molecules capable of a wide range of catalytic activity to sustain the life processes of the first protocells. For this idea to have merit, researchers must demonstrate (at a minimum) that RNA molecules inherently manifest an adequate range of catalytic activity to support a comprehensive biochemical system—this in addition to discovering an RNA molecule that can replicate itself.

Some success toward this end has come from a laboratory process called *in vitro* evolution, which has produced RNA enzymes (ribozymes) that can catalyze a number of different types of chemical reactions essential to the RNA world.[48] This work demonstrates that, in principle, life centered on RNA biochemistry is conceivable. Beyond this success, however, researchers have struggled to make a self-replicating ribozyme, a necessity for the RNA world hypothesis to have any validity.

Researchers have made ribozymes with varied properties. Some ribozymes can assist in the synthesis of ribonucleotides and can join two RNA chains together (a process called *ligation*). Other ribozymes can add ribonucleotide subunits to the end of an RNA molecule, extending the chain.[49] All of these activities are necessary for replication of RNA molecules. Yet to date, biochemists have been unable to make RNA with genuine self-replicating capability.

A team of molecular biologists from the Scripps Research Institute in La Jolla, California, recently made a significant step forward in this quest when they engineered a type of self-replicating RNA molecule that evolved to produce a molecular ecosystem of self-replicators.[50] Though the nature of this self-replication is not the type that would contribute to the origin of life (in which the RNA molecule would use ribonucleotides and build an exact replica of itself), their work still has significance for the RNA world hypothesis.

Their latest work built off of an earlier study. Using *in vitro* evolution, researchers made a ribozyme (called R3C) that serves as both a ligase—joining RNA molecules together—and a template that juxtaposes RNA molecules. In this experiment, two RNA molecules, labeled A and B, joined together (or ligated) to produce an RNA molecule, designated C. This newly made RNA molecule, in turn, served as a template bringing A and B molecules into contact with each other and a ligase joining them together. This cycle repeated over and over again. So a molecule of C can make several more copies of C. And each of these can also make several more copies of C, hence a self-replicating system.

Most recently, the researchers added a twist to the original system. In addition to using just two RNA molecules (A and B) that can combine to form C, they added two more RNA fragments (X and Y) that combine to form a larger RNA molecule, Z. In this system, C serves as a template and a ligase for the reaction that joins X and Y together to form Z, and Z operates as a template and ligase for the reaction that joins A and B together to make C. The scientists refer to this process as cross-replication.

The scientists then used *in vitro* evolution to create an ensemble of variants of A, B, X, and Y (A_1, A_2, A_3 . . . ; B_1, B_2, B_3 . . . ; X_1, X_2, X_3 . . . ; Y_1, Y_2, Y_3 . . .) and added this collection of RNA molecules into a test tube to let the cross-replication reactions proceed. Over time the more efficient self-replicators dominated the mixture. It appears that a form of molecular Darwinian evolution took place in the lab. Even more intriguing were the mistakes that occurred during cross-replication, the occasional mismatches in the pairings. (For example, instead of A_1 and B_1 combining to form C_1, they combined to form a new molecule, C_{12}.) When these mispairings took place, novel RNA molecules arose. If these new molecules were more efficient self-replicators, over time they came to dominate the mixture. Eventually, the test tube no longer contained any of the original ribozymes. Instead, researchers found a mixture of "mutated" ribozymes species much more effective as self-replicators than the original RNA molecules.

On the surface this work seems powerful evidence for the evolutionary paradigm in general and for the RNA world hypothesis specifically. It certainly would be *if* the *in vitro* evolutionary mechanism were applicable to early Earth and to the putative RNA world. The critical issue is this: the generation of ribozymes relies on *in vitro* evolution, but the production of these self-replicating ribozymes—in fact, of any ribozyme—depends on design that exists behind the scenes.

The process of *in vitro* evolution relies on detailed experimental design and researcher intervention. The protocol begins with a large pool of RNA molecules with random nucleotide sequences and hence random structures.[51] From this pool, researchers select (through the experiment's design) RNA molecules with a predetermined set of chemical properties. These selected

RNA molecules are recovered and their number amplified by the enzyme reverse transcriptase and with the polymerase chain reaction (PCR). PCR also employs an enzyme, a DNA polymerase. The new RNA sequence is then randomly altered to generate a new pool of RNA molecules using another enzyme called T7 RNA polymerase, and the process is repeated again and again until RNA molecules with the desired chemical properties emerge. Production of the RNA self-replicators also required researchers to modify the structure of ribozymes generated by *in vitro* evolution so the ribozymes could function as molecular templates and ligases.

The "evolution" of RNA molecules in the laboratory is a carefully orchestrated process devised and managed by intelligent agents. Its success hinges on thoughtful experimental design. It must be noted that the essential enzymes (protein molecules with a complex, fine-tuned structure), reverse transcriptase, and DNA polymerase molecules would never exist in an RNA world. It stretches the bounds of credulity to think that this process, or one like it, could have occurred naturally on early Earth. As thrilling as their achievements are, origin-of-life researchers have fallen short of demonstrating RNA's ability to evolve.

In the words of Leslie Orgel, "It is instructive to notice how much synthetic skill is needed to develop even the simplest cycles."[52]

The Bitter Gall

When it comes to replicator-first scenarios in general and the RNA world hypothesis in particular, origin-of-life researchers have demonstrated, in principle, that physicochemical processes do exist that can generate the building blocks of RNA, combine them to form ribonucleotides, assemble them into RNA chains, and evolve them into a collective of functional ribozymes that could sustain an RNA world. These researchers have done exquisite work, and yet they have failed to show that these processes have geochemical relevance. If it weren't for chemists (1) carefully controlling the amounts and purity of the chemical components added to the reaction mixtures; (2) adjusting the reaction conditions; and (3) stopping the reactions before the desired products decomposed, then the building-block materials would never form. When it comes to assembling RNA oligonucleotides from ribonucleotide building blocks, if not for intelligent agents (1) activating the ribonucleotides with the optimal chemical groups; (2) carefully selecting the right type of clay; and (3) pretreating it to remove inhibiting metal ions, then RNA oligonucleotides would never assemble.

If they prove anything more than the researchers' tenacity and ingenuity, efforts to provide experimental support for the RNA world scenario have demonstrated that life cannot "happen" apart from the work of an intelligent, purposeful agent.

These findings—or the limits nature places upon them—have led a number of origin-of-life researchers, including Robert Shapiro, to abandon replicator-first scenarios for life's origin and look elsewhere. In their thorough scientific quest, these researchers have turned to metabolism-first models of chemical evolution to explain the emergence of life on Earth. In the next chapter, I will discuss and evaluate these types of models.

12

A Thousand Other Miseries

I gazed on my victim, and my heart swelled with exultation and hellish triumph: clapping my hands, I exclaimed, "I, too, can create desolation; my enemy is not invulnerable; this death will carry despair to him, and a thousand other miseries shall torment and destroy him."

Frankenstein's monster in *Frankenstein*

I remember driving onto the University of Central Florida (UCF) campus. I was there to take part in a symposium on the origin of life. It was a beautiful fall day in mid-October, and I anticipated a leisurely drive through meticulously sculpted grounds and buildings. But as I made my way toward the lecture hall, I found myself in a scene of devastation. Everywhere I looked, piles of collected debris decorated the lawns and once-stately trees lay on their side, having been violently ripped from the ground. The sight was a far cry from the beauty typical of most college settings. What I was witnessing was the aftermath of Hurricane Charley, a mind-boggling example of nature's destructive force—far more devastating than the destruction Frankenstein's monster wrecked.

The devastation I happened upon at UCF wasn't limited to the campus grounds. I looked upon the shattered remains of replicator-first models for the origin of life and the RNA world hypothesis. Robert Shapiro and I, along with chemist Christopher Switzer, were on campus to present a series of talks on the current status of origin-of-life research. We were asked to address both scientific and philosophical issues. Switzer, who has done some excellent work on developing nucleic acid analogues,[1] was there to represent scientific orthodoxy on the origin of life, the RNA world hypothesis. Shapiro stood in as a skeptic of that orthodoxy. And I represented an extreme position, one that rejected *all* naturalistic chemical evolutionary explanations for life's beginning. While Switzer and Shapiro only briefly touched on the philosophical issues related to the origin-of-life problem, I spent a significant portion of my talk making a case that life's origin must stem from the work of a Creator.

I was excited for an opportunity to discuss my views at a scientific forum with these two distinguished scientists. I had heard Shapiro speak at two previous ISSOL conferences about problems with replicator-first scenarios, and I wanted a chance to interact with him about my ideas. I got much more than I had hoped for. Instead of engaging in a single conversation, I ended up spending a significant amount of time with him. Over the course of a couple days, we shared several meals together and took walks through the campus, discussing a wide range of topics, including the relationship between science and faith. At one point, Shapiro asked me to autograph his copy of the book I coauthored with Hugh Ross, *Origins of Life*.

Though a harsh critic of many origin-of-life models (his nickname in the origin-of-life community is "Dr. No"), Shapiro seemed a kindhearted, soft-spoken gentleman. We vigorously debated whether or not science could ever hope to uncover evidence for the work of a Creator, and we also found some common ground. We both agreed that significant problems exist for most origin-of-life scenarios, but we didn't see eye-to-eye when it comes to skepticism about chemical evolution. Shapiro, a committed naturalist, remains convinced that some physicochemical mechanism will be discovered to account for the start of life. At the ISSOL meetings and at the UCF origins symposium, Shapiro made it clear that he favors metabolism-first scenarios. In fact, in recent years he has become a leading advocate for this set of origin-of-life models.

In the preceding chapter, I presented my evaluation of replicator-first scenarios for life's beginnings. I argued that origin-of-life researchers have demonstrated, in principle, that physicochemical processes can generate the building blocks of RNA, combine them to form ribonucleotides, assemble them into RNA chains, and evolve these molecules into a collection of functional ribozymes able to sustain an RNA world—but only with an enormous investment of skillful, purposeful researcher involvement, and never with any realistic geochemical relevance.

In this chapter, I assess the alternative approach to replicator-first models, the metabolism-first scenarios. Again, using the framework outlined in chapter 8, I examine the geochemical relevance of these models. As in several previous chapters, I address these questions: Have origin-of-life researchers found a way, through their efforts to create life in the lab, to explain the origin of life? To what extent and why have their efforts been frustrated? And does this work impact the need for a Creator to account for life's beginnings?

Metabolism-First Scenarios

Some researchers have postulated that once prebiotic materials formed, these relatively small molecules self-organized to form chemical cycles and networks of reactions that eventually gave rise to simple metabolic systems. Once encapsulated, or sequestered, these complex web-like protometabolic systems became the first protocells.[2]

According to this view, molecular self-replicators emerged later, along with enzymes that catalyzed each step in the essential chemical cycles and networks. Some proponents of metabolism-first scenarios maintain that these cycles and networks closely resembled the metabolic pathways observed in cells today. Accordingly, metabolic pathways represent molecular fossils of sorts, purportedly providing evidence for metabolism-first models. In other words, "metabolism recapitulates biogenesis."[3]

Adherents to this view suggest that either (1) individual chemical species involved in these cycles and networks catalyzed these same reactions—a type of autocatalysis; or (2) mineral surfaces catalyzed the protometabolic pathways. Models relying on mineral catalysis are the more prominent of the two alternatives. Some metabolism-first scenarios, such as the iron-sulfur world, go so far as to propose that minerals, such as pyrite, became encapsulated within vesicles along with the protometabolic networks and thereby served as life's first catalytic agents.

To date, models that deal with this collection of ideas have received only limited attention because they are less developed than their replicator-first counterparts. But this deficiency is being addressed. In an attempt to lay out key principles, Shapiro recently identified five requirements for virtually *all* metabolism-first scenarios:[4]

1. Emergence of a boundary to segregate the protometabolic pathways from the environment
2. An energy source to power the protometabolic interactions
3. A coupling mechanism to link the available energy to the protometabolic pathways
4. Emergence of a chemical network comprised of interconnected cycles of reactions among small molecules
5. A means for the network to grow and reproduce

Here's a brief overview of the theoretical scheme: small prebiotic molecules present on the early Earth became encapsulated within a membrane system. Within the encapsulated system, a hypothetical reaction, say X → Y, generated energy. This energy was used to power a special reaction, called the driver reaction. Next, a hypothetical compound, call it A, was converted to hypothetical compound B (A → B). Once B formed it converted to C, and C converted to D, and D converted to E, which in turn generated A. The net effect was that the energy released by X → Y powered the cycle. If a feeder reaction, say F → C, existed outside the cycle, the cycle could have drawn more material into the cycle. Over time, the cycle would have expanded and become more complex as other compounds interfaced with the original cycle and in turn took part in other cycles.

Origin-of-life investigator Leslie Orgel noted that "if complex cycles analogous to metabolic cycles could have operated on primitive Earth, before the appearance of enzymes or other informational polymers, many of the obstacles to the construction of a plausible scenario for the origin of life would disappear."[5]

However, metabolism-first models can only be viewed as truly viable *if* they are chemically plausible. And chemical plausibility must be assessed based on the efficiencies and specificities of the protometabolic cycles within the context of the conditions of the early Earth.

Which Came First?

To date, metabolism-first scenarios, such as the one proposed by Shapiro, remain intriguing theoretical ideas with minimal, if any, experimental support. It is one thing to have hypothetical compound X convert into Y, releasing energy that couples to the conversion of A to B and then C to D, then have D catalyze the conversion of B to C, and so forth, on paper. But it is quite another matter to identify compounds that will behave in this way in the laboratory, let alone in the environment of early Earth.

While cognizant of this concern, Leslie Orgel has identified a number of additional challenges to the notion that metabolism came first.[6] As a case in point, he observes that cycles and networks operating on early Earth would have been highly susceptible to disruption by chemical interferents and competing side reactions. These interfering species and side reactions would have siphoned away materials and clogged up the cycles. In other words, these models rely on unrealistic chemistry.

This set of models must also address the chemical stability-instability paradox. Chemical compounds must be reactive enough to take part in protometabolic cycles and networks, but this reactivity makes them susceptible to breakdown and decomposition, which then makes the chemical cycles and networks inherently unstable, frustrating *all* metabolism-first scenarios. On the other hand, chemical compounds stable enough to withstand degradation do not enter into chemical cycles and networks because they are too chemically unreactive.

Without the availability of enzymes, protometabolic reactions cannot proceed rapidly enough to sustain a protocell—apart from the help of some sort of chemical accelerant.[7] Mineral surfaces seem the only reasonable candidates for service as prebiotic catalysts. And yet while mineral surfaces can catalyze specific reactions, to propose that a mineral will catalyze the full range of chemical reactions required for cycles or chemical networks to operate is woefully unrealistic. An attempt to increase the catalytic range by invoking the availability of many different types of mineral surfaces only creates an additional problem—the need for an efficient way to transport "metabolites" from mineral site to mineral site. These additional complex requirements raise questions about how a chemical cycle could have been maintained, become encapsulated, and evolved into a protocell's metabolic system.[8]

In a paper published posthumously, Orgel illustrates the problems with metabolism-first scenarios by applying them to the reverse citric acid cycle.[9] Certain bacteria utilize the reverse citric acid cycle to fix carbon, converting carbon dioxide and water into organic compounds. Some researchers have proposed that the reverse citric acid cycle was one of the first metabolic pathways to emerge and that its genesis predated the origin of information-based molecules such as RNA (and proteins and DNA). Again, metabolism recapitulates biogenesis.[10]

Orgel notes that the conditions of the early Earth do indeed permit the reverse citric acid cycle to operate with adequate efficiency, provided the pathway is stable for long periods of time and disruptive side reactions never reduce the cycle's overall efficiency below 50 percent. On the other hand, the reverse citric acid cycle—and, in fact, all protometabolic cycles—would have been impossible on early Earth because the catalysts needed to drive the cycle lacked the required specificity.

The reverse citric acid cycle consists of eleven steps, each one requiring a specific mineral catalyst. The cycle also depends on six fundamentally distinct chemical transformations. Inside cells, this metabolic process employs complex enzyme catalysts possessing high specificities and capacities for molecular-level discrimination among the components of the cycle. Orgel fittingly argues that it's unlikely the right types of minerals needed to carry out these reactions would coexist at particular locales on the early Earth in such a way to support all the steps in the reverse citric acid cycle.

The specificity problem becomes exacerbated if the reverse citric acid cycle is to evolve toward greater complexity, a requirement if life is to originate from a protometabolic cycle. Presumably, evolution of complexity results when additional reaction sequences are appended onto the core reactions of the cycle. As Orgel notes, "Given the difficulty of finding an ensemble of

catalysts that are sufficiently specific to enable the original cycle, it is hard
to see how one could hope to find an ensemble capable of enabling two or
more."[11]

Discrimination, or more appropriately, the lack of discrimination, also
presents a problem. Many of the compounds in the reverse citric acid cycle
share structural similarities. Enzymes inside cells can readily distinguish these
similar compounds, but mineral catalysts cannot. This lack of specificity would
have caused key components of the cycle to be siphoned off into unwanted
disruptive side reactions. Over time, this disruption would likely have driven
the efficiency of the supposed cycle below 50 percent, quenching it.

The problems identified for the reverse citric acid cycle apply to all other
conceivable protometabolic cycles as well.

The Iron-Sulfur World

Perhaps one of the best developed models in the metabolism-first arena is the
iron-sulfur world hypothesis proposed and championed almost exclusively by
Günter Wächtershäuser. This model is also referred to as the chemoautotrophic
theory for the origin of life. Like Shapiro, Wächtershäuser potently critiques
much of the work taking place in the origin-of-life research community. In
his talk at ISSOL '99, he scolded the researchers in attendance, as I recall,
for proposing scenarios that lack scientific rigor. Like Shapiro, he rejected
replicator-first models. Instead he proposed that a specific type of surface
chemistry near hydrothermal vents may have produced small molecules that
organized and led to the origin of life.

The key reaction in Wächtershäuser's model is the conversion of iron(2)
sulfide and hydrogen sulfide into iron pyrite (fool's gold). This reaction generates energy that can be used to fix carbon into organic materials.[12] Iron
pyrite precipitates in large amounts around hydrothermal vents, making this
reaction conceivably relevant to the geochemical processes of the early Earth.
It's also noteworthy that iron-sulfur complexes are critical cofactors in several key enzymes that comprise part of the electron transport chain, as well
as in proteins such as the oxidoreductases and ferredoxins. Wächtershäuser
maintains that these cofactors are relics of the iron-sulfur world and serve as
molecular fossils, so to speak.[13]

Using a mixture of iron sulfide and nickel sulfide precipitates that had
been processed into a slurry, Wächtershäuser and his longtime collaborator Claudia Huber produced acetic acid from carbon dioxide and methyl
mercaptan. (The iron sulfide and nickel sulfide precipitates were included in
the experiment to model chemistry that occurs on the surface of minerals
associated with hydrothermal vent deposits.) The intermediate in this reaction was a special type of chemical compound called an activated thioester,

which can generate acetic acid if treated with water or transfer the acetyl group (which is closely related in structure to acetic acid) to other organic compounds. The two researchers noticed that if they incorporated selenium into their system, it produced acetic acid and methyl mercaptan directly, without the activated thioester intermediate. They consider these chemical processes to represent "the primordial initiation reaction for a chemoautotrophic origin of life."[14]

Using a similar approach, Wächtershäuser and Huber have demonstrated that a series of alpha hydroxy acids and amino acids can be generated from carbon monoxide using nickel sulfide and nickel/iron sulfide catalysts. They have also shown that amino acids can react to form dipeptides, adding further experimental support for the iron-sulfur world model.[15] This reaction is considered the preamble to assembly of more complex biomolecules such as proteins.

Despite detailed chemical modeling and experimental support, the iron-sulfur world scenario has yet to captivate the attention of more than a few researchers. One reason for this skepticism is that the lab conditions required to make the iron-sulfur world chemistry work seem far from realistic for conditions on early Earth. For example, the laboratory reactions require high concentrations of reactants unlikely to have existed in nature at that time.[16] The supporting experiments also required careful regulation of the reaction pH, using magnesium hydroxide in some cases. The iron sulfide/nickel sulfide catalysts employed in these experiments also required special preparation. This type of control would never have existed in the prebiotic milieu.

Huber and Wächtershäuser also took care to exclude chemical materials likely present on early Earth, materials that would have interfered with the chemical reactions they conducted in the laboratory, thereby creating a false sense of success.[17]

A recent analysis indicates that the reactions associated with the iron-sulfur world could not have proceeded fast enough on the early Earth to generate oligomers, including peptides.[18] Nor was there any means to prevent the chemical degradation of peptides had they formed. As a case in point, Wächtershäuser and his collaborators observed that dipeptides formed with carbon monoxide and acetic acid catalyzed by iron sulfide and nickel sulfide mixtures also broke down under the reaction conditions.[19]

Although Huber and Wächtershäuser have enjoyed some success generating biologically interesting compounds, other researchers have yet to share in the same success. For example, using the conditions postulated by Wächtershäuser, Stanley Miller and his collaborator A. D. Keefe were unsuccessful in making amino acids or nucleobases from iron sulfide, hydrogen sulfide, and carbon dioxide. Their failure, they conclude, highlights the delicacy of the chemistry proposed by Wächtershäuser. This lack of chemical robustness would render it irrelevant to conditions on early Earth.[20]

What Wächtershäuser has accomplished is calling attention to the possibility that iron sulfide and related minerals may possibly have had a role in the origin of life. His team has shown in principle that these materials can react with gaseous molecules to generate biologically intriguing molecules. They have also done a good job deciphering the chemical mechanisms associated with these processes. But, as with all other aspects of the bottom-up approach to the origin of life, this wonderful laboratory work proves geochemically unrealistic. More noteworthy, it shows that if not for the design and control exerted by intelligent agents in the laboratory, the chemical reactions associated with the iron-sulfur world could not proceed with any efficiency, if they proceeded at all.

A Thousand Other Miseries

On paper, metabolism-first scenarios seem plausible. Nevertheless, a thorough chemical analysis of these models exposes fundamental and intractable flaws. Metabolism-first scenarios fall short of providing viable pathways to life. The limited experimental evidence supporting these scenarios, developed primarily in the context of the iron-sulfur world, indicates that the chemical processes associated with this model require conditions that would not have existed on the primordial planet. As Leslie Orgel has commented, metabolism-first scenarios require an "appeal to magic," a "series of remarkable coincidences," and a "near miracle."[21]

If the origin of life cannot be explained with a replicator-first approach (see chapter 11), a metabolism-first scenario remains the only alternative yet imaginable. But given the evidence cited in this chapter, this alternative seems no more viable than the first. In fact, chemist Addy Pross has argued that metabolism-first systems simply cannot generate replicator-based chemistry.[22] According to Pross's analysis, replicator systems could conceivably yield metabolism, but again, serious barriers stand in the way of replicator-first explanations for life's origin. The bottom line: inherent problems exist for both replicator-first and metabolism-first scenarios. To date researchers have found neither conceivable nor realistic chemical routes from a prebiotic soup to life. Both options—replicator-first and metabolism-first—fail.

In Orgel's last written words to the origin-of-life community, he admonishes advocates of each scenario: "Solutions offered by supporters of geneticist or metabolist scenarios that are dependent on 'if pigs could fly' hypothetical chemistry are unlikely to help."[23]

The closing chapter continues the search for explanations of life's start: the one major issue still to be addressed is the origin of cell membranes. For life to emerge from nonlife, regardless of whether by means of replicator-first or metabolism-first processes, the prebiotic system must somehow become encapsulated. What does this step involve, and how likely is it to be accomplished via chemical evolutionary mechanisms?

13

Persevere in Exile

"You propose," replied I, "to fly from the habitations of man, to dwell in those wilds where the beasts of the field will be your only companions. How can you, who long for the love and sympathy of man, persevere in this exile? You will return, and again seek their kindness, and you will meet with their detestation; your evil passions will be renewed, and you will then have a companion to aid you in the task of destruction. This may not be: cease to argue the point, for I cannot consent."

Victor Frankenstein in *Frankenstein*

The monster pleads with Frankenstein to make another like him, a female to be his companion. As part of his request, he promises to take her away and to remain till death in the jungles of South America, living off the land. "Neither you nor any other human being shall ever see us again."

For a brief moment, Frankenstein wavers, wanting to believe that the life he had created will voluntarily remain confined within the "wilds," eschewing contact with other human beings. But he can't be sure the beast will ultimately respect his own self-imposed boundaries.

Boundaries are important. They are designed to keep things separate, to keep things apart. Boundaries are critical for life. Cells require boundaries to keep their structures and chemical processes separate from the exterior environment. Cell membranes define life's boundaries.[1] Like a well-guarded border, the cell membrane keeps harmful materials from entering the cell and sequesters the beneficial compounds inside it (see appendix, page 205). And like vigilant guards, proteins embedded in membranes regulate the traffic of materials into and out of the cell. These transport proteins ensure the cell takes in the necessary nutrients and expels waste products. Membranes also serve as the site for photosynthesis and energy production. In short, the cell membrane plays an indispensable role in living systems.

I became enthralled with cell membranes during my junior year of college. Of all the remarkable biochemical systems that constitute life, these molecular boundaries seemed to me the most fascinating. In graduate school, I decided to focus my studies on cell membrane systems. I reveled in the opportunity to spend virtually all my waking hours doing experiments and thinking about membrane systems, structure, and function. The biochemistry and biophysics of cell membranes became my specialty. As a graduate student and postdoctoral fellow, I worked on model systems made up of only phospholipids and the intact bacterial membranes and their lipid components.

The more I learned about the intricacies and wonders of these paradoxically hardy and delicate structures, the more I puzzled over the question of how cell membranes emerged in the origin-of-life process. The typical cell membrane consists of a single bilayer of phospholipids (see appendix, page 205). When added to water, phospholipid molecules spontaneously aggregate into bilayers. Most scientists assume that once membrane components appeared on early Earth, they readily self-assembled to form the first cell membranes.[2] This explanation seemed simple, and yet I learned from firsthand experience what biochemists who specialize in cell membrane research have known for years: the bilayers that assemble from purified phospholipids display complex properties. Phospholipids don't form *single* bilayer structures like those that define cell membranes. Instead, the phospholipid bilayers that form spontaneously organize into sheets (multilamellar bilayers) or spherical structures (resembling an onion) that consist of stacks of *multiple* bilayers.[3] These aggregates only superficially resemble the cell membrane's single-bilayer structure.

Phospholipids can be forced to form structures composed of a *single* bilayer, like those that make up cell membranes. These artificially induced aggregates arrange into hollow spherical structures called liposomes, or unilamellar vesicles. But liposomes do not form spontaneously. Rather, they result *only* by extensive manipulation on the part of researchers in the laboratory.[4] And once induced to form, these structures exist only briefly (a few days) before reverting back to multilayered sheets and vesicles.[5] Thus, biochemists refer to liposomes as metastable systems.

So the question remains: how is it that cell membranes are made up of a stable single-bilayer phase given that bilayer-forming lipids spontaneously form either multiple-bilayer sheets or relatively unstable single-bilayer vesicles (liposomes)? I stumbled upon the answer one day while poking through stacks of journals in the chemistry library at the University of Virginia looking for papers on the interaction between proteins and phospholipid bilayers. I came across an article written by Norman Gershfeld, a biochemist from the National Institutes of Health. He had spent years in relative obscurity intensely focused on this very question, and at that time, his insight satisfied my intellectual curiosity.

But fifteen years later it played an important part in a critique I coauthored (with chemist Jackie Thomas) on chemical evolutionary models for the origin of cell membranes, published in the journal *Origins of Life and Evolution of Biospheres*.[6]

A Giant Leap along Life's Path

The origin of cell membranes represents one of the most critical steps in the emergence of protocells. From an evolutionary standpoint, this stage of the origin-of-life process would have been complex, involving (1) the formation of boundaries; and (2) the encapsulation of either information-rich self-replicators (according to the replicator-first scenario) or protometabolic pathways (according to the metabolism-first scenario). Once these two stages were completed, transport processes across the primordial cell membranes must have developed to get necessary materials in and out of the protocell. And so must have a means for these protocellular entities to grow and divide.

Once again, using the framework outlined in chapter 8, I offer an evaluation of the geochemical relevance of this aspect of chemical evolution. How far have researchers come in finding a realistic way to account for this key stage in the origin of life? And how does this work impact efforts to solve the mystery of life's beginnings?

Finding the Building Materials

In the quest to identify bilayer-forming molecules, researchers have attempted to discover chemical pathways that can form long amphiphilic hydrocarbon chains from simple compounds. These scientists have also investigated chemical routes with the potential to yield more complex phospholipids.

One such route has been known since the 1930s. This process (the Fischer-Tropsch reaction) converts carbon monoxide and hydrogen into long-chain hydrocarbons in the presence of iron or nickel at high temperatures. Origin-of-life workers have also identified modifications to this process (for example, the inclusion of carbonates) that yield amphiphilic compounds such as fatty acids and fatty alcohols rather than long-chain hydrocarbons.[7] Fatty acids make up the phospholipid tail region.

Some researchers initially questioned the applicability of the Fischer-Tropsch reaction to early Earth's conditions since this process requires gaseous carbon monoxide and hydrogen plus high temperatures and pressures.[8] Until recently, chemists were convinced the reaction could not occur in the presence of water. This notion has now been overturned. Scientists from Oregon State University found they could produce numerous compounds containing long-chain hydrocarbons in a Fischer-Tropsch–type reaction under aqueous conditions at relatively moderate temperatures (from 302 to 482°F or 150 to 250°C) if they started with oxalic acid.[9] Their findings seemed promising because these conditions are potentially relevant to early Earth. In many ways they resemble conditions found at deep-sea hydrothermal vents. However, as other researchers point out, the hydrogen sulfide present at hydrothermal vents would likely inhibit Fischer-Tropsch reactions.[10]

Along similar lines, two origin-of-life scientists have demonstrated that under hydrothermal vent temperatures and pressures, pyruvic acid forms a complex mixture of organic materials.[11] Some of these compounds are amphiphilic and can form vesicles. It remains to be seen if these reactions are relevant to an early Earth setting and could have taken place under plausible geothermal conditions.

Origin-of-life investigator Arthur Weber has proposed a synthetic cycle to account for prebiotic fatty acid production.[12] This complex cycle starts with glycolaldehyde (a compound thought to have existed on early Earth) and proceeds through six steps that involve either loss of water or the addition of hydrogen. While each reaction of the cycle is feasible, the complexity of the cycle, including the catalytic requirements for each step and the need for the cycle to "turn" at least seven times to produce a fatty acid capable of forming membrane lipids, calls into question the relevance of the glycolaldehyde pathway as a meaningful source of prebiotic fatty acids.[13]

Once formed, fatty acids must react with glycerin and phosphate to form phospholipids. Origin-of-life researchers suggest that this reaction could have occurred on early Earth if these three compounds were heated moderately (150°F or 65°C) to dryness.[14] The relevance of this reaction remains questionable because it requires complete dehydration. If *any* water is present, it fails. In fact, water's presence reverses the proposed reaction and thereby breaks down phospholipids. Further, phospholipid-forming reactions also require reactant concentrations unlikely to have occurred on early Earth.

Chemists Charles B. Thaxton, Walter L. Bradley, and Roger L. Olsen identified an additional problem confounding natural-process phospholipid production.[15] Two key ingredients needed for phospholipid formation (fatty acids and phosphates) form water-insoluble complexes with calcium and magnesium ions. The tendency of these two compounds to physically associate with calcium and magnesium is so great that, once formed, fatty acids and phosphates would have precipitated out of any possible early Earth environment. In effect, the precipitation of the fatty acid and phosphate complexes would have rendered these compounds unavailable for prebiotic formation of the phospholipids so vital to cell membranes.

In the face of tough questions about the possibility of prebiotic synthesis, some researchers have appealed to the infall of extraterrestrial materials to early Earth as the source of bilayer-forming compounds.[16] Analysis of carbon-containing meteorites (carbonaceous chondrites such as the Murchison meteorite) initially indicated the presence of compounds consisting of long hydrocarbon chains, but subsequent analysis demonstrated that these compounds resulted from terrestrial contamination.[17]

Recent laboratory experiments have rejuvenated support for an extraterrestrial source of amphiphilic materials on early Earth.[18] Scientists from NASA Ames Research Center, the SETI Institute, and the University of California, Santa Cruz, demonstrated in simulation studies that ultraviolet light irradiation of artificial cometary and interstellar ice (water, methanol, ammonia, and carbon monoxide) can produce a complex mixture of compounds that include bilayer-forming materials. This result has led to speculation that the infall of these materials might have provided the compounds needed to form the first cell membranes. However, additional testing and further assessment will determine the degree to which these findings are relevant at all.

A Proposed Chain of Construction Events

Even though phospholipids comprise the dominant lipid species of contemporary cell membranes, origin-of-life researchers suggest that simpler lipids may have assembled to form the first ones.

Amphiphilic compounds all form aggregates when added to water. These aggregates take on a variety of forms, depending on the amphiphile's molecular structure.[19] Phospholipids with *two* long hydrocarbon chains can form bilayers. Amphiphilic compounds with a *single* long hydrocarbon chain tend to form spherical structures called *micelles*, generally regarded as having no relevance to the first protocells because they lack an internal aqueous compartment.

Despite their tendency to form nonbilayer micelles, some amphiphilic compounds with just one long hydrocarbon chain *can* form bilayers, but only under highly specific solution conditions (for example, pH and temperature) when mixed with the right materials.[20] Some origin-of-life researchers regard these results as the key to explaining the first appearance of cell membranes. The findings' significance increases based on the observation that lipid-like materials extracted from the Murchison meteorite form bilayer structures under specific solution conditions.[21] Similar bilayer structures also form from extracts of simulated cometary and interstellar ice irradiated with ultraviolet light.[22] Origin-of-life researchers point to these compounds as possibly the first cell membrane components and as evidence that the materials necessary to form the first protocell boundary structures were present on early Earth. They further suggest that these results may show the ease with which bilayers can spontaneously form, once the right components appear. However, it must be noted that this formation has yet to be observed under natural conditions.

Encapsulation

Researchers hypothesize that once bilayer-forming compounds appeared on early Earth, cycles of dehydration and rehydration led to the encapsulation of large self-replicating molecules (proteins, DNA, and RNA) and subunit molecules within the bilayer's confines. Lab experiments show that bilayer vesicles made of phospholipids can encapsulate DNA molecules during drying and subsequent water addition.[23] So researchers presume that once formed, bilayer vesicles containing self-replicating molecules could have spontaneously begun to carry out the chemical processes needed to sustain growth and self-replication and could have acquired transport and energy transduction capabilities.[24]

Membrane Transport

Lipid bilayers are generally impermeable to the types of molecules needed to maintain the activities of encapsulated self-replicators. But a few researchers have shown that if the chain length of the bilayer-forming lipids is carefully adjusted, an adequate supply of the compounds required to sustain the self-replicator can pass through the bilayer.[25]

Growth and Fission

Once primitive cell membranes formed, they would have had to grow and spontaneously divide without the aid of biomolecular machinery.[26] Researchers have attempted to solve this problem by showing that adding membrane components to preexisting vesicles (in the laboratory) caused these structures to grow and then divide when the original "parent" aggregate reached an unstable size.[27]

More Careful Consideration

These studies on the origin of cell membranes may seem to support the possibility that these structures readily self-assembled on early Earth and that once formed, these primitive bilayers spontaneously acquired the functional attributes of contemporary biological membrane systems. However, careful examination of this work more realistically suggests otherwise.

Challenges to Primitive Membrane Emergence

The proposed composition of the first primitive membranes—aromatic hydrocarbons mixed with octanoic and nonanoic acid—presents an immediate problem. Although Murchison meteorite extracts and laboratory simulation studies show that these compounds form bilayer structures, such results offer no real help.

Neither octanoic nor nonanoic acid would likely have occurred at levels sufficient for origin-of-life scenarios. Researchers have recovered only extremely low levels of these compounds from the Murchison meteorite.[28] Moreover, the abundance of individual amphiphilic species decreases exponentially with increasing chain length.[29] While extraterrestrial infall could have delivered some octanoic and nonanoic acid to early Earth, the levels would have been far too low to participate in primitive membrane structures. Octanoic and nonanoic acids can form bilayer structures only at relatively high concentrations.[30]

In addition to the concentration requirements, octanoic and nonanoic acids also demand exacting environmental conditions. These compounds can form bilayers only at very specific pH levels.[31] Octanoic and nonanoic bilayers become unstable if solution pH deviates from near-neutral values. Solution temperature is critical for bilayer stability as well.[32] Yet another complication is solution salt level. Research shows that modeled versions of primitive membranes fall apart in the presence of salt. These structures display stability only in pure water.[33]

Octanoic and nonanoic bilayer stability also requires the availability of just-right molecular companions. The presence of nonanol (a nine-carbon alcohol) extends the survivable pH range for nonanoic acid bilayers.[34] (The increased stability results from specific interactions between the nonanoic acid headgroup and nonanol.) But only when nonanol is present at specific levels does bilayer stability result.

To date, no studies have been conducted on the long-term stability of octanoic and nonanoic acid bilayers. These bilayers may or may not manifest long-term stability under the conditions that would allow them to form. Nevertheless, the strict requirements needed for bilayer formation make it unlikely that these compounds could ever have contributed to the formation of the first protocellular membranes. Formation of nonanoic acid bilayers (or bilayers comprised of any amphiphile with a single hydrocarbon chain) is improbable, given the multiple just-right conditions that must be met simultaneously. If any bilayer structures did form, any environmental fluctuations or compositional deviations would have destabilized them and caused them to revert to micelle structures.

The instability of primitive bilayers in salt may represent an even greater problem. To imagine any salt-free aqueous environment on early Earth is difficult to say the least. In fact, primitive bilayer stability is compromised at salt levels far below those in today's oceans. Early Earth's oceans were from one and a half to two times saltier than modern seas.[35] This complication makes the unguided emergence of primitive membranes even less likely.

Challenges to Encapsulation

At first glance, the results of the encapsulation studies completed to date may seem promising. But more thorough investigation raises questions of relevance. Only a few of these studies have focused on fatty acids. Most made use of phospholipids systems instead. But this discrepancy represents more than a minor oversight because, as most scientists concur, fatty acid vesicles would have served as the first primitive membrane systems.

The encapsulation studies with phospholipids exemplify the expression "the devil's in the details." Researchers have noted that if encapsulation of DNA or proteins is to occur, the concentration of phospholipids and DNA (or proteins) must be carefully adjusted. Investigators have also noted that the ratio of phospholipids and DNA (or proteins) also must be judiciously chosen.[36] In one study, the research team noted that encapsulation was inhibited by the presence of salts.[37] The concentration dependence and the sensitivity to environmental conditions suggest that the laboratory procedures used to encapsulate DNA and proteins probably have little or no meaning in the context of the early Earth.

The limited work done on encapsulation by fatty acid vesicles again shows the unlikelihood that this process occurred on its own. The essential dehydration-hydration cycle is far too exacting. Unless the just-right conditions exist (including temperature and salinity, for example), bilayers will not re-form upon rehydration of dehydrated lipids.

Challenges to Transport

While laboratory experiments show how transport could have conceivably occurred across primitive cell membranes, these studies too lack geochemical relevance. Instead, they reveal that the identity of the compounds comprising fatty acid or phospholipid vesicles must be carefully managed and selected or transport cannot take place across the vesicle bilayers.[38] This compositional control, readily available in laboratory experiments under the command of biochemists, would not have been present in nature alone.

Challenges to Growth and Fission

To date, studies on the growth and fission of fatty acid vesicles have involved the use of unsaturated fatty acids. These compounds would not have been available on early Earth.[39] Another problem arises when the mechanisms for vesicle growth and division are considered in the context of the RNA world.

Most ribozymes require the presence of calcium and magnesium to operate. But these materials cause fatty acids to precipitate. Only if saturated fatty acids are mixed with fatty acids that have a glycerol group attached to them are the vesicles they form tolerant to magnesium.[40] And these vesicles grow very inefficiently. This strict dependence on lipid identity for vesicle growth and fission raises questions as to whether or not this process could have occurred in any meaningful way on early Earth.

From Primitive to Contemporary Membranes

At some point cell membranes composed of phospholipids must have emerged. This necessity is real, whether the pathway that leads to the first contemporary cell membranes begins with primitive membranes comprised of simple amphiphiles or whether the initial cell membranes appeared anew as phospholipid bilayers. Naturalistic scenarios that attempt to explain the formation of the first phospholipid-containing biological membranes face enormous obstacles.

Robust chemical pathways leading to phospholipids have yet to be identified. And the first phospholipids likely possessed a tendency to form nonbilayer aggregates that could not have performed as a barrier.

One can reasonably assume that the first phospholipid species on early Earth and, hence, the first contemporary cell membranes consisted of phosphatidylethanolamines (PEs) and phosphatidylglycerols (PGs). These two phospholipid classes have ethanolamine and glycerol as headgroups, respectively. PEs and PGs are the primary phospholipid classes found in bacterial membranes, and bacteria were among the first life-forms to appear on Earth.[41]

Since PEs and PGs stand as the dominant phospholipid species in bacterial membranes, origin-of-life scenarios must account specifically for the formation of biological membranes comprised of these two phospholipid types. Herein lies the problem. While phospholipids do self-assemble into bilayers, they also form nonbilayer structures. Phospholipids display rich and complex phase behavior. They tend to form specific aggregate types based on the headgroup structure (see figure 13.1). Headgroup characteristics determine a specific phospholipid's overall molecular shape, which in turn dictates the type of aggregate it forms.

PEs tend to form nonbilayer phases, and in the presence of calcium, PGs also form nonbilayer structures.[42] Cardiolipin (a derivative of PGs also present in bacterial membranes) likewise readily forms nonbilayers. Finally, the presence of PGs in PE aggregates increases their tendency to form nonbilayer aggregates.[43]

While biochemists remain uncertain as to the full biological significance of these nonbilayer structures, they agree that if the nonbilayer structures do play a role in cell membrane processes, they must quickly pass in and out of existence. But these nonbilayer phases compromise the cell membrane's

FIGURE 13.1.

Nonbilayer Structures Formed by Phospholipid Aggregates

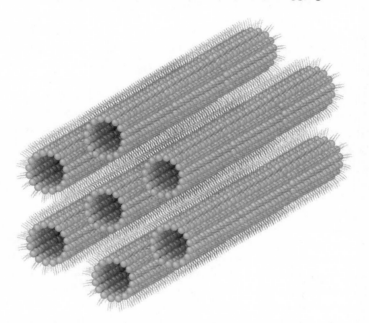

Note the nonbilayer structure formed by phosphatidylethanolamine. Phil Chien

structural integrity and barrier function.[44] Permanent or long-lived nonbilayer phases would have rapidly led to cell death.

In the early 1980s, Swedish researchers conducted experiments that high-lighted the relationship between bilayer stability, lipid composition, and lipid shape.[45] These workers showed that the bacterium *Acholeplasma laidlawii* can adjust its membrane's lipid composition as environmental conditions change. These observed changes preserved the proper lipid shape, thereby maintaining bilayer stability. If the lipid composition was not altered as environmental conditions changed, the bacteria's cell membrane adopted a nonbilayer structure that led to the cell's demise.

With respect to the origin of life and the emergence of the first protocell, calcium's presence in the early Earth's environment and the tendency of PEs and PE/PG mixtures to form nonbilayer aggregates mean that these phospholipids may not have readily formed bilayers. If they did not, this failure frustrates the pathway leading to the first cell membranes. Moreover, fluctuating environmental conditions and altered bilayer composition would have given early bilayers comprised of PE and PG the potential to transition to nonbilayer phases. This transition would have inhibited the origin-of-life process.

Fine-Tuned Molecular Aggregates

Even if the first phospholipids on Earth were among those that readily form bilayers, they still cannot be credited with making possible the spontaneous assembly of cell membrane systems. As I already noted, bilayer-forming phospholipids display complex properties. Phospholipid bilayers spontaneously stack into sheets (multilamellar bilayers) or spherical structures (resembling an onion) that consist of multiple-bilayer sheets.[46] These aggregates only superficially resemble the cell membrane's single-bilayer structure.

Given that the cell membrane is made up of a stable single-bilayer phase, how is it that bilayer-forming lipids yield multiple-bilayer sheets or relatively unstable single-bilayer vesicles (liposomes)? During the 1980s and early 1990s, National Institutes of Health researcher Norman Gershfeld successfully answered this question.

As it turns out, stable single-bilayer phases similar to those that constitute cell membranes form only under unique conditions.[47] (Chemists refer to phenomena that occur under a unique set of conditions as critical phenomena.) Formation of single-bilayer vesicles occurs only at a specific temperature (the critical temperature). Pure phospholipids spontaneously transform into stable single bilayers from either multiple-bilayer sheets or unstable liposomes only at the critical temperature.[48] This temperature depends, in turn, on the specific phospholipid or the bilayer's phospholipid composition.[49]

Gershfeld and his team made some helpful observations along these lines. For example, they noted that phospholipids extracted from both rat and squid nervous system tissue will assemble into single-bilayer structures at critical temperatures that correspond to the physiological temperatures of their respective organisms.[50] Gershfeld's group also observed that for the cold-blooded sea urchin *L. pictus*, the cell membrane composition of the earliest cells in the embryo varies in response to the environmental temperature. This variation serves to maintain a single bilayer phase, with a critical temperature matching the environmental conditions.[51] Gershfeld's team noted that the bacterium *E. coli* also adjusted its cell membrane phospholipid composition to maintain a single-bilayer phase.[52]

These studies highlight the biological importance of the critical bilayer phenomena. So do other studies that indicate the deadly effects of the cell membrane's deviation from critical conditions. Gershfeld's team identified a correlation between the rupture of human red blood cells and incubation at temperatures exceeding 98.6°F (37°C, the normal human body temperature). Transformation of the cell membrane from a single bilayer to multiple-bilayer stacks accompanies the rupture of red blood cells—a loss of the cell membrane's critical state.[53] The team even provided evidence that cell membrane defects at the sites of neurodegeneration may play a role in Alzheimer's dis-

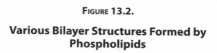

FIGURE **13.2.**

Various Bilayer Structures Formed by Phospholipids

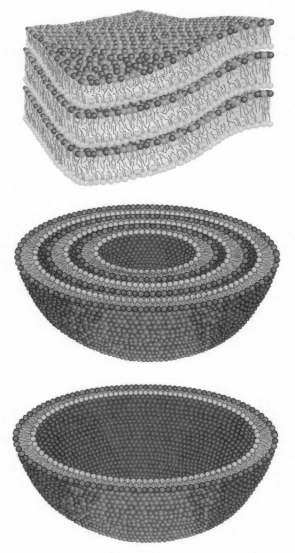

Typically, phospholipids assemble into stacks of bilayer sheets or spherical multilamellar bilayer vesicles. The formation of single lamellar bilayer vesicles, which directly resemble the bilayer structure of cell membranes, happens only as a result of researcher manipulation and is only temporarily stable. Phil Chien ease.[54] Presumably, collapse of the cell membrane's single bilayer into multiple bilayers results from altered membrane phospholipid composition.

Gershfeld and his team's work indicates that cell membranes are highly fine-tuned molecular structures dependent on an exacting set of physical and chemical conditions. Their findings underscore the unlikelihood that chemical and physical processes operating on early Earth could have produced the precise phospholipid composition to form the stable single-bilayer phase that universally defines cell membranes. Even if chance events had somehow arrived at this just-right phospholipid composition, any fluctuations in temperature would have destroyed the single-bilayer structure. With the loss of this structure, the first protocells would have fallen apart.

I Cannot Consent

In the effort to account for the origin of cell membranes, origin-of-life researchers have demonstrated that, in principle, physicochemical processes do exist that can (1) generate the building blocks of primitive cell membranes; (2) lead to self-assembly into vesicles; (3) encapsulate information-rich molecules and protometabolic networks; (4) establish transport across the membrane; and (5) produce vesicle growth and division. Some success has been achieved in identifying the mechanistic basis for the different stages of membrane evolution. However, amid all these astounding accomplishments they have failed to show any geochemical relevance.

Each stage of the process from prebiotic amphiphiles to functioning primitive membranes depends heavily on the concentration of the lipids, their exact identity, and environmental conditions (including temperature, pH, and salt levels, among others). If it weren't for chemists' diligence in the laboratory, no primitive membrane vesicles would form, encapsulate materials, or grow and divide. If anything, attempts to provide experimental support for the chemical evolution of cell membranes has effectively demonstrated that the work of an intelligent, purposeful agent is required for life's origin.

In their pursuit to understand life's genesis, origin-of-life researchers work in tandem with synthetic biologists, particularly with those seeking to engineer life from the bottom up. Some of the most prominent figures in origin-of-life research are also investigating questions in synthetic biology. To understand the origin of life, either how it began long ago or how to make it now, researchers go into the lab and manipulate chemicals, attempting to identify chemical reactions and physical mechanisms that can generate life's building blocks from simple compounds. In turn, they conduct experiments to learn how these building-block materials can assemble into more complex molecules that aggregate and evolve, either on their own or with experimenter help, to form living systems. In a sense, they are doing the same work. They are trying to create (or more appropriately re-create) life in the lab. The only difference: origin-of-life scientists are constrained by the conditions and resources available on the primordial Earth. Synthetic biologists are free to use whatever means they can discover or devise to reach the end goal.

Many origin-of-life researchers express hope that attempts to create artificial life in the lab will provide them with important clues as to how life may have originated. At the same time, many synthetic biologists are starting to apply what they have learned from those studying origin-of-life questions and problems. As origin-of-life scientists discover chemical routes that can yield life's building blocks and assemble these materials into more complex systems, they can use this knowledge to jump-start the efforts to create artificial life. In effect, the quest for artificial life and the investigation into the origin-of-life question are deeply intertwined endeavors.

It is noteworthy, then, that the conclusion coming from origin-of-life research so closely mirrors the implications of the work taking place in synthetic biology: to generate, sustain, and manipulate a living entity requires the intense involvement of highly intelligent beings. As evolutionary biologist Simon Conway Morris has pointed out, "Many of the experiments designed to explain one or other [sic] step in the origin of life are either of tenuous relevance to any believable prebiotic setting or involve an experimental rig in which the hand of the researcher becomes for all intents and purposes the hand of God."[55]

Up to this point, I have focused on the implications of synthetic biology and origin-of-life research on the creation-evolution controversy. Next I turn my attention to another issue regarding the creation of life in the laboratory: should Christians condemn this type of work, or should we support these efforts?

Epilogue

Borne Away by the Waves

> He sprung from the cabin-window, as he said this, upon the ice-raft which lay close to the vessel. He was soon borne away by the waves and lost in darkness and distance.
>
> Robert Walton in *Frankenstein*

When Victor Frankenstein dies and his creature vanishes into the icy darkness of the Arctic night, the secret for making life from inanimate materials is lost. Fortunately, this is fiction, not reality. Origin-of-life researchers and synthetic biologists have carefully documented their progress over the last decade in attempting to generate life from simple materials in a bottom-up fashion or reengineer existing life-forms from the top down, yielding microbes with nonnatural properties.

These advances have nearly reached a critical mass. Movement toward the generation of artificial life through laboratory manipulation is taking place at an ever-increasing pace. It is just a matter of time before Craig Venter and Hamilton Smith produce *Mycoplasma laboratorium* and multiple variants derived from this minimal life-form. And other investigators, including Jack Szostak, are hot on their heels. In the next few years, the production of a variety of protocells from the bottom up will undoubtedly be accomplished. And when these milestones are achieved, the floodgates will open. The rapid pace of discovery and invention will quickly translate these "firsts" into turnkey operations. The generation of new life-forms will soon become "old hat."

The prospect of creating life in the lab yields excitement—as well as consternation. For most in the scientific community, the production of artificial life will be welcomed with open arms, and for good reason. The creation of artificial life *will* be a boon for science and technology. The creation of artificial life will help shed light onto life's fundamental structures and processes and also provide insight into the very nature of life itself. Attempts to create life will help scientists better define what life is. The ability to create novel, non-natural life-forms from scratch and redesign and reengineer existing microbes represents the next revolution in technology. These human inventions will have industrial applications and uses in agriculture and biomedicine that at this juncture seem nearly limitless. The technology associated with the capacity to create artificial life will transform our world in unimaginable ways.

At the same time, however, the creation of life in the lab will raise concerns. For the first time mere humans will possess the "elixir of life," control over life itself—power and authority that many people would maintain are safe *only* in the hands of God. The idea of humans creating life conjures images of Frankenstein's monster or worse.

And yet from a Christian perspective there is considerable reason to desire the types of technological advances synthetic biology will make possible. Scripture teaches that humans are to serve as Earth's caretakers (see Gen. 1:26–28; 2:15). The opportunity to design and reengineer microbes to produce renewable sources of clean energy, for example, will help us to carry out this mandate.

The Bible also teaches that we are to love our neighbors as ourselves (see Matt. 22:39). This command compels work in biomedical research, for example. Biomedical advances provide the means to treat diseases and debilitating injuries, and the use of artificial life toward this end will play an ever-increasing role in these endeavors. Surely providing treatment, comfort, and hope for the sick is one way we can love our neighbors. Again, artificial microbes will play a role in finding new therapies and possible cures for sicknesses that impact countless lives today.

So is it wrong for Christians to support research and technology that encourages humans to assume God's role as Creator? As we think through the response to this question, let's keep in mind the implications of this research for the creation-evolution controversy. While some may suggest the creation of artificial life makes the need for a Creator obsolete, in reality it does the opposite. As both the top-down and bottom-up approaches demonstrate, only by deliberate effort, inordinate ingenuity, and astonishing skill can synthetic biologists even begin the process of making artificial life. This work reinforces God's status as Creator, whether skeptics like it or not, because it empirically demonstrates that even the simplest life-form cannot arise without the involvement of an intelligent, intentional agent. When Christians support work in synthetic biology, they are encouraging scientific advance that adds to the weight of evidence for God's existence.

The attempts of scientists and biotechnologists to "play God" are really no different from any other human creative activity. Everything we do as human beings can be rightly understood as "playing God" because we are made "in God's image" (see Gen. 1:27). In this sense, we create because we bear the image of a God who is the Creator. And since God made life, it was only a matter of time before we would discover how to make life from the materials and templates he provided.

The ability to create artificial life comes with great risks, just as does the acquisition of any new power God has allowed us to discover and use. If and when we use that newfound capability as a means to wrongly supplant God, as did those who built the Tower of Babel (see Gen. 11:1–9), we will pay a terrible price. But if we use it for good, recognizing that the ability to make artificial life comes from the Creator, this work can bring glory to God. It all comes down to one's worldview—and a willingness to be guided by God's goodness. Humility is key, because with humility comes the all-important reverence for God and an awareness of the innate moral weakness of human nature.

The ability to create artificial life will usher in a brave new world, but it need not bring a future of icy darkness, a world that Christians fear or eschew. It can be one that we engage and embrace and influence for good.

An Introduction to Biochemistry

Like all other matter, life consists of atoms that combine to form molecules.[1] Many of the most important biomolecules are large macromolecules that interact to form life's basic structures both inside the cell and in the extracellular surroundings. The two major classes of macromolecules are proteins and the nucleic acids, DNA and RNA.

Living systems also depend on the chemistry of small molecules. The cell membrane matrix is comprised of relatively small molecules called lipids that aggregate into molecular sheets called bilayers. Small molecules also play an important role in the myriad chemical reactions necessary to sustain life. These reactions take place inside and outside the cell. The ensemble of chemical reactions that generate life's subcellular structures and support life's activities is referred to as metabolism.

Life's Large Molecules

Proteins

Proteins take part in essentially every cellular and extracellular structure and activity. Proteins help form structures inside the cell and in the cell's surrounding matrix. Some proteins dissolve in the cytosol and the lumen of organelles. Others aggregate to form larger structures, like the cytoskeleton. Proteins also associate with the cell membrane in a variety of ways (see page 205).

Figure A.1

Protein Structure

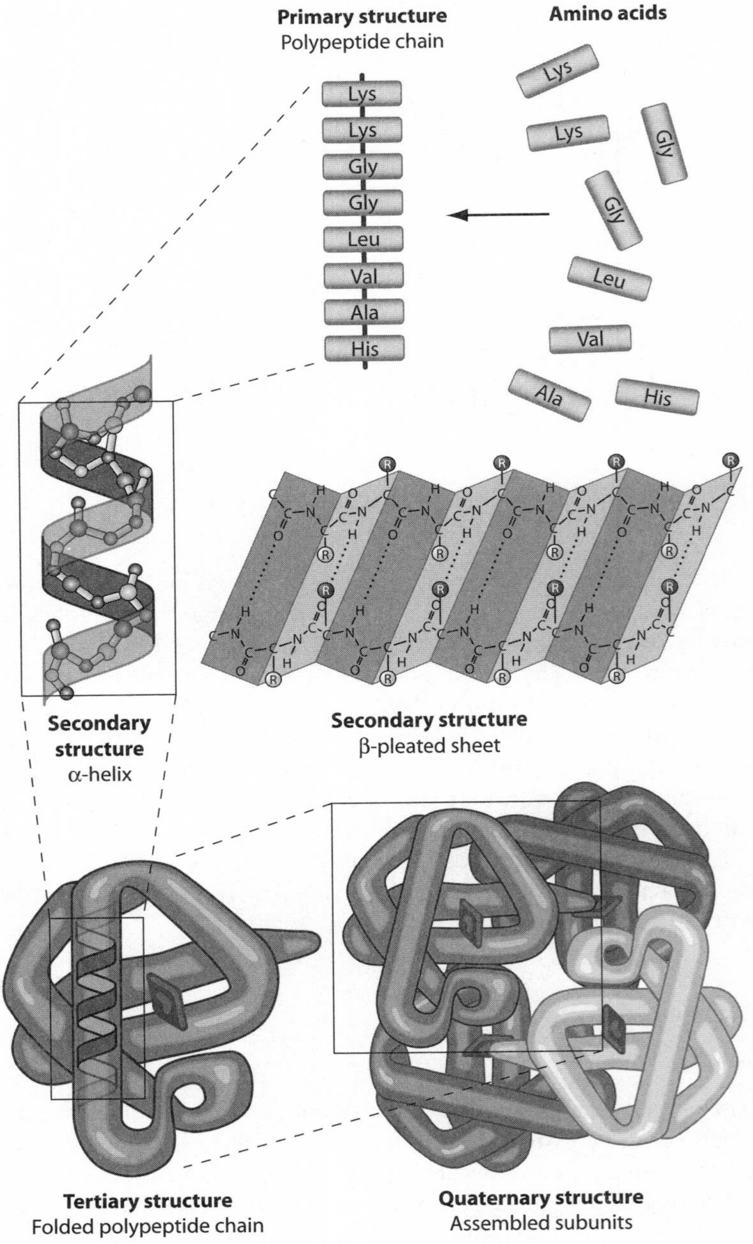
Primary structure
Polypeptide chain
Amino acids
Lys
Lys
Gly
Gly
Leu
Val
Ala
His
Secondary structure
α-helix
Secondary structure
β-pleated sheet
Tertiary structure
Folded polypeptide chain
Quaternary structure
Assembled subunits

Proteins catalyze (assist and speed up) chemical reactions, harvest chemical energy, serve in the cell's defense systems, and store and transport molecules to name just a few of their roles.

Molecules called polypeptides make up proteins. Some proteins consist of a single polypeptide. Others form when one or more of the same or different polypeptides interact to form a complex.

Polypeptides are chain-like molecules that fold into precise three-dimensional structures. The polypeptide's three-dimensional architecture determines the way it interacts with other polypeptides and consequently determines the protein's function.

Polypeptides form when the cellular machinery links together smaller subunit molecules (called amino acids) in a head-to-tail fashion. Generally speaking, cells employ twenty different amino acids to make polypeptides. The amino acids that make up the cell's polypeptide chains possess a variety of chemical and physical properties. In principle, the twenty amino acids can link up in any possible amino acid combinations to form a polypeptide.

Each amino acid sequence imparts the polypeptide with a unique chemical and physical profile along its chain. Because some amino acids attract one another while others repel, the chemical and physical profile determines how the polypeptide chain folds and therefore how it interacts with other polypeptide chains to form a functional protein. The amino acid sequence of a polypeptide ultimately determines its function, given that the amino acid sequence determines the polypeptide's structure, and structure dictates function (see figure A.1).

Because proteins are such large, complex molecules, biochemists categorize aspects of protein structure into four levels. A protein's *primary* structure is the linear sequence of amino acids that makes up each of its polypeptide chains. The *secondary* structure refers to the three-dimensional arrangement of the polypeptide chain's backbone and the interactions between chemical groups that make up its backbone. Three of the most common secondary structures are the random coil, alpha-helix, and beta-pleated sheet. *Tertiary* structure describes the overall shape of a polypeptide chain and the location of each of its atoms in three-dimensional space. The structure and spatial orientation of the chemical groups that extend from the polypeptide backbone is also part of the tertiary structure. *Quaternary* structure arises when individual polypeptide chains interact to form a functional protein.

DNA

DNA consists of chain-like molecules known as polynucleotides. Two polynucleotide chains align in an antiparallel fashion to form a DNA molecule. (The two strands are arranged parallel to one another with the starting point of one strand in the polynucleotide duplex located adjacent to the ending point of the other strand and vice versa.) The two polynucleotide chains in the pair twist around each other, forming the well-known DNA double helix. The cell's machinery forms polynucleotide chains by linking together four different subunit molecules called nucleotides. The four nucleotides used to build DNA chains are adenosine (A), guanosine (G), cytidine (C), and thymidine (T) (see figure A.2).

When the two DNA strands align, the adenine (A) side chains of one strand always pair with thymine (T) side chains from the other strand. Likewise, the guanine (G) side chains from one DNA strand always pair with cytosine (C) side chains from the other strand.

When the side chains pair, they form cross bridges between the two DNA strands. The length of the A-T and G-C cross bridges is nearly identical. Adenine and guanine are both composed of two rings, and thymine and cytosine are composed of one ring. Each cross bridge consists of three rings.

FIGURE A.2

DNA Structure

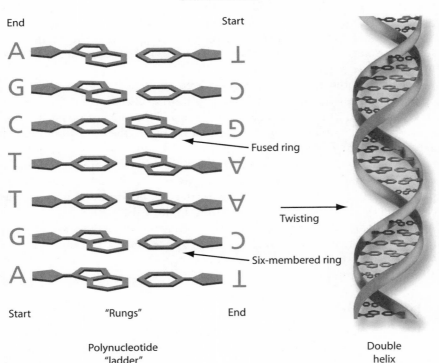

DNA stores the information necessary to make all the polypeptides used by the cell. The sequence of nucleotides in the DNA strands specifies the sequence of amino acids in polypeptide chains. Scientists refer to the sequence of nucleotides along the DNA strand that codes for the amino acid sequence of a particular polypeptide as a gene. Through the use of genes, DNA stores the information functionally expressed in the amino acid sequences of polypeptide chains.

Central Dogma of Molecular Biology

This concept describes how the information stored in the DNA becomes functionally expressed through the amino acid sequence and activity of poly-

FIGURE **A.3**

Central Dogma of Molecular Biology

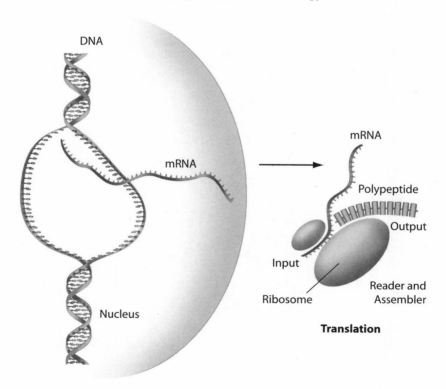

DNA

mRNA

mRNA

Polypeptide

Output

Input

Reader and
Assembler

Ribosome

Nucleus

Translation

Transcription

peptide chains (see figure A.3). DNA does not leave the nucleus to direct the synthesis of polypeptide chains. Rather the cellular machinery copies the gene's sequence by assembling another polynucleotide, called messenger RNA (mRNA). The mRNA, a single-stranded molecule, is similar (but not identical) in composition to DNA. An important difference between DNA and mRNA is the use of uridine (U) in place of thymidine (T) to form the mRNA chain. Scientists refer to the process of making mRNA from DNA as transcription.

Once assembled, mRNA migrates from the cell's nucleus into the cytoplasm. At a structural component of the cell called the ribosome, mRNA directs the synthesis (assembly) of polypeptide chains. The information content of the polynucleotide sequence is translated into the polypeptide amino acid sequence.

FIGURE A.4

Phospholipid Structure

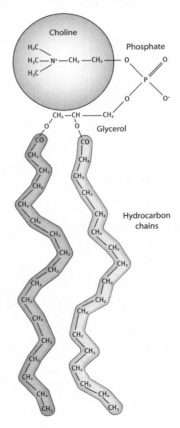

Life's Small Molecules

The Cell Membrane

Two classes of biomolecules interact to form cell membranes: small molecules, called lipids, and proteins. Lipids, a structurally heterogeneous group of compounds, share water insolubility as a defining property. But lipids readily dissolve in organic solvents. Cholesterol, triglycerides, saturated and unsaturated fats, oils, and lecithin are examples of lipids familiar to many.

Phospholipids are the cell membrane's major lipid component. A phospholipid's molecular shape roughly resembles a distorted balloon with two ropes tied to it (see figure A.4). Biochemists describe phospholipids by their two regions, each with markedly different physical properties. The head region, corresponding to the "balloon," is soluble in water or is hydrophilic ("water-loving"). The phospholipid tails, corresponding to the "ropes" tied to the balloon, are insoluble in water or are hydrophobic ("water-hating").

Chemists refer to molecules such as phospholipids that possess molecular regions with dual solubility characteristics as amphiphilic ("ambivalent in its likes"). Soaps and detergents are amphiphilic compounds known to virtually everyone.

Amphiphilicity has great biological importance. Phospholipids' dual-solubility properties play the key role in cell membrane structure. When added to water, phospholipids spontaneously organize into sheets that are two molecules thick called bilayers. When organized into a bilayer, phospholipid molecules align into two monolayers with the phospholipid headgroups adjacent to one another and the phospholipid tails packed together closely. The monolayers, in turn, come together so the phospholipid tails of one monolayer contact the phospholipid tails of its companion monolayer. This tail-to-tail arrangement ensures that the water-soluble headgroups contact water and the water-insoluble tails sequester from water (see figure A.5).

FIGURE A.5

Phospholipid Bilayer

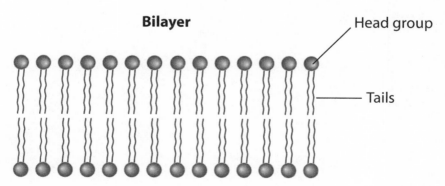

Proteins associate with the cell membrane in a variety of ways. Some, called peripheral proteins, bind to the inner or outer membrane surfaces. Others, called integral proteins, embed into the cell membrane. Some integral proteins insert only partially into the membrane interior, others penetrate nearly halfway into the membrane's core, and others span the entire membrane (see figure A.6).

Membrane proteins serve the cell in numerous capacities. Some proteins function as receptors, binding compounds that allow the cell to communicate with its external environment. Some catalyze chemical reactions at the cell's interior and exterior surfaces. Some proteins shuttle molecules across the cell membrane; others form pores and channels through the membrane. Some membrane proteins impart structural integrity to the cell membrane itself.

The cell membrane's inner and outer monolayers differ in composition, structure, and function. Because of this difference, biochemists refer to cell membranes as asymmetric. The phospholipid classes on the inner and outer membrane surfaces are unique; the membrane proteins likewise are specific to either the inner or outer membrane surfaces. Proteins that span the cell membrane possess a specific orientation. Because of protein asymmetry, the functional characteristics of the inner and outer surfaces vary.

Since the early 1970s, the "fluid mosaic" model has provided the framework to understand membrane structure and function. This model views the phospholipid bilayer as a two-dimensional fluid that serves simultaneously as both a cellular barrier and a solvent for integral membrane proteins. The

FIGURE A.6

Membrane Proteins

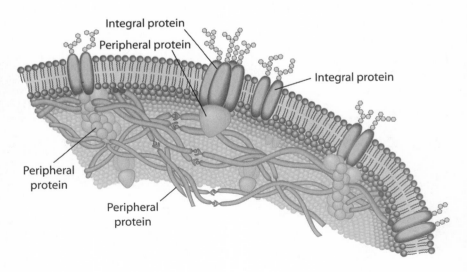

Integral protein

Peripheral protein

Integral protein

Peripheral protein

Peripheral protein

fluid mosaic model shows how the membrane proteins and lipids freely diffuse laterally throughout the cell membrane. Beyond modeling the bilayer structure and asymmetry, the fluid mosaic model fails to account for the structural and functional organization of cell membranes (see figure A.7).

In recent years, scientists have revised the fluid mosaic model. They found that most proteins are confined to domains within the membrane instead of diffusing freely in the phospholipid bilayers. Other proteins diffuse throughout the membrane, but instead of moving randomly, these proteins move in a directed fashion. Phospholipids also organize into domains with certain phospholipid classes laterally segregated in the bilayer. The fluidity of the bilayer also varies from region to region in the cell membrane.

Metabolism

This term refers to the myriad chemical reactions in an organism necessary to sustain its life. Metabolic activity enables life-forms to extract energy from their environment and make life's component parts. These processes allow organisms to grow, reproduce, maintain biological systems and structures, and respond to environmental changes.

Metabolic reactions include the production and breakdown of proteins and RNA molecules, DNA replication, and the assembly of cell membranes and cell walls. Metabolism also involves reactions of small molecules. For example, compounds, such as glucose and other sugar molecules, break down into smaller molecules to release energy for the cell's operations. A significant number of metabolic reactions produce small molecules that are used by the

FIGURE A.7

Fluid Mosaic Model

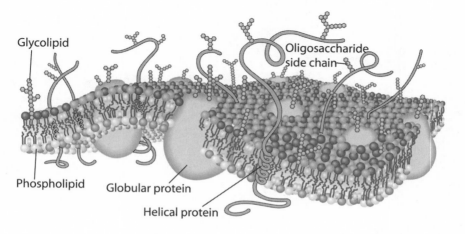

cell's machinery as building blocks to assemble proteins, DNA, the RNAs, and cell membrane bilayers. Some metabolic activities prepare materials the cell no longer needs—cellular waste—for elimination. Other reactions detoxify materials harmful to the cell.

Metabolic processes within the cell's interior are often organized into "pathways," sequences of chemical reactions that transform a starting compound into a final product via a series of small, stepwise chemical changes. Each step in a metabolic route is mediated by a protein (called an enzyme) that assists in the chemical transformation.

Metabolic pathways can be linear, branched, or circular. The chemical components that are part of a particular metabolic sequence sometimes take part in other metabolic pathways. These shared compounds cause metabolic pathways to be intricately interconnected and networked together.

Notes

Chapter 1 Waking Up in Frankenstein's Dream

1. J. D. Watson and F. H. C. Crick, "Molecular Structure of Nucleic Acids: A Structure for Deoxyribose Nucleic Acid," *Nature* 171 (April 25, 1953): 737–38; J. D. Watson and F. H. C. Crick, "Genetic Implications of the Structure of Deoxyribonucleic Acid," *Nature* 171 (May 30, 1953): 964–67.

2. Stanley L. Miller, "A Production of Amino Acids under Possible Primitive Earth Conditions," *Science* 117 (May 15, 1953): 528–59; Stanley L. Miller, "Production of Some Organic Compounds under Possible Primitive Earth Conditions," *Journal of the American Chemical Society* 77 (May 12, 1955): 2351–61.

3. Iris Fry, *The Emergence of Life on Earth* (New Brunswick, NJ: Rutgers University Press, 2000), 79–83.

4. John Horgan, *The End of Science* (New York: Broadway, 1997), 138–42.

5. Stanley L. Miller, J. William Schopf, and Antonio Lazcano, "Oparin's 'Origin of Life': Sixty Years Later," *Journal of Molecular Evolution* 44 (April 1997): 351–53.

6. Fry, *Emergence of Life*, 83–88.

7. William J. Cromie, "Creating Life in a Lab," *Harvard University Gazette*, September 12, 1996, http://news.harvard.edu/gazette/1996/09.12/CreatingLifeina.html.

8. Alan W. Schwartz and Sherwood Chang, "From Big Bang to Primordial Planet: Setting the Stage for the Origin of Life," in *Life's Origin*, ed. J. William Schopf (Berkeley: University of California Press, 2002), 73.

9. Fazale Rana and Hugh Ross, *Origins of Life* (Colorado Springs: NavPress, 2004), 116–19.

10. Stuart Kauffman, "Self-Replication: Even Peptides Do It," *Nature* 382 (August 8, 1996): 496–97; David H. Lee et al., "A Self-Replicating Peptide," *Nature* 382 (August 8, 1996): 525–28.

11. M. Reza Ghadiri, "From Peptide Replicators to Self-Organized Networks," abstract in *ISSOL '99 Book of Program and Abstracts*, comp. and ed. Lois Lane (La Jolla, CA: ISSOL, 1999), 49.

209

12. Seth Borenstein, "Artificial Life Likely in 3 to 10 Years," *AP News* (August 20, 2007), http://www.thefreelibrary.com/Artificial+life+likely+in+3+to+10+years-a01611383640.

13. For a fascinating account of Craig Venter's role in the Human Genome Project, see James Shreeve, *The Genome War* (New York: Ballantine, 2005).

14. For a lay-level discussion of Craig Venter's work, see Alice Park, "Scientist Creates Life—Almost," *Time*, January 24, 2008, http://www.time.com/time/health/article/0,8599,1706552,00.html. The scientific articles include: Clyde A. Hutchison III et al., "Global Transposon Mutagenesis and a Minimal Mycoplasma Genome," *Science* 286 (December 10, 1999): 2165–69; Carole Lartigue et al., "Genome Transplantation in Bacteria: Changing One Species to Another," *Science* 317 (August 3, 2007): 632–38; Daniel G. Gibson et al., "Complete Chemical Synthesis, Assembly, and Cloning of a *Mycoplasma genitalium* Genome," *Science* 319 (February 29, 2008): 1215–20.

15. Daniel G. Gibson et al., "Creation of a Bacterial Cell Controlled by a Chemically Synthesized Genome," *Science* 329 (July 2, 2010): 52–56.

16. Borenstein, "Artificial Life Likely in 3 to 10 Years."

Chapter 2 Life Is like Music

1. Antonio Lazcano, "The Transition from Nonliving to Living," in *Early Life on Earth*, ed. Stefan Bengston (New York: Columbia University Press, 1994), 61; quoted in Radu Popa, *Between Necessity and Probability: Searching for the Definition and Origin of Life* (Berlin: Springer-Verlag, 2004), 201.

2. Radu Popa collects these quotes in *Between Necessity and Probability*.

3. Michael J. Katz, *Templets and the Explanation of Complex Patterns* (Cambridge: Cambridge University Press, 1986), 84; quoted in Popa, 200.

4. Imre Friedmann, "Short Definitions of Life," in *Fundamentals of Life*, ed. Gyula Pályi, Claudia Zucchi, and Luciano Caglioti (New York: Elsevier, 2002), 30; quoted in Popa, 200.

5. Noam Lahav in Pályi et al., 41; quoted in Popa, 204.

6. Shneior Lifson, quoted in Popa, 200. Popa seems to draw from several unnamed sources, but the original source for the last half of the quote is Shneior Lifson, "Chemical Selection, Diversity, Teleonomy and the Second Law of Thermodynamics," *Biophysical Chemistry* 26 (May 9, 1987): 310.

7. Paul C. Lauterbur in Pályi et al., 41; quoted in Popa, 204.

8. See Fazale Rana and Hugh Ross, *Origins of Life* (Colorado Springs: NavPress, 2004); Fazale Rana, *The Cell's Design* (Grand Rapids: Baker, 2008).

9. See Discovery Institute—Center for Science and Culture, "A Scientific Dissent from Darwinism," http://www.dissentfromdarwin.org (accessed July 30, 2010).

10. For an interesting discussion of how the inability to define life creates problems for the search for life on other bodies in our solar system, see Peter Ward, *Life as We Do Not Know It: The NASA Search for (and Synthesis of) Alien Life* (New York: Penguin, 2005).

Chapter 3 Blessed by a New Species

1. Mark D. Adams et al., "3,400 New Expressed Sequence Tags Identify Diversity of Transcripts in Human Brain," *Nature Genetics* 4 (July 1993): 256–67.

2. For a biographical account of Venter's life and role in the Human Genome Project, see James Shreeve, *The Genome War* (New York: Ballantine Books, 2005).

3. Robert D. Fleischmann et al., "Whole-Genome Random Sequencing and Assembly of *Haemophilus influenzae* Rd," *Science* 269 (July 28, 1995): 496–512.

4. Mark D. Adams et al., "The Genome Sequence of *Drosophila melanogaster*," *Science* 287 (March 24, 2000): 2185–95.

5. Shannon J. Williamson et al., "The Sorcerer II Global Ocean Sampling Expedition: Metagenomic Characterization of Viruses within Aquatic Microbial Samples," *PLoS ONE* 3 (January 23, 2008), e1456, doi:10.1371/journal.pone.0001456, http://www.plosone.org/article/info:doi%2F10.1371%2Fjournal.pone.0001456.

6. André Goffeau, "Life with 482 Genes," *Science* 270 (October 20, 1995): 445–46; Claire M. Fraser et al., "The Minimal Gene Complement of *Mycoplasma genitalium*," *Science* 270 (October 20, 1995): 397–403.

7. Clyde A. Hutchinson III et al., "Global Transposon Mutagenesis and a Minimal Mycoplasma Genome," *Science* 286 (December 10, 1999): 2165–69; John I. Glass et al., "Essential Genes of a Minimal Bacterium," *Proceedings of the National Academy of Sciences, USA* 103 (January 10, 2006): 425–30.

8. Daniel G. Gibson et al., "Complete Chemical Synthesis, Assembly, and Cloning of a *Mycoplasma genitalium* Genome," *Science* 319 (February 29, 2008): 1215–20; Daniel G. Gibson et al., "Creation of a Bacterial Cell Controlled by a Chemically Synthesized Genome," *Science* 329 (July 2, 2010): 52–56.

9. Carole Lartigue et al., "Genome Transplantation in Bacteria: Changing One Species to Another," *Science* 317 (August 3, 2007): 632–38; Gibson et al., "Creation of a Bacterial Cell."

10. Hamilton O. Smith et al., "Generating a Synthetic Genome by Whole Genome Assembly: φX174 Bacteriophage from Synthetic Oligonucleotides," *Proceedings of the National Academy of Sciences, USA* 100 (December 23, 2003): 15440–45.

11. Daniel G. Gibson et al., "One-Step Assembly in Yeast of 25 Overlapping DNA Fragments to Form a Complete Synthetic *Mycoplasma genitalium* Genome," *Proceedings of the National Academy of Sciences, USA* 105 (December 23, 2008): 20404–9.

12. Lartigue et al., "Genome Transplantation in Bacteria."

13. Carole Lartigue et al., "Creating Bacterial Strains from Genomes That Have Been Cloned and Engineered in Yeast," *Science* 325 (September 25, 2009): 1693–96.

14. Gibson et al., "Creation of a Bacterial Cell."

Chapter 4 Treading in the Steps Already Marked

1. Alan G. Atherly, Jack R. Girton, and John F. McDonald, *The Science of Genetics* (Fort Worth: Saunders College Publishing, 1999), 354.

2. James Shreeve, *The Genome War* (New York: Ballantine, 2005), 95–103.

3. George Malacinski, *Essentials of Molecular Biology*, 4th ed. (Sudbury, MA: Jones and Bartlett, 2003), 346–69.

4. Andreas Meyer, Rene Pellaux, and Sven Panke, "Bioengineering Novel *in vitro* Metabolic Pathways Using Synthetic Biology," *Current Opinion in Microbiology* 10 (June 2007): 246–53.

5. Kechun Zhang et al., "Expanding Metabolism for Biosynthesis of Nonnatural Alcohols," *Proceedings of the National Academy of Sciences, USA* 105 (December 30, 2008): 20653–58.

6. Victoria Hale et al., "Microbially Derived Artemisinin: A Biotechnology Solution to the Global Problem of Access to Affordable Antimalarial Drugs," *American Journal of Tropical Medicine and Hygiene* 77 (December 2007): 198–202.

7. Dae-Kyun Ro et al., "Production of the Antimalarial Drug Precursor Artemisinic Acid in Engineered Yeast," *Nature* 440 (April 13, 2006): 940–43.

8. Lubert Stryer, *Biochemistry*, 3rd ed. (New York: W. H. Freeman, 1988), 739–42.

9. Ibid., 733–35.

10. Ibid., 746–64.

11. Lei Wang, Jianming Xie, and Peter G. Schultz, "Expanding the Genetic Code," *Annual Review of Biophysics and Biomolecular Structure* 35 (June 2006): 225–49.

12. Chang C. Liu et al., "Protein Evolution with an Expanded Genetic Code," *Proceedings of the National Academy of Sciences, USA* 105 (November 18, 2008): 17688–93.

13. Some examples are: J. C. Francis and P. E. Hansche, "Directed Evolution of Metabolic Pathways in Microbial Populations. I. Modification of the Acid Phosphatase pH Optimum in *S. cerevisiae*," *Genetics* 70 (January 1972): 59–73; J. C. Francis and Paul E. Hansche, "Directed Evolution of Metabolic Pathways in Microbial Populations. II. A Repeatable Adaptation in *Saccharomyces cerevisiae*," *Genetics* 74 (June 1973): 259–65; Paul E. Hansche, "Gene Duplication as a Mechanism of Genetic Adaptation in *Saccharomyces cerevisiae*," *Genetics* 79 (April 1975): 661–74; Celeste J. Brown, Kristy M. Todd, and R. Frank Rosenzweig, "Multiple Duplications of Yeast Hexose Transport Genes in Response to Selection in a Glucose-Limited Environment," *Molecular Biology and Evolution* 15 (August 1998): 931–42.

14. Shinichi Kinoshita et al., "6–Aminohexanoic Acid Cyclic Dimer Hydrolase. A New Cyclic Amide Hydrolase Produced by *Acromobacter guttatus* KI72," *European Journal of Biochemistry* 80 (November 1977): 489–95; Shinichi Kinoshita et al., "Purification and Characterization of 6–Aminohexanoic-Acid-Oligomer Hydrolase of *Flavobacterium* sp. KI72," *European Journal of Biochemistry* 116 (June 1981): 547–51; Susumu Ohno, "Birth of a Unique Enzyme from an Alternative Reading Frame of the Preexisted, Internally Repetitious Coding Sequence," *Proceedings of the National Academy of Sciences, USA* 81 (April 1984): 2421–25.

15. Carl Zimmer, *Microcosm* (New York: Pantheon, 2008), 172.

16. See Gretchen Vogel, "Tracking the History of the Genetic Code," *Science* 281 (July 17, 1998): 329–31; Stephen J. Freeland and Laurence D. Hurst, "The Genetic Code Is One in a Million," *Journal of Molecular Evolution* 47 (September 1998): 238–48; Stephen J. Freeland et al., "Early Fixation of an Optimal Genetic Code," *Molecular Biology and Evolution* 17 (April 2000): 511–18.

17. Robin D. Knight, Stephen J. Freeland, and Laura F. Landweber, "Selection, History and Chemistry: The Three Faces of the Genetic Code," *Trends in Biochemical Sciences* 24 (June 1, 1999): 241–47; Guo-Cheng Yuan et al., "Genome-Scale Identification of Nucleosome Positions in *S. cerevisiae*," *Science* 309 (July 22, 2005): 626–30; Edward A. Sekinger, Zarmik Moqtaderi, and Kevin Struhl, "Intrinsic Histone-DNA Interactions and Low Nucleosome Density Are Important for Preferential Accessibility of Promoter Regions in Yeast," *Molecular Cell* 18 (June 10, 2005): 735–48.

18. F. H. C. Crick, "The Origin of the Genetic Code," *Journal of Molecular Biology* 38 (December 28, 1968): 367–79.

19. Syozo Osawa et al., "Evolution of the Mitochondrial Genetic Code I. Origin of AGR Serine and Stop Codons in Metazoan Mitochondria," *Journal of Molecular Evolution* 29 (September 1989): 202–7; Dennis W. Schultz and Michael Yarus, "On the Malleability in the Genetic Code," *Journal of Molecular Evolution* 42 (May 1996): 597–601; Eörs Szathmáry, "Codon Swapping as a Possible Evolutionary Mechanism," *Journal of Molecular Evolution* 32 (February 1991): 178–82.

20. Fazale Rana, *The Cell's Design* (Grand Rapids: Baker, 2008), 173–78.

21. Hubert P. Yockey, *Information Theory and Molecular Biology* (Cambridge: Cambridge University Press, 1992), 180–83.

22. Manfred Eigen et al., "How Old Is the Genetic Code? Statistical Geometry of tRNA Provides an Answer," *Science* 244 (May 12, 1989): 673–79.

23. See Fazale Rana and Hugh Ross, *Origins of Life* (Colorado Springs: NavPress, 2004) for a comprehensive list of references to the scientific literature.

24. Yockey, *Information Theory*, 184–196; Alfonso Jiménez-Sánchez, "On the Origin and Evolution of the Genetic Code," *Journal of Molecular Evolution* 41 (December 1995): 712–16; Huan-Lin Wu et al., "Evolution of the Genetic Triplet Code via Two Types of Doublet Codons," *Journal of Molecular Evolution* 61 (July 2005): 54–64.

25. Yockey, *Information Theory*, 184–196.

Chapter 5 Becoming Acquainted with the Principals—and Principles

1. *MedGadget*, "Harvard Scientists Doing God's Work," September 8, 2008, http://www.medgadget.com/archives/2008/09/harvard_scientists_doing_gods_work.html.

2. Steen Rasmussen et al., eds., *Protocells* (Cambridge, MA: MIT Press, 2008).

3. David W. Deamer, "A Giant Step towards Artificial Life?" *Trends in Biotechnology* 23 (July 1, 2005): 336–38.

4. Ibid., 336.

5. See Szostak Lab, 2007, http://genetics.mgh.harvard.edu/szostakweb (accessed September 18, 2009).

6. Thomas Oberholzer, Knud H. Nierhaus, and Pier Luigi Luisi, "Protein Expression in Liposomes," *Biochemical and Biophysical Research Communications* 261 (August 1999): 238–41.

7. Jacquelyn A. Thomas and Fazale R. Rana, "The Influence of Environmental Conditions, Lipid Composition, and Phase Behavior on the Origin of Cell Membranes," *Origins of Life and Evolution of Biospheres* 37 (June 2007): 267–85; David W. Deamer, "Membrane Compartments in Prebiotic Evolution," in *The Molecular Origins of Life*, ed. André Brack (Cambridge: Cambridge University Press, 1998), 189–205.

8. Thomas and Rana, "Influence of Environmental Conditions," 267–85; Deamer, "Membrane Compartments," 189–205.

9. Martin M. Hanczyc, Sheref S. Mansy, and Jack W. Szostak, "Mineral Surface Directed Membrane Assembly," *Origins of Life and Evolution of Biospheres* 37 (February 2007): 67–82; Martin M. Hanczyc, Shelly M. Fujikawa, and Jack W. Szostak, "Experimental Models of Primitive Cellular Compartments: Encapsulation, Growth, and Division," *Science* 302 (October 2003): 618–22.

10. Irene A. Chen and Jack W. Szostak, "A Kinetic Study of the Growth of Fatty Acid Vesicles," *Biophysical Journal* 87 (August 1, 2004): 988–98.

11. Martin M. Hanczyc and Jack W. Szostak, "Replicating Vesicles as Models of Primitive Cell Growth and Division," *Current Opinion in Chemical Biology* 8 (December 2004): 600–64.

12. Irene A. Chen, Kourosh Saleni-Ashtiani, and Jack W. Szostak, "RNA Catalysis in Model Protocell Vesicles," *Journal of the American Chemical Society* 127 (September 28, 2005): 13213–19.

13. Irene A. Chen, Richard W. Roberts, and Jack W. Szostak, "The Emergence of Competition between Model Protocells," *Science* 305 (September 3, 2004): 1474–76.

14. Hanczyc, Fujikawa, and Szostak, "Experimental Models of Primitive Cellular Compartments"; Ting F. Zhu and Jack W. Szostak, "Coupled Growth and Division of Model Protocell Membranes," *Journal of the American Chemical Society* 131 (April 22, 2009): 5705–13.

15. Gali Steinberg-Yfrach et al., "Light-Driven Production of ATP Catalysed by F_0F_1-ATP Synthase in an Artificial Photosynthetic Membrane," *Nature* 392 (April 2, 1998): 479–82.

16. Irene A. Chen and Jack W. Szostak, "Membrane Growth Can Generate a Transmembrane pH Gradient in Fatty Acid Vesicles," *Proceedings of the National Academy of Sciences, USA* 101 (May 25, 2004): 7965–70.

17. M. G. Sacerdote and Jack W. Szostak, "Semipermeable Lipid Bilayers Exhibit Diastereoselectivity Favoring Ribose," *Proceedings of the National Academy of Sciences, USA* 102 (April 26, 2005): 6004–8.

18. Sheref S. Mansy et al., "Template-Directed Synthesis of a Genetic Polymer in a Model Protocell," *Nature* 454 (July 3, 2008): 122–25.

19. Sheref S. Mansy and Jack W. Szostak, "Thermostability of Model Protocell Membranes," *Proceedings of the National Academy of Sciences, USA* 105 (September 9, 2008): 13351–55.

20. Pierre-Alain Monnard, Andrej Luptak, and David W. Deamer, "Models of Primitive Cellular Life: Polymerases and Templates in Liposomes," *Philosophical Transactions of the Royal Society* B 362 (October 29, 2007): 1741–50.

21. For example, see Ching-Hsuan Tsai, Jingyang Chen, and Jack W. Szostak, "Enzymatic Synthesis of DNA on Glycerol Nucleic Acid Templates without Stable Duplex Formation between Product and Template," *Proceedings of the National Academy of Sciences, USA* 104 (September 11, 2007): 14598–603; Jesse J. Chen et al., "Enzymatic Primer-Extension with Glycerol-Nucleoside Triphosphates on DNA Templates," *PLoS ONE* 4 (March 3, 2009), doi:10.1371/journal.pone.0004949, http://www.plosone.org/article/info:doi%2F10.1371%2Fjournal.pone.0004949; Jesse J. Chen, Xin Cai, and Jack W. Szostak, "N2'→P3' Phosphoramidate Glycerol Nucleic Acid as a Potential Alternative Genetic System," *Journal of the American Chemical Society* 131 (February 18, 2009): 2119–21.

22. John C. Chaput and Jack W. Szostak, "Evolutionary Optimization of a Nonbiological ATP Binding Protein for Improved Folding Stability," *Chemical Biology* 11 (June 1, 2004): 865–74; Kristopher Josephson, Matthew C. T. Hartman, and Jack W. Szostak, "Ribosomal Synthesis of Unnatural Peptides," *Journal of the American Chemical Society* 127 (August 24, 2005): 11727–35; Florian P. Seebeck and Jack W. Szostak, "Ribosomal Synthesis of Dehydroalanine-Containing Peptides," *Journal of the American*

Chemical Society 128 (June 7, 2006): 7150–51; Matthew D. Smith et al., "Structural Insights into the Evolution of a Non-Biological Protein: Importance of Surface Residues in Protein Fold Optimization," *PLoS ONE* 2 (May 23, 2007), doi:10.1371/journal.pone.0000467, http://www.plosone.org/article/info:doi%2F10.1371%2Fjournal.pone.0000467; Sheref S. Mansy et al., "Structure and Evolutionary Analysis of a Non-Biological ATP-Binding Protein," *Journal of Molecular Biology* 371 (August 10, 2007): 501–13; Matthew C. T. Hartman et al., "An Expanded Set of Amino Acid Analogs for the Ribosomal Translation of Unnatural Peptides," *PLoS ONE* 2 (October 3, 2007), doi:10.1371/journal.pone.0000972, http://www.plosone.org/article/info:doi%2F10.1371%2Fjournal.pone.0000972; Alexander O. Subtelny, Matthew C. T. Hartman, and Jack W. Szostak, "Ribosomal Synthesis of N-Methyl Peptides," *Journal of the American Chemical Society* 130 (May 14, 2008): 6131–36.

23. Vincent Noireaux and Albert Libchaber, "A Vesicle Bioreactor as a Step toward an Artificial Cell Assembly," *Proceedings of the National Academy of Sciences, USA* 101 (December 24, 2004): 17669–74.

Chapter 6 A Scientist's Splendor

1. T. W. Graham Solomons, *Organic Chemistry*, 2nd ed. (New York: Wiley, 1980), 48–49.

2. Steen Rasmussen et al., eds., *Protocells* (Cambridge, MA: MIT Press, 2008).

3. F. Albert Cotton and Geoffrey Wilkinson, *Advanced Inorganic Chemistry*, 5th ed. (New York: Wiley, 1988), 234–304.

4. Paul Davies, "Are Aliens among Us?" *Scientific American* (December 2007): 63–69.

5. Matheshwaran Saravanan, Kommireddy Vasu, and Valakunja Nagaraja, "Evolution of Sequence Specificity in a Restriction Endonuclease by a Point Mutation," *Proceedings of the National Academy of Sciences, USA* 105 (July 29, 2008): 10344–47.

6. For a detailed discussion of biochemical chicken-and-egg systems like restriction endonuclease–methylase pairs, I recommend my book *The Cell's Design* (Grand Rapids: Baker, 2008).

7. Devin Strickland, Keith Moffat, and Tobin R. Sosnick, "Light-Activated DNA Binding in a Designed Allosteric Protein," *Proceedings of the National Academy of Sciences, USA* 105 (August 5, 2008): 10709–14.

8. Lin Jiang et al., "De Novo Computational Design of Retro-Aldol Enzymes," *Science* 319 (March 7, 2008): 1387–91; Daniela Röthlisberger et al., "Kemp Elimination Catalysts by Computational Enzyme Design," *Nature* 453 (2008): 190–95.

9. Jiang et al., "De Novo Computational Design," 1391.

10. For example, see Ching-Hsuan Tsai et al., "Enzymatic Synthesis of DNA on Glycerol Nucleic Acid Templates without Stable Duplex Formation between Product and Template," *Proceedings of the National Academy of Sciences, USA* 104 (September 11, 2007): 14598–603; Jesse J. Chen et al., "Enzymatic Primer-Extension with Glycerol-Nucleoside Triphosphates on DNA Templates," *PLoS ONE* 4 (March 23, 2009): doi:10.1371/journal.pone.0004949, http://www.plosone.org/article/info:doi%2F10.1371%2Fjournal.pone.0004949; Jesse J. Chen, Xin Cai, and Jack W. Szostak, "N2′→P3′ Phosphoramidate Glycerol Nucleic Acid as a Potential Alternative Genetic System," *Journal of the American Chemical Society* 131 (February 18, 2009): 2119–21.

11. For example, see Stephanie A. Havemann et al., "Incorporation of Multiple Sequential Pseudothymidines by DNA Polymerases and their Impact on DNA Duplex Structure," *Nucleosides, Nucleotides, and Nucleic Acids* 27 (March 2008): 261–78.

12. See my book *The Cell's Design* for a discussion of why DNA's structure is optimal.

Chapter 7 The Particulars of Life's Formation

1. Iris Fry, *The Emergence of Life on Earth* (New Brunswick, NJ: Rutgers University Press, 2000), 79–83.

2. John Horgan, *The End of Science* (New York: Broadway Books, 1997), 138–42.

3. For representative presentations of the textbook description for the origin of life that span the last fifteen years, see Karen Arms and Pamela S. Camp, *Biology*, 3rd ed. (Philadelphia: Saunders College Publishing, 1987), 412–28; Sylvia S. Mader, *Inquiry into Life*, 6th ed. (Dubuque, IA: William C. Brown, 1991), 552–62; Richard Cowen, *History of Life*, 3rd ed. (Malden, MA: Blackwell Science, 2000), 1–18.

4. Ibid.

5. Stanley L. Miller, J. William Schopf, and Antonio Lazcano, "Oparin's 'Origin of Life': Sixty Years Later," *Journal of Molecular Evolution* 44 (April 1997): 351–53.

6. The concept for figure 7.2 was taken and expanded from Christopher P. McKay, "Life in Comets," in *Comets and the Origin and Evolution of Life*, ed. Paul J. Thomas, Christopher F. Chyba, and Christopher P. McKay (New York: Springer, 1997), 275; Tom Fenchell, Gary M. King, and T. H. Blackburn, *Bacterial Biogeochemistry*, 2nd ed. (San Diego: Academic Press, 1998), 255.

7. Fazale Rana and Hugh Ross, *Origins of Life* (Colorado Springs: NavPress, 2004).

8. James F. Kasting and Lisa L. Brown, "The Early Atmosphere as a Source of Biogenic Compounds," in *The Molecular Origins of Life*, ed. André Brack (Cambridge: Cambridge University Press, 1998), 35–36.

9. Rafael Navarro-González, Mario J. Molina, and Luisa T. Molina, "Production of Reactive Nitrogen in Explosive Volcanic Clouds," abstract in *ISSOL '99 Abstracts*, comp. and ed. Lois Lane (La Jolla, CA: ISSOL, 1999), 34.

10. Christopher Wills and Jeffrey Bada, *The Spark of Life* (Cambridge, MA: Perseus, 2000), 97–101; Leslie E. Orgel, "The Origin of Life—A Review of Facts and Speculations," *Trends in Biochemical Sciences* 23 (December 1, 1998): 491–95.

11. Karl O. Stetter, "Hyperthermophiles and Their Possible Role as Ancestors of Modern Life," in *Molecular Origins of Life*, 315–35.

12. Michael Hagmann, "Between a Rock and a Hard Place," *Science* 295 (March 15, 2002), 2006–7; Noam Lahav, *Biogenesis* (New York: Oxford University Press, 1999), 266–81; Orgel, "Origin of Life," 491–95.

13. Lahav, *Biogenesis*, 169–71; J. Oró and Antonio Lazcano, "Comets and the Origin and Evolution of Life," in *Comets and the Origin and Evolution of Life*, 3–27; Christopher F. Chyba and Carl Sagan, "Comets as a Source of Prebiotic Organic Molecules for the Early Earth," in *Comets and the Origin and Evolution of Life*, 147–73.

14. James P. Ferris and David A. Usher, "Origins of Life" in *Biochemistry*, Geoffrey Zubay, coordinating author (Reading, MA: Addison-Wesley, 1983), 1191–1241.

15. Wills and Bada, *Spark of Life*, 101–3.

16. Lahav, *Biogenesis*, 168–69; James P. Ferris, "Catalyzed RNA Synthesis for the RNA World," in *Molecular Origins of Life*, 255–68.

17. Christian de Duve, "Clues from Present-Day Biology: The Thioester World," in *Molecular Origins of Life*, 219–36.

18. Harold J. Morowitz, *Beginnings of Cellular Life* (New Haven: Yale University Press, 1992).

19. Fry, *Emergence of Life on Earth*, 100–102.

20. Antonio Lazcano, "The RNA World, Its Predecessors, and Its Descendents," in *Early Life on Earth: Nobel Symposium No. 84*, ed. Stefan Bengtson (New York: Columbia University Press, 1994), 70–80.

21. Fry, *Emergence of Life on Earth*, 135–137.

22. Arthur J. Zaug and Thomas R. Cech, "The Intervening Sequence of RNA of *Tetrahymena* Is an Enzyme," *Science* 231 (January 31, 1986): 470–75; Thomas R. Cech, "A Model for the RNA-Catalyzed Replication of RNA," *Proceedings of the National Academy of Sciences, USA* 83 (June 1, 1986): 4360–63.

23. Thomas R. Cech, "The Ribosome Is a Ribozyme," *Science* 289 (August 11, 2000): 878–79.

24. Kenneth D. James and Andrew D. Ellington, "Catalysis in the RNA World," in *Molecular Origins of Life*, 269–94.

25. Alexis Madrigal, "Self-Replicating Chemicals Evolve into Lifelike Ecosystem," *WIRED Science*, January 8, 2009, http://blog.wired.com/wiredscience/2009/01/replicatingrna.html.

26. Elizabeth Finkel, "DNA Cuts Its Teeth—As an Enzyme," *Science* 286 (December 24, 1999): 2441–42; Stephen W. Santoro and Gerald F. Joyce, "A General Purpose RNA-Cleaving DNA Enzyme," *Proceedings of the National Academy of Sciences, USA* 94 (April 29, 1997): 4262–66; Terry L. Sheppard, Phillip Ordoukhanian, and Gerald F. Joyce, "A DNA Enzyme with N-Glycosylase Activity," *Proceedings of the National Academy of Sciences, USA* 97 (July 5, 2000): 7802–7; Stuart Kauffman, "Even Peptides Do It," *Nature* 382 (August 8, 1996): 496–97; D. H. Lee et al., "A Self-Replicating Peptide," *Nature* 382 (August 8, 1996): 525–28.

27. Alan W. Schwartz, "Origins of the RNA World," in *Molecular Origins of Life*, 237–54.

28. David W. Deamer, "Membrane Compartments in Prebiotic Evolution," in *Molecular Origins of Life*, 189–205; David W. Deamer, Elizabeth H. Mahon, and Giovanni Bosco, "Self-Assembly and Function of Primitive Membrane Structures," in *Early Life on Earth*, 107–23.

29. Deamer, "Membrane Compartments," 189–205; Deamer, Mahon, and Bosco, "Self-Assembly," 107–123.

30. Carl Woese, "The Universal Ancestor," *Proceedings of the National Academy of Sciences, USA* 95 (June 9, 1998): 6854–59.

31. Carl Woese, "Interpreting the Universal Phylogenetic Tree," *Proceedings of the National Academy of Sciences, USA* 97 (July 18, 2000): 8392–96; W. Ford Doolittle, "Phylogenetic Classification and the Universal Tree," *Science* 284 (June 25, 1999): 2124–28.

Chapter 8 Conquering the Challenges

1. Alexis Madrigal, "Self-Replicating Chemicals Evolve into Lifelike Ecosystem," *WIRED Science*, January 8, 2009, http://blog.wired.com/wiredscience/2009/01/replicatingrna.html.

2. For a detailed discussion of this work, see the book I authored with Hugh Ross, *Origins of Life* (Colorado Springs: NavPress, 2004).

3. Charles B. Thaxton, Walter L. Bradley, and Roger L. Olsen, *The Mystery of Life's Origin* (Dallas: Lewis & Stanley, 1984), 18–21, 99–112.

4. Rana and Ross, *Origins of Life*, 63–79.

Chapter 9 Promised Impossibilities

1. Brian Hiatt, "U2: Hymns for the Future," *Rolling Stone*, March 19, 2009, 52.

2. Nicolas Wade, "Stanley Miller, Who Examined Origins of Life, Dies at 77," *New York Times*, May 23, 2007, http://www.nytimes.com/2007/05/23/us/23miller.html?ex=1337572800&en=25058a5b0dfca07d&ei=5088&partner=rssnyt&emc=rss.

3. Stanley L. Miller, "The Formation of Organic Compounds on the Primitive Earth," *Annals of the New York Academy of Sciences* 69 (August 1957): 260–74.

4. Sherwood Chang, "The Planetary Setting of Prebiotic Evolution," in *Early Life on Earth: Nobel Symposium No. 84*, ed. Stefan Bengtson (New York: Columbia University Press, 1994), 10–23; Donald R. Lowe, "Early Environments: Constraints and Opportunities for Early Evolution," in *Early Life on Earth*, 24–35; Kenneth M. Towe, "Earth's Early Atmosphere: Constraints and Opportunities for Early Evolution," in *Early Life on Earth*, 36–47.

5. Françios Raulin, "Atmospheric Prebiotic Synthesis," abstract in *ISSOL '99 Abstracts*, comp. and ed. Lois Lane (La Jolla, CA: ISSOL, 1999), 32.

6. Gordon Schlesinger and Stanley L. Miller, "Prebiotic Synthesis in Atmospheres Containing CH_4, CO, and CO_2. I. Amino Acids," *Journal of Molecular Evolution* 19 (September 1983): 376–82; Gordon Schlesinger and Stanley L. Miller, "Prebiotic Synthesis in Atmospheres Containing CH_4, CO, and CO_2. II. Hydrogen Cyanide, Formaldehyde, and Ammonia," *Journal of Molecular Evolution* 19 (September 1983): 383–90.

7. Stanley L. Miller, "The Endogenous Synthesis of Organic Compounds," in *The Molecular Origins of Life*, ed. André Brack (Cambridge: Cambridge University Press, 1998), 59–85.

8. Feng Tian et al., "A Hydrogen-Rich Early Earth Atmosphere," *Science* 308 (May 13, 2005): 1014–17.

9. David C. Catling, "Comment on 'A Hydrogen-Rich Early Earth Atmosphere,'" *Science* 311 (January 6, 2006): 38.

10. Shin Miyakawa et al., "Prebiotic Synthesis from CO Atmospheres: Implications for the Origins of Life," *Proceedings of the National Academy of Sciences, USA* 99 (November 12, 2002): 14628–31.

11. Sidney W. Fox and Klaus Dose, *Molecular Evolution and the Origin of Life* (San Francisco: Freeman, 1972), 44–45; I. S. Shklovskii and Carl Sagan, *Intelligent Life in the Universe* (San Francisco: Holden-Day, 1966), 231.

12. For references to the appropriate scientific literature, see Jonathan Wells, *Icons of Evolution* (Washington, DC: Regnery, 2000), 264–66.

13. Ivan G. Draganić, "Oxygen and Oxidizing Free-Radicals in the Hydrosphere of Early Earth," abstract in *ISSOL '99 Abstracts*, 34; I. G. Draganić, A. Negron-Mendoza, and S. I. Vujosevic, "Radiation Chemistry of Water in Chemical Evolution Exploration," abstract in *ISSOL '02 Book of Abstracts*, comp. and ed. Alicia Negron-Mendoza et al. (Oaxaca, MEX: ISSOL, 2002), 139.

14. Horst Rauchfuss, *Chemical Evolution and the Origin of Life*, trans. Terence N. Mitchell (Berlin: Springer-Verlag, 2008), 110–11; Charles S. Cockell and John A. Raven, "Ozone and Life on the Archaean Earth," *Philosophical Transactions of the Royal Society* A 365 (July 15, 2007): 1889–1901.

15. H. James Cleaves and Stanley L. Miller, "Oceanic Protection of Prebiotic Organic Compounds from UV Radiation," *Proceedings of the National Academy of Sciences, USA* 95 (June 23, 1998): 7260–63.

16. Carl Sagan and Christopher Chyba, "The Early Faint Sun Paradox: Organic Shielding of Ultraviolet-Labile Greenhouse Gases," *Science* 276 (May 23, 1997): 1217–21.

17. Miller, "Endogenous Synthesis," 59–85.

18. Ibid.

19. Rauchfuss, *Chemical Evolution*, 112–13.

20. Miller, "Endogenous Synthesis," 59–85.

21. Jeffrey L. Bada and Antonio Lazcano, "Prebiotic Soup—Revisiting the Miller Experiment," *Science* 300 (May 2, 2003): 745–46.

22. Noam Lahav, *Biogenesis* (New York: Oxford University Press, 1999), 138–39.

23. Rafael Navarro-González, Mario J. Molina, and Luisa T. Molina, "Production of Reactive Nitrogen in Explosive Volcanic Clouds," abstract in *ISSOL '99 Abstracts*, comp. and ed. Lois Lane (La Jolla, CA: ISSOL, 1999), 34; Christopher Wills and Jeffrey Bada, *The Spark of Life: Darwin and the Primeval Soup* (Cambridge, MA: Perseus, 2000), 74–76.

24. Rauchfuss, *Chemical Evolution*, 108–10.

25. Ibid., 110.

26. John W. Delano, "Cr Oxygen Barometry: Oxidation State of Mantle-Derived Volatiles through Time," abstract in *ISSOL '99 Abstracts*, 35; John W. Delano, "Redox History of the Earth's Interior Since ~3900 Ma: Implications for Prebiotic Molecules," *Origins of Life and Evolution of Biospheres* 31 (August 2001): 311–41.

27. Adam P. Johnson et al., "The Miller Volcanic Spark Discharge Experiment," *Science* 322 (October 17, 2008): 404.

28. For example, J. P. Amend and E. L. Shock, "Energetics of Amino Acid Synthesis in Hydrothermal Ecosystems," *Science* 281 (September 11, 1998): 1659–62; Sarah Simpson, "Life's First Scalding Steps," *Science News* 155 (January 9, 1999): 24–26; Ei-ichi Imai et al., "Elongation of Oligopeptides in a Simulated Submarine Hydrothermal System," *Science* 283 (February 5, 1999): 831–33; George Cody et al., "Primordial Carbonylated Iron-Sulfur Compounds and the Synthesis of Pyruvate," *Science* 289 (August 25, 2000): 1337–40.

29. Alexander Smirnov and Martin A. A. Schoonen, "Evaluating Experimental Artifacts in Hydrothermal Prebiotic Synthesis Experiments," *Origins of Life and Evolution of Biospheres* 33 (April 2003): 117–27.

30. Stanley L. Miller and Jeffrey L. Bada, "Submarine Hot Springs and the Origin of Life," *Nature* 334 (August 18, 1988): 609–11; Matthew Levy and Stanley L. Miller,

"The Stability of the RNA Bases: Implications for the Origin of Life," *Proceedings of the National Academy of Sciences, USA* 95 (July 7, 1998): 7933–38.

31. H. James Cleaves and John H. Chalmers, "Extremophiles May Be Irrelevant to the Origin of Life," *Astrobiology* 4 (March 2004): 1–9.

32. Martin A. A. Schoonen and Yong Xu, "Nitrogen Reduction under Hydrothermal Vent Conditions: Implications for the Prebiotic Synthesis of C-H-O-N Compounds," *Astrobiology* 1 (June 2001): 133–142.

33. Cleaves and Chalmers, "Extremophiles May Be Irrelevant," 1–9.

34. Lahav, *Biogenesis*, 139.

35. Fazale Rana and Hugh Ross, *Origins of Life* (Colorado Springs: NavPress, 2004).

Chapter 10 The Agony of Reflections

1. Jon Cohen, "Getting All Turned Around over the Origins of Life on Earth," *Science* 267 (1995): 1265.

2. G. F. Joyce et al., "Chiral Selection in Poly(C)-Directed Synthesis of Oligo(G)," *Nature* 310 (August 16, 1984): 602–4; G. F. Joyce et al., "The Case for an Ancestral Genetic System Involving Simple Analogues of the Nucleotides," *Proceedings of the National Academy of Sciences, USA* 84 (July 1, 1987): 4398–4402; Gerald F. Joyce, "RNA Evolution and the Origins of Life," *Nature* 338 (March 16, 1989): 217–24; Eörs Szathmáry, "The First Two Billion Years," *Nature* 387 (June 12, 1997): 662–63.

3. Mike D. Reynolds, *Falling Stars* (Mechanicsburg, PA: Stackpole Books, 2001), 141.

4. Keith A. Kvenvolden, James G. Lawless, and Cyril Ponnamperuma, "Nonprotein Amino Acids in the Murchison Meteorite," *Proceedings of the National Academy of Sciences, USA* 68 (February 1971): 486–90.

5. J. R. Cronin, Sandra Pizzarello, and Dale P. Cruikshank, "Organic Matter in Carbonaceous Chondrites, Planetary Satellites, Asteroids and Comets," in *Meteorites and the Early Solar System*, ed. John F. Kerridge and Mildred S. Matthews (Tucson: University of Arizona Press, 1988), 819–57.

6. Keith A. Kvenvolden, "Chirality of Amino Acids in the Murchison Meteorite—A Historical Perspective," abstract in *ISSOL '99 Abstracts*, comp. and ed. Lois Lane (La Jolla, CA: ISSOL, 1999), 41.

7. Ibid.

8. John R. Cronin, "Clues from the Origin of the Solar System: Meteorites," in *The Molecular Origins of Life*, ed. André Brack (Cambridge: Cambridge University Press, 1998), 119–46.

9. John R. Cronin and Sandra Pizzarello, "Enantiomeric Excesses in Meteoritic Amino Acids," *Science* 275 (February 14, 1997): 951–55; M. H. Engel and S. A. Macko, "Isotopic Evidence for Extraterrestrial Non-Racemic Amino Acids in the Murchison Meteorite," *Nature* 389 (September 18, 1997): 265–68; S. Pizzarello and J. R. Cronin, "Alanine Enantiomers in the Murchison Meteorite," *Nature* 394 (July 16, 1998): 236.

10. Sandra Pizzarello, Yongsong Huang, and Marcelo R. Alexandre, "Molecular Asymmetry in Extraterrestrial Chemistry: Insights from a Pristine Meteorite," *Proceedings of the National Academy of Sciences, USA* 105 (March 11, 2008): 3700–3704.

11. Daniel P. Glavin and Jason P. Dworkin, "Enrichment of the Amino Acid L-Isovaline by Aqueous Alteration on CI and CM Meteorite Parent Bodies," *Proceedings of the National Academy of Sciences, USA* 106 (April 7, 2009): 5487–92.

12. Joyce et al., "Chiral Selection," 602–4; Joyce et al., "Ancestral Genetic System," 4398–4402; Joyce, "RNA Evolution," 217–24; Szathmáry, "First Two Billion Years," 662–63.

13. Donna G. Blackmond, "Asymmetric Autocatalysis and Its Implications for the Origin of Homochirality," *Proceedings of the National Academy of Sciences, USA* 101 (April 20, 2004): 5732–36.

14. Ibid.

15. Sandra Pizzarello and Arthur L. Weber, "Prebiotic Amino Acids as Asymmetric Catalysts," *Science* 303 (February 20, 2004): 1151.

16. Arthur L. Weber and Sandra Pizzarello, "The Peptide-Catalyzed Stereospecific Synthesis of Tetroses: A Possible Model for Prebiotic Molecular Evolution," *Proceedings of the National Academy of Sciences, USA* 103 (August 22, 2006): 12713–17.

17. Jeffrey L. Bada, "Origins of Homochirality," *Nature* 374 (April 13, 1995): 594.

18. Robert Irion, "Did Twisty Starlight Set Stage for Life?" *Science* 281 (July 31, 1998): 627.

19. Atsushi Nemoto et al., "Enantiomeric Excess of Amino Acids in Hydrothermal Environments," *Origins of Life and Evolution of Biospheres* 35 (April 2005): 167–74.

20. Bada, "Origins of Homochirality," 594. For an example of Miller's work on PNA as the first genetic material, see Kevin E. Nelson, Matthew Levy, and Stanley L. Miller, "The Prebiotic Synthesis of the Components of Peptide Nucleic Acid, A Possible First Genetic Material," in *ISSOL '99 Abstracts*, 55.

21. Kevin E. Nelson, Matthew Levy, and Stanley Miller, "Peptide Nucleic Acids Rather Than RNA May Have Been the First Genetic Molecule," *Proceedings of the National Academy of Sciences, USA* 97 (April 11, 2000): 3868–71.

22. Horst Rauchfuss, *Chemical Evolution and the Origin of Life*, trans. Terence N. Mitchell (Berlin: Springer-Verlag, 2008), 247–55.

23. G. L. J. A. Rikken and E. Raupach, "Enantioselective Magnetochiral Photochemistry," *Nature* 405 (June 22, 2000): 932–35.

24. Rauchfuss, *Chemical Evolution*, 249.

25. Robert M. Hazen, *Genesis: The Scientific Quest for Life's Origin* (Washington, DC: Joseph Henry Press, 2005), 169.

26. Robert M. Hazen, "Life's Rocky Start," *Scientific American*, April 2001, 77–85.

27. Rauchfuss, *Chemical Evolution*, 247–55.

28. Robert M. Hazen, Timothy R. Filley, and Glenn A. Goodfriend, "Selective Adsorption of L- and D-Amino Acids on Calcite: Implications for Biochemical Homochirality," *Proceedings of the National Academy of Sciences, USA* 98 (May 1, 2001): 5487–90; Hazen, *Genesis*, 167–87.

29. Hazen, Filley, and Goodfriend, "Selective Adsorption," 5487–90.

30. Hazen, "Life's Rocky Start," 77–85; Evgenii I. Klabunovskii, "Can Enantiomorphic Crystals Like Quartz Play a Role in the Origin of Homochirality on Earth?" *Astrobiology* 1 (June 2001): 127–31.

31. Cristobal Viedma, "Enantiomeric Crystallization from DL-Aspartic and DL-Glutamic Acids: Implications for Biomolecular Chirality in the Origin of Life," *Origins of Life and Evolution of Biospheres* 31 (December 2001): 501–9.

32. Ronald Breslow and Mindy S. Levine, "Amplification of Enantiomeric Concentrations under Credible Prebiotic Conditions," *Proceedings of the National Academy of Sciences, USA* 103 (August 29, 2006): 12979–80.

33. ScienceDaily, "Meteorites Delivered the 'Seeds' of Earth's Left-Hand Life, Experts Argue," April 7, 2008, http://www.sciencedaily.com/releases/2008/04/080406114742 .htm.

34. For example, Jose J. Flores, William A. Bonner, and Gail A. Massey, "Asymmetric Photolysis of (RS)-Leucine with Circularly Polarized Ultraviolet Light," *Journal of the American Chemical Society* 99 (May 1977): 3622–25; G. Balavoine, A. Moradpour, and H. B. Kagan, "Preparation of Chiral Compounds with High Optical Purity by Irradiation with Circularly Polarized Light, a Model Reaction for the Prebiotic Generation of Optical Activity," *Journal of the American Chemical Society* 96 (August 17, 1974): 5152–58.

35. Rikken and Raupach, "Enantioselective Magnetochiral Photochemistry," 932–35.

Chapter 11 United by No Link

1. Christopher Wills and Jeffrey Bada, *The Spark of Life* (Cambridge, MA: Perseus, 2000), 101–2.

2. For a technical description of Cairns-Smith's model, see A. G. Cairns-Smith and H. Hartman, *Clay Minerals and the Origin of Life* (Cambridge: Cambridge University Press, 1986). For a more accessible description, see A. G. Cairns-Smith, *Seven Clues to the Origin of Life* (Cambridge: Cambridge University Press, 1985).

3. Wills and Bada, *Spark of Life*, 101–2.

4. Robert M. Hazen, *Genesis* (Washington, DC: Joseph Henry Press, 2005), 156–58.

5. James P. Ferris, "Catalyzed RNA Synthesis for the RNA World," in *The Molecular Origins of Life*, ed. André Brack (Cambridge: Cambridge University Press, 1998), 255–68; James P. Ferris, "From Building Blocks to the Polymers of Life," in *Life's Origin*, ed. J. William Schopf (Berkeley: University of California Press, 2002), 113–39.

6. James Ferris, "Prebiotic Chemistry, Catalysis and RNA Synthesis," abstract in *ISSOL '02 Abstracts* (Oaxaca, MEX: ISSOL, 2002), 40.

7. Leslie E. Orgel, "Prebiotic Chemistry and the Origin of the RNA World," *Critical Reviews in Biochemistry and Molecular Biology* 39 (March–April 2004): 99–123.

8. R. A. Sanchez, J. P. Ferris, and L. E. Orgel, "Cyanoacetylene in Prebiotic Synthesis," *Science* 154 (November 11, 1966): 784–85; Michael P. Robertson and Stanley L. Miller, "An Efficient Prebiotic Synthesis of Cytosine and Uracil," *Nature* 375 (June 29, 1995): 772–74; Michael P. Robertson and Stanley L. Miller, "Corrections: An Efficient Prebiotic Synthesis of Cytosine and Uracil," *Nature* 377 (September 21, 1995): 257; Stanley L. Miller, "The Endogenous Synthesis of Organic Compounds," in *Molecular Origins of Life*, 59–85.

9. Robert Shapiro, "Prebiotic Cytosine Synthesis: A Critical Analysis and Implications for the Origin of Life," *Proceedings of the National Academy of Sciences, USA* 96 (April 13, 1999): 4396–4401.

10. Matthew Levy and Stanley L. Miller, "The Stability of the RNA Bases: Implications for the Origin of Life," *Proceedings of the National Academy of Sciences, USA* 95 (July 7, 1998): 7933–38.

11. Shapiro, "Prebiotic Cytosine Synthesis," 4396–4401.

12. Miller, "Endogenous Synthesis," 59–85; Stanley L. Miller and Antonio Lazcano, "Formation of the Building Blocks of Life," in *Life's Origin*, 78–112; Orgel, "Prebiotic Chemistry," 99–123.

13. Robert Shapiro, "The Prebiotic Role of Adenine: A Critical Analysis," *Origin of Life and Evolution of the Biosphere* 25 (June 1995): 83–98.

14. H. James Cleaves II and Stanley L. Miller, "The Prebiotic Synthesis of Nucleoside Analogues from Mixed Formose Reactions: Implications for the First Genetic Material," in *ISSOL '02 Abstracts*, 102.

15. Norman W. Gabel and Cyril Ponnamperuma, "Model for Origin of Monosaccharides," *Nature* 216 (November 4, 1967): 453–55; A. G. Cairns-Smith, P. Ingram, and G. L. Walker, "Formose Production by Minerals: Possible Relevance to the Origin of Life," *Journal of Theoretical Biology* 35 (June 1972): 601–4; Alan W. Schwartz and R. M. de Graaf, "The Prebiotic Synthesis of Carbohydrates: A Reassessment," *Journal of Molecular Evolution* 36 (February 1993): 101–6; Miller, "Endogenous Synthesis," 59–85.

16. Schwartz and de Graaf, "Prebiotic Synthesis," 101–6; Miller, "Endogenous Synthesis," 59–85.

17. Orgel, "Prebiotic Chemistry," 99–123.

18. Ibid.

19. A. Seetharama Acharya and James M. Manning, "Reaction of Glycolaldehyde with Proteins: Latent Crosslinking Potential of α-Hydroxyaldehydes," *Proceedings of the National Academy of Sciences, USA* 80 (June 1, 1983): 3590–94; Miller, "Endogenous Synthesis," 59–85.

20. Rosa Larralde, Michael P. Robertson, and Stanley L. Miller, "Rates of Decomposition of Ribose and Other Sugars: Implications for Chemical Evolution," *Proceedings of the National Academy of Sciences, USA* 92 (August 29, 1995): 8158–60.

21. Ron Cowen, "Did Space Rocks Deliver Sugar?" *Science News*, December 22, 2001, 388; Mark A. Sephton, "Life's Sweet Beginnings?" *Nature* 414 (December 20, 2001): 857–58; George Cooper et al., "Carbonaceous Meteorites as a Source of Sugar-Related Organic Compounds for the Early Earth," *Nature* 414 (December 20, 2001): 879–83.

22. A. Ricardo et al., "Borate Minerals Stabilize Ribose," *Science* 303 (January 9, 2004): 196.

23. Orgel, "Prebiotic Chemistry," 99–123.

24. M. G. Sacerdote and J. W. Szostak, "Semipermeable Lipid Bilayers Exhibit Diastereoselectivity Favoring Ribose," *Proceedings of the National Academy of Sciences, USA* 102 (April 26, 2005): 6004–8.

25. Anthony D. Keefe and Stanley L. Miller, "Are Polyphosphates or Phosphate Esters Prebiotic Reagents?" *Journal of Molecular Evolution* 41 (December 1995): 693–702.

26. Ibid.; Ramanarayanan Krishnamurthy, "Challenges in 'Prebiotic' Chemistry," in *ISSOL '02 Abstracts*, 46.

27. Keefe and Miller, "Polyphosphates?" 693–702; Charles B. Thaxton, Walter L. Bradley, and Roger L. Olsen, *The Mystery of Life's Origin* (Dallas: Lewis and Stanley, 1984), 56.

28. Leslie Orgel, "The RNA World and the Origin of Life," in *ISSOL '02 Abstracts*, 39.

29. Orgel, "Prebiotic Chemistry," 99–123.

30. Matthew P. Powner, Béatrice Gerland, and John D. Sutherland, "Synthesis of Activated Pyrimidine Ribonucleotides in Prebiotically Plausible Conditions," *Nature* 459 (May 14, 2009): 239–42.

31. Richard Van Noorden, "RNA World Easier to Make," *Nature News*, May 13, 2009, http://www.nature.com/news/2009/090513/full/news.2009.471.html.

32. Orgel, "Prebiotic Chemistry," 99–123.

33. Ibid.

34. Ibid.

35. Gözen Ertem and James P. Ferris, "Synthesis of RNA Oligomers on Heterogeneous Templates," *Nature* 379 (January 18, 1996): 238–40; James P. Ferris et al., "Synthesis of Long Prebiotic Oligomers on Mineral Surfaces," *Nature* 381 (May 2, 1996): 59–61.

36. R. Lipkin, "Early Life: In the Soup or on the Rocks?" *Science News*, May 4, 1996, 278.

37. Orgel, "Prebiotic Chemistry," 99–123.

38. Robert Shapiro, "A Replicator Was Not Involved in the Origin of Life," *IUBMB Life* 49 (March 2000): 173–76; Robert Shapiro, "The Homopolymer Problem in the Origin of Life," abstract in *ISSOL '99 Abstracts*, comp. and ed. Lois Lane (La Jolla, CA: ISSOL, 1999), 48.

39. Robert Shapiro, "Small Molecule Interactions Were Central to the Origin of Life," *Quarterly Review of Biology* 81 (June 2006): 105–125.

40. Ferris, "Prebiotic Chemistry," in *ISSOL '02 Abstracts*, 40; Gözen Ertem, "Montmorillonite, Oligonucleotides, RNA and Origin of Life," in *ISSOL '02 Abstracts*, 59.

41. Leslie E. Orgel, "NSCORT 2000 Progress Report," http://exobio.ucsd.edu/00Orgel.htm (accessed August 7, 2001; site now discontinued).

42. Mitsuhiko Akaboshi et al., "Dephosphorylating Activity of Rare Earth Elements and Its Implication in the Chemical Evolution," in *ISSOL '99 Abstracts*, 63; Mitsuhiko Akaboshi et al., "Inhibition of Rare Earth Catalytic Activity by Proteins," *Origin of Life and Evolution of the Biosphere* 30 (January 2000): 25–32.

43. Orgel, "Prebiotic Chemistry," 99–123.

44. Gerald F. Joyce et al., "The Case for an Ancestral Genetic System Involving Simple Analogues of the Nucleotides," *Proceedings of the National Academy of Sciences, USA* 84 (July 1, 1987): 4398–4402; Igor A. Koslov, Stefan Pitsch, and Leslie E. Orgel, "Oligomerization of Activated D- and L-Guanosine Mononucleotides on Templates Containing D- and L-Deoxycytidylate Residues," *Proceedings of the National Academy of Sciences, USA* 95 (November 10, 1998): 13448–52.

45. Samanta Pino et al., "Nonenzymatic RNA Ligation in Water," *Journal of Biological Chemistry* 283 (December 26, 2008): 36494–503.

46. Shapiro, "Replicator Was Not Involved," 173–76; Shapiro, "Homopolymer Problem," in *ISSOL '99 Abstracts*, 48.

47. Shapiro, "Replicator Was Not Involved," 173–176; Robert Shapiro, "Monomer World," in *ISSOL '02 Abstracts*, 60.

48. Some examples are: Laura F. Landweber and Irina D. Pokrovskaya, "Emergence of a Dual-Catalytic RNA with Metal-Specific Cleavage and Ligase Activities: The Spandrels of RNA Evolution," *Proceedings of the National Academy of Sciences, USA* 96 (January 5, 1999): 173–78; Peter J. Unrau and David P. Bartel, "RNA-Catalysed Nucleotide Synthesis," *Nature* 395 (September 17, 1998): 260–63; Charles Wilson and Jack W. Szostak, "*In Vitro* Evolution of a Self-Alkylating Ribozyme," *Nature* 374 (April 27, 1995): 777–82; Theodore M. Tarasow, Sandra L. Tarasow, and Bruce E. Eaton, "RNA-Catalysed Carbon-Carbon Bond Formation," *Nature* 389 (September

4, 1997): 54–57; Jeff Rodgers and Gerald F. Joyce, "A Ribozyme That Lacks Cytidine," *Nature* 402 (November 18, 1999): 323–25; Jon R. Lorsch and Jack W. Szostak, "In Vitro Evolution of New Ribozymes with Polynucleotide Kinase Activity," *Nature* 371 (September 1, 1994): 31–36.

49. Wendy K. Johnston et al., "RNA-Catalyzed RNA Polymerization: Accurate and General RNA-Templated Primer Extension," *Science* 292 (May 18, 2001): 1319–25; Michael S. Lawrence and David P. Bartel, "Processivity of Ribozyme-Catalyzed RNA Polymerization," in *ISSOL '02 Abstracts*, 59.

50. Tracey A. Lincoln and Gerald F. Joyce, "Self-Sustained Replication of an RNA Enzyme," *Science* 323 (February 27, 2009): 1229–32.

51. Laura F. Landweber, "Experimental RNA Evolution," *Trends in Ecology and Evolution* 14 (September 1, 1999): 353–58; David P. Bartel and Peter J. Unrau, "Constructing an RNA World," *Trends in Cell Biology* 9 (December 1, 1999): M9–M13; Martin C. Wright and Gerald F. Joyce, "Continuous In Vitro Evolution of Catalytic Function," *Science* 276 (April 25, 1997): 614–17; David P. Bartel and Jack W. Szostak, "Isolation of New Ribozymes from a Large Pool of Random Sequences," *Science* 261 (September 10, 1993): 1411–18.

52. Leslie Orgel, "Self-Organizing Biochemical Cycles," *Proceedings of the National Academy of Sciences, USA* 97 (November 7, 2000): 12503–7.

Chapter 12 A Thousand Other Miseries

1. For example, see Thazha P. Prakash, Christopher Roberts, and Christopher Switzer, "Activity of 2',5'-Linked RNA in the Template-Directed Oligomerization of Mononucleotides," *Angewandte Chemie*, international ed. in English 36 (August 4, 1997): 1522–23.

2. Harold J. Morowitz, *Beginnings of Cellular Life* (New Haven: Yale University Press, 1992); Robert Shapiro, "Monomer World," abstract in *ISSOL '02 Abstracts*, comp. and ed. Alicia Negron-Mendoza et al. (Oaxaca, MEX: ISSOL, 2002), 60.

3. Morowitz, *Beginnings of Cellular Life*, 155.

4. Robert Shapiro, "Small Molecule Interactions Were Central to the Origin of Life," *Quarterly Review of Biology* 81 (June 2006): 105–25.

5. Leslie E. Orgel, "The Implausibility of Metabolic Cycles on the Prebiotic Earth," *PLoS Biology* 6 (January 22, 2008), doi:10.1371/journal.pbio.0060018, http://www .plosbiology.org/article/info%3Adoi%2F10.1371%2Fjournal.pbio.0060018.

6. Leslie E. Orgel, "Self-Organizing Biochemical Cycles," *Proceedings of the National Academy of Sciences, USA* 97 (November 7, 2000): 12503–7.

7. Richard Wolfenden and Mark J. Snider, "The Depth of Chemical Time and the Power of Enzymes as Catalysts," *Accounts of Chemical Research* 34 (December 2001): 938–45.

8. Orgel, "Self-Organizing Biochemical Cycles," 12503–7.

9. Orgel, "The Implausibility of Metabolic Cycles on the Prebiotic Earth."

10. Eric Smith and Harold J. Morowitz, "Universality in Intermediary Metabolism," *Proceedings of the National Academy of Sciences, USA* 101 (September 7, 2004): 13168–73.

11. Orgel, "The Implausibility of Metabolic Cycles on the Prebiotic Earth."

12. Horst Rauchfuss, *Chemical Evolution and the Origin of Life*, trans. Terence N. Mitchell (Berlin: Springer-Verlag, 2008), 193–204.

13. Ibid.

14. Claudia Huber and Günter Wächtershäuser, "Activated Acetic Acid by Carbon Fixation on (Fe,Ni)S Under Primordial Conditions," *Science* 276 (April 11, 1997): 245–47.

15. Claudia Huber and Günter Wächtershäuser, "α-Hydroxy and α-Amino Acids under Possible Hadean, Volcanic Origin-of-Life Conditions," *Science* 314 (October 27, 2006): 630–32; Claudia Huber and Günter Wächtershäuser, "Peptides by Activation of Amino Acids with CO on (Ni,Fe)S Surfaces: Implications for the Origin of Life," *Science* 281 (July 31, 1998): 670–72.

16. Christopher Wills and Jeffrey Bada, *The Spark of Life* (Cambridge, MA: Perseus, 2000), 96–101.

17. Orgel, "The Implausibility of Metabolic Cycles on the Prebiotic Earth."

18. David S. Ross, "A Quantitative Evaluation of the Iron-Sulfur World and Its Relevance to Life's Origins," *Astrobiology* 8 (November 2, 2008): 267–72.

19. Claudia Huber et al., "A Possible Primordial Peptide Cycle," *Science* 301 (August 15, 2003): 938–40.

20. Rauchfuss, *Chemical Evolution*, 193–204.

21. Orgel, "Self-Organizing Biochemical Cycles," 12503–7.

22. Addy Pross, "Causation and the Origin of Life: Metabolism or Replication First?" *Origins of Life and Evolution of Biospheres* 34 (June 2004): 307–321.

23. Orgel, "The Implausibility of Metabolic Cycles on the Prebiotic Earth."

Chapter 13 Persevere in Exile

1. Robert C. Bohinski, *Modern Concepts in Biochemistry*, 4th ed. (Boston: Allyn and Bacon, 1983), 8–28.

2. Geoffrey Zubay, *Origins of Life on the Earth and in the Cosmos*, 2nd ed. (San Diego: Academic Press, 2000), 371–76.

3. Danilo D. Lasic, "The Mechanism of Vesicle Formation," *Biochemical Journal* 256 (November 15, 1988): 1–11.

4. Ibid.

5. For example, see Barry R. Lentz, Tamra J. Carpenter, and Dennis R. Alford, "Spontaneous Fusion of Phosphatidylcholine Small Unilamellar Vesicles in the Fluid Phase," *Biochemistry* 26 (August 1987): 5389–97.

6. Jacquelyn A. Thomas and Fazale R. Rana, "The Influence of Environmental Conditions, Lipid Composition, and Phase Behavior on the Origin of Cell Membranes," *Origins of Life and Evolution of Biospheres* 37 (June 2007): 267–85.

7. Zubay, *Origins of Life on the Earth*, 347.

8. Ibid.; Stanley L. Miller and Jeffrey L. Bada, "Submarine Hot Springs and the Origin of Life," *Nature* 334 (August 18, 1998): 609–11; Nils G. Holm and Eva M. Andersson, "Hydrothermal Systems," in *The Molecular Origins of Life*, ed. André Brack (Cambridge: Cambridge University Press, 1998), 86–99.

9. Ahmed I. Rushdi and Bernd R. T. Simoneit, "Lipid Formation by Aqueous Fischer-Tropsch-Type Synthesis over a Temperature Range of 100 to 400°C," *Origin of Life and Evolution of the Biosphere* 31 (February 2001): 103–18.

10. Miller and Bada, "Submarine Hot Springs," 609–11.

11. Robert M. Hazen and David W. Deamer, "Hydrothermal Reactions of Pyruvic Acid: Synthesis, Selection, and Self-Assembly of Amphiphilic Molecules," *Origins of Life and Evolution of Biospheres* 37 (April 2007): 143–52.

12. Zubay, *Origins of Life on the Earth*, 348–50; Arthur L. Weber, "Origin of Fatty Acid Synthesis: Thermodynamics and Kinetics of Reaction Pathways," *Journal of Molecular Evolution* 32 (February 1991): 93–100.

13. Leslie E. Orgel, "Self-Organizing Biochemical Cycles," *Proceedings of the National Academy of Sciences, USA* 97 (November 7, 2000): 12503–7.

14. Zubay, *Origins of Life on the Earth*, 350; W. R. Hargreaves, S. Mulvihill, and D. W. Deamer, "Synthesis of Phospholipids and Membranes in Prebiotic Conditions," *Nature* 266 (March 3, 1977): 78–80; J. Eichberg et al., "Cyanamide Mediated Syntheses under Plausible Primitive Earth Conditions. IV. The Synthesis of Acylglycerols," *Journal of Molecular Evolution* 10 (September 1977): 221–30; D. E. Epps et al., "Cyanamide Mediated Syntheses under Plausible Primitive Earth Conditions. V. The Synthesis of Phosphatidic Acids," *Journal of Molecular Evolution* 11 (December 1978): 279–92; D. E. Epps et al., "Cyanamide Mediated Synthesis under Plausible Primitive Earth Conditions. VI. The Synthesis of Glycerol and Glycerophosphates," *Journal of Molecular Evolution* 14 (December 1979): 235–41; M. Rao, J. Eichberg, and J. Oró, "Synthesis of Phosphatidylcholine under Possible Primitive Earth Conditions," *Journal of Molecular Evolution* 18 (May 1982): 196–202; M. Rao, J. Eichberg, and J. Oró, "Synthesis of Phosphatidylethanolamine under Possible Primitive Earth Conditions," *Journal of Molecular Evolution* 25 (May 1987): 1–6.

15. Charles B. Thaxton, Walter L. Bradley, and Roger L. Olsen, *The Mystery of Life's Origin* (Dallas: Lewis and Stanley, 1984), 56, 177–178.

16. David W. Deamer, Elizabeth H. Mahon, and Giovanni Bosco, "Self-Assembly and Function of Primitive Membrane Structures," in *Early Life on Earth: Nobel Symposium No. 84*, ed. Stefan Bengtson (New York: Columbia University Press, 1994), 107–23; David W. Deamer, "Membrane Compartments in Prebiotic Evolution," in *Molecular Origins of Life*, 189–205.

17. John R. Cronin, "Clues from the Origin of the Solar System: Meteorites," in *Molecular Origins of Life*, 119–46.

18. Jason P. Dworkin et al., "Self-Assembling Amphiphilic Molecules: Synthesis in Simulated Interstellar/Precometary Ices," *Proceedings of the National Academy of Sciences, USA* 98 (January 30, 2001): 815–19; Ron Cowen, "Life's Housing May Come from Space," *Science News*, February 3, 2001, 68.

19. J. N. Israelachvili, S. Marcelja, and Roger G. Horn, "Physical Principles of Membrane Organization," *Quarterly Review of Biophysics* 13 (May 1980): 121–200.

20. William R. Hargreaves and David W. Deamer, "Liposomes from Ionic, Single-Chain Amphiphiles," *Biochemistry* 17 (September 1978): 3759–68.

21. Deamer, Mahon, and Bosco, "Self-Assembly and Function," 107–23; Deamer, "Membrane Compartments," 189–205; D. W. Deamer and R. M. Pashley, "Amphiphilic Components of the Murchison Carbonaceous Chondrite: Surface Properties and Membrane Formation," *Origins of Life and Evolution of the Biosphere* 19 (January 1989): 21–38; David W. Deamer, "Boundary Structures Are Formed by Organic Components of the Murchison Carbonaceous Chondrite," *Nature* 317 (October 31, 1985): 792–94.

22. Dworkin et al., "Self-Assembling Amphiphilic Molecules," 815–19.

23. Deamer, Mahon, and Bosco, "Self-Assembly and Function," 107–23; David W. Deamer and Gail L. Barchfeld, "Encapsulation of Macromolecules by Lipid Vesicles under Simulated Prebiotic Conditions," *Journal of Molecular Evolution* 18 (May 1982): 203–6; David W. Deamer, "The First Living Systems: A Bioenergetic Perspective," *Microbiology and Molecular Biology Reviews* 61 (June 1997): 239–61.

24. Deamer, Mahon, and Bosco, "Self-Assembly and Function," 107–23; Deamer, "Membrane Compartments," 189–205.

25. Deamer, "Membrane Compartments," 189–205.

26. Martin M. Hanczyc, Shelly M. Fujikawa, and Jack W. Szostak, "Experimental Models of Primitive Cellular Compartments: Encapsulation, Growth, and Division," *Science* 302 (October 24, 2003): 618–22.

27. Martin M. Hanczyc and Jack W. Szostak, "Replicating Vesicles as Models of Primitive Cell Growth and Division," *Current Opinion in Chemical Biology* 8 (December 2004): 660–64.

28. Deamer, Mahon, and Bosco, "Self-Assembly and Function," 107–23; Deamer, "Membrane Compartments," 189–205.

29. James G. Lawless and George U. Yuen, "Quantification of Monocarboxylic Acids in the Murchison Carbonaceous Meteorite," *Nature* 282 (November 22, 1979): 396–98.

30. Deamer, Mahon, and Bosco, "Self-Assembly and Function," 107–23; Deamer, "Membrane Compartments," 189–205.

31. Deamer, "Boundary Structures," 792–94.

32. Hargreaves and Deamer, "Liposomes," 3759–68.

33. Matt Kaplan, "A Fresh Start," *New Scientist*, May 11, 2002, 7.

34. Charles L. Apel, David W. Deamer, and Michael N. Mautner, "Self-Assembled Vesicles of Monocarboxylic Acids and Alcohols: Conditions for Stability and for the Encapsulation of Biopolymers," *Biochimica et Biophysica Acta* 1559 (February 10, 2002): 1–9.

35. Kaplan, "A Fresh Start," 7.

36. I. Baeza et al., "Studies on Precellular Evolution: The Encapsulation of Polyribonucleotides by Liposomes," *Advances in Space Research* 6 (January 1986): 39–43; Deamer and Barchfeld, "Encapsulation of Macromolecules," 203–6; R. L. Shew and D. W. Deamer, "A Novel Method for Encapsulation of Macromolecules in Liposomes," *Biochimica et Biophysica Acta* 816 (June 11, 1985): 1–8.

37. Shew and Deamer, "A Novel Method," 1–8.

38. Apel, Deamer, and Mautner, "Self-Assembled Vesicles," 1–9; Ajoy C. Chakrabarti and David W. Deamer, "Permeability of Lipid Bilayers to Amino Acids and Phosphate," *Biochimica et Biophyisica Acta* 111 (November 9, 1992): 171–77; Deamer, "The First Living Systems," 239–61.

39. Thomas and Rana, "Influence of Environmental Conditions," 267–85.

40. Irene A. Chen, Kouroush Salehi-Ashtiani, and Jack W. Szostak, "RNA Catalysis in Model Protocell Vesicles," *Journal of the American Chemical Society* 127 (September 28, 2005): 13213–19.

41. Shlomo Rottem, "Transbilayer Distribution of Lipids in Microbial Membranes," in *Membrane Lipids of Prokaryotes*, ed. Shmuel Razin and Shlomo Rottem (New York: Academic Press, 1982), 235–61.

42. John M. Seddon, "Structure of the Inverted Hexagonal (H_{II}) Phase, and Non-Lamellar Phase Transitions of Lipids," *Biochimica et Biophysica Acta* 1031 (Febru-

ary 28, 1990): 1–69; Göran Lindblom and Leif Rilfors, "Cubic Phases and Isotropic Structures Formed by Membrane Lipids—Possible Biological Relevance," *Biochimica et Biophysica Acta* 988 (May 9, 1989): 221–56.

43. Fazale R. Rana, "Structure and Function of Outer Membranes and LPS from Wild-Type and LPS-Mutant Strains of *Salmonella typhimurium* and Their Interaction with Magainins and Polymyxin B" (PhD dissertation, Ohio University, 1990). Also see references therein.

44. Seddon, "Hexogonal (H_{II}) Phase," 1–69.

45. Aake Wieslander et al., "Lipid Bilayer Stability in Membranes: Regulation of Lipid Composition in *Acholeplasma laidlawii* as Governed by Molecular Shape," *Biochemistry* 19 (August 1980): 3650–55.

46. Lasic, "Mechanism of Vesicle Formation," 1–11.

47. N. L. Gershfeld, "The Critical Unilamellar Lipid State: A Perspective for Membrane Bilayer Assembly," *Biochimica et Biosphysica Acta* 988 (December 6, 1989): 335–50.

48. For example, see Norman L. Gershfeld et al., "Critical Temperature for Unilamellar Vesicle Formation in Dimyristoyl phosphatidylcholine Dispersions from Specific Heat Measurements," *Biophysical Journal* 65 (September 1993): 1174–79.

49. N. L. Gershfeld, "Spontaneous Assembly of a Phospholipid Bilayer as a Critical Phenomenon: Influence of Temperature, Composition, and Physical State," *Journal of Physical Chemistry* 93 (June 1989): 5256–61.

50. Lionel Ginsberg, Daniel L. Gilbert, and Norman L. Gershfeld, "Membrane Bilayer Assembly in Neural Tissue of Rat and Squid as a Critical Phenomenon: Influence of Temperature and Membrane Proteins," *Journal of Membrane Biology* 119 (January 1991): 65–73.

51. K. E. Tremper and N. L. Gershfeld, "Temperature Dependence of Membrane Lipid Composition in Early Blastula Embryos of *Lytechinus pictus*: Selective Sorting of Phospholipids into Nascent Plasma Membranes," *Journal of Membrane Biology* 171 (September 1999): 47–53.

52. A. J. Jin et al., "A Singular State of Membrane Lipids at Cell Growth Temperatures," *Biochemistry* 38 (October 5, 1999): 13275–78.

53. N. L. Gershfeld and M. Murayama, "Thermal Instability of Red Blood Cell Membrane Bilayers: Temperature Dependence of Hemolysis," *Journal of Membrane Biology* 101 (December 1988): 67–72.

54. Lionel Ginsberg, John H. Xuereb, and Norman L. Gershfeld, "Membrane Instability, Plasmalogen Content and Alzheimer's Disease," *Journal of Neurochemistry* 70 (June 1998): 2533–38.

55. Simon Conway Morris, *Life's Solution* (Cambridge: Cambridge University Press, 2003), 41.

Appendix

1. Details about life's chemistry can be found in any introductory biochemistry textbook. For this appendix, Robert C. Bohinski, *Modern Concepts in Biochemistry*, 4th ed. (Boston: Allyn and Bacon, 1983) was consulted.

Index

About the Author

Dr. Fazale Rana is the vice president of research and apologetics at Reasons To Believe. Research in biochemistry provided him with evidence that life must have a Creator. Acting on a personal challenge to read the Bible, he found scriptural evidence that convinced him of the Creator's identity.

After graduating with highest honors from West Virginia State College (WVSC) with a BS degree in chemistry, Dr. Rana earned a PhD in chemistry with an emphasis in biochemistry at Ohio University (OU). A presidential scholar, Dr. Rana was elected into two honor societies at WVSC and won the Donald Clippinger Research Award two different years at OU. He conducted postdoctoral work at the Universities of Virginia and Georgia. Before joining Reasons To Believe, he worked for seven years on product development for Procter & Gamble. Dr. Rana also holds an adjunct faculty position at Biola University, teaching in the Master of Science and Religion and the Christian Apologetics programs.

Several articles by Dr. Rana have been published in peer-reviewed scientific journals such as *Biochemistry, Applied Spectroscopy, FEBS Letters, Journal of Microbiological Methods,* and *Journal of Chemical Education.* Recently he published an article on cell membrane origins in *Origins of Life and Evolution of Biospheres.* He has delivered numerous presentations at international scientific meetings. Dr. Rana also has two patents, authored a chapter on molecular convergence and intelligent design for *The Nature of Nature* (edited by Bruce L. Gordon and William A. Dembski), and co-wrote a chapter on antimicrobial peptides for *Biological and Synthetic Membranes* (edited by D. Allan Butterfield). In addition, he is author of *The Cell's Design* and coauthor with Hugh Ross of *Origins of Life* and *Who Was Adam?*

Dr. Rana travels around the country to speak at churches, business firms, and university campuses on science and faith issues. He is also a frequent guest on radio and television programs.

Dr. Rana and his wife, Amy, live in Southern California.

About Reasons To Believe

Uniquely positioned within the science-faith discussion since 1986, Reasons To Believe (RTB) openly communicates that science and faith are, and always will be, allies, not enemies. Distinguished for bridging the gap between science and faith respectfully and with integrity, RTB welcomes dialogue with both skeptics and believers. Addressing topics such as the origin of the universe, the origin of life, and the history and destiny of humanity, RTB's website offers a vast array of helpful resources. Through their books, "Today's New Reason to Believe" blog, podcasts, and speaking events, RTB scholars present powerful reasons from science to believe in the God of the Bible as Creator.

For more information contact us via:
www.reasons.org
731 E. Arrow Highway
Glendora, CA 91740
(800) 482-7836
Or email us at customerservice@reasons.org

REASONS TO BELIEVE
Bridging the gap between science and faith.

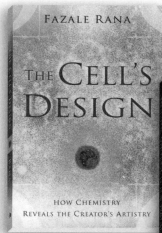
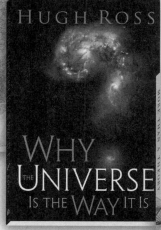
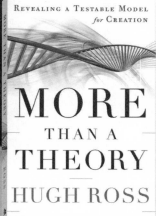